W9-BNE-375

Behind the
Headlines _11/17/99_

Behind the
Headlines

Stories About People and Events Which Shaped St. Louis

G. Duncan Bauman

as told to
Mary Kimbrough

The Patrice Press
Tucson, Arizona

Copyright © 1999
G. Duncan Bauman

All rights reserved. No portion of this publication may be reproduced, stored in a retrieval system, or transmitted in any form or by any means, electronic, mechanical, photocopying, or recording, without the prior permission of the author or publisher.

Library of Congress Cataloging-in-Publication Data

Bauman, G. Duncan (George Duncan), 1912-
  Behind the headlines / G. Duncan Bauman as told to Mary Kimbrough.
    p. cm.
  Includes index.
  ISBN 1-880397-31-5
    1. Bauman, G. Duncan (George Duncan), 1912– 2. Newspaper publishing–Missouri–Saint Louis–History–20th century.
3. Publishers and publishing–Missouri–Saint Louis–Biography.
4. St. Louis globe-democrat (Saint Louis, Mo.: 1875). 5. Saint Louis (Mo.)–Politics and government–20th century.
I. Kimbrough, Mary. II. Title.
Z473.B28 1999
070.5'092-dc21
[B]   99-038421

Unless otherwise noted, all photographs are from the *Globe-Democrat* archives at the St. Louis Mercantile Library.

The Patrice Press
P. O. Box 85639
Tucson AZ 85754-5639
1-800-367-9242
http: //www.patricepress.com

Printed in the United States of America

To my parents,
Peter W. and Mae Duncan Bauman,
for being with me all the way
and especially for providing me with a Jesuit education,
thus enabling me to meet the challenges of my newspaper career.

Contents

Foreword

Duncan Bauman thinks there isn't anything a human being can do that is more satisfying than being in print media. When a young man and thinking about his lifetime career, the courtroom and the city room battled for his mind and his heart.

The city room won. The typewriter and the Linotype finally prevailed over the judge's bench and the jury box.

As a matter of fact, Bauman was already established in the newspaper business and had left the Chicago *Herald-Examiner* to join the *St. Louis Globe-Democrat* long before he received his J.D. degree from the Washington University School of Law in 1948. Printer's ink had seeped into his bloodstream and now, a half-century later, it still is an essential part of his being.

As publisher and editor of the *St. Louis Globe-Democrat*, he was a nationally known newspaper executive and a respected St. Louis mover and shaker and policy maker. He traveled the world and dined at the White House, walked with diplomats and talked with tycoons. Local observers called him one of the most powerful men in St. Louis.

Like his colleagues in the elite fraternity of men and women who sit behind the desk where the buck stops, he carried in his mind volumes of inside information which for one reason or another did not make its way into the paper. And like them, he was compelled to do a daily balancing act between pragmatism and full disclosure. Might a story hurt someone unnecessarily? Will it offend an advertiser? Does it violate canons of good taste? And above all, is it true, without a doubt?

For Duncan Bauman there were even more considerations. As a

trusted member of community boards and organizations, privy to inside information, he withheld that information from his own reporters as a matter of integrity. (But he was sure to demand first dibs on the story when it was ready to break. He battled the competition, the *St. Louis Post-Dispatch*, and gave no quarter.)

In his journey from reporter's beat to executive suite, from news cub to civic leader, a part of him stayed behind forever in the gaudy, Runyonesque world of *The Front Page*, that lusty, legendary chapter of American journalism now vanished in an era of computers and cold type. It was on William Randolph Hearst's *Herald-Examiner* that Bauman read his first byline, relished his first taste of journalism, and learned his sometimes painful lessons in obeying Hearst's command: "Get it right—but get it first!"

In retirement, he remembers those lessons and the blood-tingling exhilaration of the "scoop." To talk to him about his life and career, you sense that he is still "Dunc Bauman, boy reporter," even after becoming a community activist and powerful publisher.

He may not have run out of the executive office to leap aboard a speeding fire engine or telephone police headquarters for information on a crime, but he wanted to know where that fire was and whether a suspect had been caught. He had the spirit of a reporter and nothing could dampen it.

Selected by his peers as 1983 *Globe-Democrat* Man of the Year, he was praised by William H. Webster, former director of the Federal Bureau of Investigation, as the epitome of "the very best of St. Louis citizenship."

"He is a deeply caring person and doesn't hesitate to put himself on the line for the people and the community and the country he cares so much about," Webster said.

A man of sturdy conscience and deep religious conviction, an ardent patriot who flies the flag every day from a pole in his front yard, he might be forced to put aside his personal opinions in determining publication or placement, but he always insisted that news and editorial matter in the *Globe-Democrat* be consistent with sound moral principles.

Armed with the fighting instincts of a bulldog, Bauman always came out swinging, whether he was outraged at some official or at labor or management or malfeasance at any level of responsibility, or if he were stumping for support of a favored project. But if he found later that he had backed the wrong side or individual in a political race or civic project, he would admit it and go back into battle. As a newsman, he lived, worked—and occasionally swore—with gusto. On the other hand, he inherited an attitude of courtesy and respect, along with his staunch Roman Catholic faith and political philosophy from his parents, Peter W. and Mae Bauman.

His wife, Nora, became so enmeshed in his career that she often referred to the *Globe-Democrat* family as "we" or "us" and frequently called Duncan "the boss." She died February 12, 1990, after fifty-two years of marriage; two years later, he married the former Lucy Hencke Hume. Bauman continues to be active in dozens of community and religious activities, and he keeps up with the news, sometimes with optimism and often with indignation.

But his still-crowded retirement calendar can't turn off the memories of his days in the city room and it can't squelch his opinion that "there isn't anything a human being can do that is more satisfying than being in print media."

Mary Kimbrough
St. Louis, Mo.
November 1999

Preface and Acknowledgments

For better or worse, this is my century and this is my world.

If I could have chosen a time in which to live, it would be the twentieth century.

It was a time of radical change—a reporter's paradise.

I saw the era's early years and now I am seeing its twilight days. In a sense, I grew up with the century itself. I know it well. I remember its first brief flights into the sky and I have seen its journeys into space. I remember our first telephone, my own crystal set radio, my first car, my first television.

Some insist, as Charles Dickens wrote of another era, that the twentieth century has been the best of times, the worst of times—the spring of hope, the winter of despair. Perhaps they are right. It was not all bad, to be sure, neither was it all good. Like every other era in the history of mankind, it rode a roller coaster.

I have seen small towns flourish and wither away. I have seen human mobility move families around the nation like pawns on a chessboard, changing neighborhoods from little islands of friends to isolated plots populated by strangers who hardly speak.

I have seen peaceful farmland transformed into traffic-clogged and polluted suburbs. I have seen the death of Mom and Pop stores and the warm-hearted corner druggist, the birth of supermarkets, the growth of corporate power, the spread of urban sprawl. Medical science has made unbelievable strides, but, unfortunately, the kindly family doctor who brought his black bag to the home-bound invalid has disappeared in the huge, impersonal conglomerate of insured and computerized health care.

Nations have been created, only to be gobbled up by greedy dictators. I have seen a war which we thought would "end all wars," only to be followed by periods of uneasy peace and vicious battles that broke the spirit and scarred the faces of men and of their homelands.

Women have gained the vote and risen to political power. Megamergers have swallowed smaller companies, downsized corporate personnel and given rise to home-based businesses.

I have seen man find his way to the North and South Poles, conquer the oceans, take his first steps on the moon, opening long-closed minds to the vision of space colonization.

Technology has erased time constraints, moving the human voice across the globe in milliseconds. Transportation time tables have been reduced from weeks or months to hours. Society is computerized, mechanized, and tranquilized. Bland recorded "options" have replaced responsive telephone operators.

I was born at the end of an era that was called by some the Age of Optimism, the Age of Innocence, the Age of Confidence. According to the Time-Life book, *This Fabulous Century*, it was "a time when Americans were optimistic and self-confident to an extreme; they did not merely hope for the best, they fully expected it."

For the moment, the century's problems and excruciating social headaches could be ignored.

But then came the century's second decade and my first. Reality set in and the age of innocence disappeared. In the year of my birth, 1912, Walter Weyl wrote in *The New Democracy*, "America is in a period of clamor, of bewilderment, of an almost tremulous unrest. We are hastily reviewing all our social conceptions. We are profoundly disenchanted."

Tremendous challenges have confronted both century and career. With others of my generation and with my journalism colleagues, I have been both blessed and cursed by those challenges. That disenchantment of the early century has given birth to human progress. Unrest has brought radical change in human thought and action. As a people, we have stumbled and fallen, only to pick ourselves up and start again. We have made grievous mistakes but we have chalked up triumphs, both grand and miniscule. Amid charges of irresponsibility, we of the press have been forced to examine the priorities and ethics of our profession. And many times, we have been found wanting.

Even so, I could not have chosen to follow a more exciting career or to be born into a more exciting time. I have not only lived through turbulent times. I have been privileged to report them.

For better or worse, this is my century and this is my world.

It has always been my conviction that no one ever achieves a major goal in life without help from someone, known or unknown, and, without a doubt, help from God. Whatever I may have been able to accomplish in life has invariably been with God's help.

In the writing of the acknowledgments for this book I fervently hope that I have not left anyone out who should have been recognized for his or her help, but if I have I apologize now.

Mary Kimbrough, a former writer for the *Globe-Democrat*, one of the best writers on our staff, has been the focal point. She has done a superb job. I cannot say enough about the help given me by Lucy, my wife. At times the project has been frustrating and discouraging but she has provided the patience, encouragement, help and editing skill which prodded me on. Our grandnephew, Michael Beatty, has assisted with research and typing. My former secretary at the *Globe,* Sandy Britton, transcribed tapes of my dictation in an expeditious, error-free and prompt manner. Our grandson, Andrew R. Hume, gave sound advice.

All of my former co-workers who were asked for remembrances were enthusiastically forthcoming: Martin Duggan, Ted Schafers, Jack Flach, and Dennis MacCarthy. Mary Ellen Davis, formerly head of the morgue at the *Globe-Democrat* and now the guardian of the morgue which rests in the Mercantile Library at the University of Missouri-St. Louis in the Thomas Jefferson Library building, happily assisted in searching the morgue for information not available anywhere else. John Hoover, director of the Mercantile Library, was warmly and enthusiastically willing to help, as was Charles Brown.

My stepdaughter, Linda Pauley, an imaginative and skilled producer of computer printed products, explored alternative cover designs which enabled us to make a choice. Amour Krupnik, formerly in charge of the *Globe-Democrat's* computer installation, artist and the paper's layout designer, provided the original cover designs. George Peek provided the final version.

The wonderful experiences and rewards of my adult life would not have been possible without the confidence of a rare, rare man, S. I.

Newhouse, Sr., who trusted me with the unique opportunity to be publisher of the *St. Louis Globe-Democrat* for nearly twenty years.

Not the less of those to whom appreciation is due are Gregory Franzwa, former St. Louisan and director of the Patrice Press, and Betty Burnett, also a former St. Louisan and Franzwa's editor.

–G. Duncan Bauman
St. Louis, Mo.
November 1999

- 1 -

"30"

This is the final edition of the Globe-Democrat, *the newspaper Abraham Lincoln said was worth more to the North during the Civil War than 10 regiments of soldiers, the newspaper that helped a young aviator named Charles A. Lindbergh make history, the newspaper that numbered a young Theodore Dreiser among its reporters, the newspaper that lived up to its slogan, 'Fighting FOR St. Louis.'*

That was written for what we thought would be the final edition of the *Globe-Democrat.* It never ran.

We were prepared to close on December 31, 1983, but the paper refused to die quickly or neatly. It lived on another three years because of government intervention and poor business judgments, years which were filled with rumors, decisions, countermanding decisions, swings from pessimism to optimism and back again, uncertainty, and, finally, two changes of ownership.

The *Globe-Democrat,* which traced its ancestry to the *Missouri Democrat,* lived to the extraordinary age of 131 years. It did not expire suddenly, as though with a fatal heart attack, but suffered a lingering demise. Its first death announcement was, in Mark Twain's words, reacting to the erroneous news of his own dying, "greatly exaggerated."

The grim odyssey began for me in the fall of 1983 when owner Si Newhouse called me to his New York office to discuss the

1

"30" was the reporter's traditional editing mark to indicate the end of a story.

paper's future. Ostensibly, we were doing quite well. Our advertising revenue was up and our daily circulation was around 60,000 ahead of our long-time rival, the St. Louis *Post-Dispatch.*

Si's father, S.I. Newhouse, had bought the paper in 1955 from E. Lansing Ray as part of a media empire that eventually included newspapers, magazines and television stations.

Lansing Ray's son and namesake had suffered a severe head wound in World War II, but even though he returned to St. Louis, he was unable to take over the responsibility of the paper and died of a cerebral hemorrhage in 1946. After that Ray seemed to be emotionally unable to carry on. I remember when Arthur Weis and I went to his home at 3 o'clock one morning to discuss a labor crisis with him. Weis was vice president of the company and I was handling our labor negotiations.

What we needed was support from him, a way to settle the matter without giving in to the union. But what we got was a plaintive question, "Why do they do this to me?"

From the start, Newhouse made it clear that he would not interfere with the paper's editorial policies. His concern with the business side didn't mean that he had no interest in St. Louis or in Missouri. In fact, on nearly every one of his frequent visits he would ask about city and state politics.

However, he was not one to haggle over union demands, and four years after he bought the paper, during a devastating ninety-five-day strike by the Newspaper Guild, he sold our plant to the *Post-Dispatch.* We moved the *Globe* a block away to the Illinois Terminal Building at 710 N. Tucker Blvd. With no presses or composing room, he contracted with the *Post* to do our printing and gave up our Sunday edition.

As the heir to the Newhouse empire, after his father's death in 1977, young Si was also a close watcher of the bottom line, but I know that both he and his father were sincerely interested in St. Louis and wanted the paper to succeed. In fact, the elder Newhouse spoke with me a number of times about his wish to buy the *Post* and kept asking if I knew how he could obtain additional stock.

On that autumn day in 1983, talking with young Si about the paper's financial position, I had to admit that the future did not look good.

The profit margins were insufficient by industry standards. We were making only about one percent. Our outlay was considerable. The telephone bill was $15,000 a week and our wire services $25,000 a week. We could raise advertising rates, of course, but it wouldn't do much good. Some of our major advertisers said to us, "'If you raise the rates, we will just cut down on our advertising. We will still spend our $2 million [or whatever they were spending], but we won't increase it."

While we made a little money that last year of Newhouse ownership, we knew we would be saddled with horrendous extra costs in the future, which would be impossible to bear. When I first came to the *Globe* in 1939, newsprint was $40 a ton. It rose to $650 a ton and we used tens of thousands of tons. We tried many ways to save money. For example, we trimmed an eighth of an inch off our page size and saved $1 million.

The most serious problem facing us was the escalating cost of labor. This dated back to the Great Depression of the early 1930s when business was bad and workers were laid off nationwide. Trade unions, fighting for their existence, became truculent and combative. Various work rules were agreed to by the publishers to preserve jobs, but those rules turned out to be atrociously restrictive and difficult, and ultimately played a major role in the death of many metropolitan newspapers, including the *Globe-Democrat*.

Publishers in those days capitulated to those requirements because of union pleas to keep people at work and the publishers' vain determination not to miss a single day of publication. It was to their credit from the standpoint of heart. But it was stupid from the standpoint of rational thinking.

Unions remained very strong through the years and there were ten different unions by the 1980s. Because of their number and vigor—and because St. Louis is a pro-union city—they exerted a great deal of influence on our mechanical operation.

The Newspaper Guild, perhaps not as truculent or intractable as most unions, negotiated pay scales and working policies for employees in the newsroom, circulation, advertising, and business departments. Reporters, desk men and women, photographers, artists and copy boys and girls, salesmen and women were required to join the Guild; only a handful of top editors, business office heads, advertising and circulation executives and heads of production were exempt.

In my years in the business, newspaper production methods

advanced from a "hot" type to "cold" type, from Linotypes to computers, from handset headlines to high-tech.

In the old days, a typewritten story, edited and headlined, would be sent down a chute from the fifth floor city room to the fourth floor composing room. When the *Globe-Democrat* was sold to S.I. Newhouse and we moved into new quarters where there was no composing room or press room, I designed a pneumatic tube system through which our copy traveled beneath the street to the *Post-Dispatch* more than a block away.

In the composing room, the copy was set in type on the Linotype machine and arranged with other articles and ads by a make-up man on a steel table in a steel form the size of a page. Each page, a metal image of what the reader would see in his newspaper in a few hours, was then covered by a thick paper mat and pressed by the stereotyper and hardened into a semi-circular form.

This paper mat, bent to form a half circle, was put into a machine which made a lead reproduction of the mat, also in a half-circle, the exact size of a full page in the newspaper, about three quarters of an inch thick and very heavy, weighing probably forty pounds.

This half-circle lead plate was then, along with a counterpart, locked onto a press cylinder. The press cylinder was encircled by the two plates. Each single turn of the press cylinder or roller then printed two pages of the newspaper. Obviously, if we were running a forty-page paper, forty of these half-cylinder plates were cast and mounted on twenty press rollers to print an edition of the paper. Each press roller accommodated two plates, or two pages, of the paper.

Each press was designed to run a paper of up to sixty-four pages at the rate of 50,000 papers per hour. Because of the start-up time, when the press starts slowly, and the stop time, when the press slows down gradually, the press rarely met its 50,000-per-hour rating, usually printing more like 35,000 or 40,000 in that time. Our final press run each day was about 200,000 copies. We started at 12:30 A.M. and the run had to be completed by 3 A.M. We usually ran three presses but we preferred to stay with two. At the time we announced our closing we were selling about 280,000 copies per day.

It was always hot and noisy in the pressroom, and the smell of

Arteaga Photos

Ted Schafers, right, at work in the Globe-Democrat *newsroom in 1963. Dennis McCarthy is seated in upper center, with cigarette. George Killenberg, managing editor, is standing at upper right.*

molten metal permeated the air. Today, when computers transport reporters' stories from one location to another to be edited and headlined, there are no big machines. The story comes to the make-up man in a paper strip the width of the newspaper column and is pasted on stiff cardboard, then photographed.

To step into a modern composing room, you might mistake it for a business office. It is clean and quiet and the employees are neatly dressed, instead of wrapped in the stained aprons they used to wear.

But the physical atmosphere is not the only element of change. Under terms of the old union contracts, we were not permitted to move personnel from one department to another in the composing room. Some employees might be standing idle, but we had to bring in extra men to do a specific job—at time and a half. And because they might not be familiar with our composing room, their work could be less than productive.

When we got close to the deadline, we might need an extra news make-up man. If an advertising make-up man was standing there doing nothing, we could not transfer him, even temporarily, but had to bring a man in from the union hiring hall at premium time to do the work that someone else, who was already on the floor and getting paid, could have done.

Another provision of the Typographical Union's contract conceded by publishers during the 1930s was the useless production of national advertising type which was thrown away after it was produced. The printers called this "reproduction." Management called it "bogus" or "deadhorse," because the practice was so futile—and smelly—costing millions of dollars each year. I cannot imagine why the publishers then could not have been aware of the disastrous consequences of this concession.

What this meant was that when we received a national ad, say an ad from an automobile company, a food manufacturer, a drug company or a cigarette company, which had already been set and was in the form of a mat ready for casting, we were compelled to set this type and then throw it away. Also, we were required to set all this national advertising received in one year within the same year. Toward the end of this time, if we had not kept current with the "deadhorse," we had to bring in printers from the hiring hall at extra expense to set the type. We did get a modicum of relief, but not much, before we closed.

Then there was what is called "manning." Labor contracts established the number of individuals, for example, to work on a specific press relative to the hours and the number of pages in that particular edition. Color printing required more workers. If we had a four-color run of fifty-six pages straight or sixty-four pages collect, we had to have twenty-two men on each press. With three presses, that meant sixty-six men in the press room. A non-union paper operated that same press with seven men. So we were compelled to have forty-five too many. In the 1970s, they were making maybe $35,000 to $40,000 a year. When you're running every night, with forty-five men you don't need, that gets to be quite a financial burden.

In the mail room, if we wanted to stuff advertising inserts, the union required us to hire extra workers, even though it could have been handled by the regular staff.

This cost us the first reprint ever distributed in St. Louis. I went to Detroit to see the advertising executives at K Mart to try to persuade them to use ROP—Run of Paper—for their ads, rather than as an extra insert. But they insisted on the insert.

We could not afford to take their ads because it would cost us too much to stuff the insert. It went to the non-union suburban papers and we never got K Mart ads.

When the *Post-Dispatch* built its new plant in Northwest County, it didn't have a dock. This meant that papers already mechanically bundled and labeled were moved by conveyors into the trucks without a need for dockhands. But both papers, the *Post* and the *Globe,* wound up keeping dockhands on the payroll because of Teamster contract stipulations, which the union would not change. The dockhands did no work.

Ironically, after the *Globe-Democrat* shut down, the unions eliminated ninety-five percent of these counterproductive rules. The *Post-Dispatch* today does not have the burdensome manning or some of the other restrictions.

Because of changes in production costs with the introduction of cold type and computers, a newspaper today could be produced for less than half of what it cost the *Globe-Democrat* in 1983. If we had had the benefits of union concessions made after our demise we probably would still be operating.

But in the fall of 1983, it wasn't too hard to predict what was going to happen. Although we were viable, the future was not promising. Much against my feelings, I agreed with the tentative decision to close.

A few weeks after our meeting in New York, Si called to say the *Globe-Democrat* would cease publishing December 31, 1983. He felt he was not receiving an adequate return on his investment and, as disappointed as I was, I knew that his concern—and the announced closing—were necessary.

On November 7, 1983, I called the staff together to announce

It was a sad day for St. Louis and the staff when it heard that the Globe-Democrat *planned to close after December 31, 1983.*

that our last issue would come out on December 31. The shock waves reverberated. Most of those staffers had worked with pride and efficiency for years, some more than fifty years. It was always a source of great satisfaction to me to see that even though some readers, especially those who disagreed with our conservative editorial policy, considered us the "second" paper, our people believed it to be "first," and they were always joyous when they had "beaten" the *Post-Dispatch.*

They wouldn't go down without a cheer for what they and their predecessors had done. Led by George A. Killenberg, who served as city editor, managing editor, and executive editor successively, and Amour Krupnik, an assistant managing editor and graphic artist, they put together an eight-page "Final Edition," recalling the many scoops and major stories which had been published in the past years.

But eight pages could never tell the whole story. Just below the masthead were the words, "An Old Friend Says Goodbye."

But it was not to be. At least, not yet.

In line with his character, young Newhouse wanted all the i's dotted and the t's crossed. His law firm had consulted the Department of Justice in compliance with the Newspaper Preservation Act and it said there was no objection to the closing.

The Newspaper Preservation Act (NPA) had been passed by the Congress in 1970 to protect the weaker paper in a two-newspaper city. The government, as well as newspaper owners, felt it was important that two voices be heard.

The Sherman Anti-Trust Act and the Robinson-Patman Act were specters that haunted newspapers. Some owners sought to relieve themselves of unnecessary financial burdens by creating Joint Operating Agreements (JOAs), such as the *Globe-Democrat* and the *Post-Dispatch* signed in 1959. But in earlier days, they had no legal protection. The NPA gave papers the privilege of signing those JOAs without the fear of being found guilty at some later date of violating the Sherman Anti-Trust Act or Robinson-Patman.

I was privy to the lobbying for Congressional approval of the NPA. Senator Stuart Symington was one of the protagonists. He talked to many of his colleagues to seek their support.

So we were set to close our doors on December 31, 1983, but Jeffrey Gluck, a young magazine publisher from Columbia, Mo., made an offer for the paper. The Department of Justice ignored our arguments that he was not qualified, did not have adequate financing and was not sufficiently experienced in the newspaper business to handle a metropolitan paper. It ordered us to sell to Gluck. We continued publishing until he took over on February 25, 1984. Some employees opted to stay with Gluck but the majority retired or went to new jobs.

We had to provide an equitable settlement for our carriers. We agreed to pay cash for the undepreciated value of their route investments. For example, if a carrier had owned a route for two years and could depreciate the value of the route in ten years, we paid him eight-tenths of his original investment. Some carriers demanded more and the litigation went on for years.

Union contracts stipulated the conditions of our settlement with regular employees and treated the few non-union employees in the same manner as union. Severance pay for some ran as high as fifty-five weeks of full salary plus unused vacation benefits. We also provided health insurance for a period after the settlement.

On that day, for the last time, I walked out of the corner office which had been my home for nearly two decades. I moved slowly through the deserted city room, where I had started work in the early 1940s, and memories deluged me.

With Dick Ramage and Rosemarie Taylor, we opened a small office downstairs in the Illinois Terminal Building where we would clean up the tag-ends of the *Globe-Democrat's* long tenure in St. Louis and do our best to take care of all the employees.

Dick, an exemplary staffer who had served in many departments of the paper, postponed his own plans to try to find jobs for others. For many weeks, he posted job opportunities just outside the city room. Later, through my health care contacts, he was referred to the Metropolitan Hospital Association of St. Louis where he worked for some time. He is now retired.

Rosemarie, a quiet, efficient young woman, with long service in our accounting department, stayed on to help employees with health care, pensions and other employee benefits. She continued that work for the *Globe-Democrat* for the benefit of its retirees at the *Post-Dispatch,* from which she only recently retired.

Jeffrey Gluck lasted less than two years as owner-publisher. On September 26, 1985, he filed for bankruptcy, listing debts at $8 million and assets at $4.3 million. It was said that the *Globe-Democrat* issued 8,000 "insufficient funds" checks during his operation. Three months later, after his ill-fated afternoon tabloid had failed, he suspended publication of the *Globe* and the once-proud paper again was ignominiously offered for sale.

Gluck's tenure at the newspaper had underscored what we had told the government, that he did not have the experience or the talent to manage a metropolitan paper. The former *Globe* employees who stayed with him in hopes of a great revival of the paper's glory days and the new ones he hired had gone through months of bounced paychecks, unpaid health insurance and daily questioning about whether the Gluck *Globe* could possibly survive. Finally, fourteen staffers took him to court, a legal move that forced him to file for bankruptcy.

After he left St. Louis, Gluck moved from city to city, buying or starting up at least nine publications. To the best of my knowledge, none survived.

On January 16, 1986, two hopeful businessmen, John B. Prentis II and William B. Franke, bought the *Globe-Democrat*. Unfortunately, despite their ambitious plans, they had to give up within a few months. They were seeking a new plan of industrial bonds, which they contended were essential to construction of a new printing plant. But the Missouri Supreme Court refused to hear their friendly lawsuit over the bonds, and in late October, 1986, they announced that the *Globe-Democrat* would stop the presses, close its doors, and disappear forever.

Its history is now in the files at the Mercantile Library of St. Louis, located in the Thomas Jefferson Library at the University of Missouri-St. Louis, home of the *Globe* morgue.

On page one of our final edition, the ghost that never saw the light of day, were illustrations of front pages which announced major local and world news in the newspaper's 131-year history:

Opening of the Louisiana Purchase Exposition
White-Star Steamer Titanic Sinks
Germany Has Surrendered
Lindbergh Flew 1,000 Miles Through Sleet Storm
Invasion of Europe Begun
President Roosevelt Dead
War Ends, Japan Accepts
Kennedy Assassinated in Dallas
Men Walk on Moon
Nixon Resigns

Also on page one was a letter from President Ronald Reagan:

Since 1852, the newspaper has been a shining example of the very best in American journalism. Fair, honest and thorough. *The Globe-Democrat* has been an important part of our nation's history by bringing the world to its readers.

Literally millions of readers, myself included, have come to look to *The Globe-Democrat* as the bearer of that which we prize above all else—the truth. I salute all of you who have been a part of this noble part of America and join you in bidding a fond farewell to a trusted friend.

And so we wrote "30" to the *Globe-Democrat*. Its story is ended. But what a story it was!

- 2 -

AN "INDEPENDENT" NEWSPAPER

T he *Globe-Democrat* story began in the turbulent days before the Civil War when St. Louis was becoming a major city of the nation and its newspapers—nearly two dozen of them—were busy gathering political power and competing for readers with often questionable tactics.

Editors had good causes on which to hang their bowlers and derbies. St. Louis, a thriving river town, a gateway to the wilderness of the West, lay astride the philosophical line dividing north and south. Despite its Southern bloodlines, it was becoming a melange of dilettantes and frontiersmen, of free men and slaves, groomed plutocrats and grizzled pioneers, boatmen and bankers, laborers and hard-nosed Northern business men, most of whom held strong views on one side or the other of the slavery question.

Publishers were as diverse and divided as the population and their enmity was often so bitter that they fought their own civil war. Newspapers ate each other up and editors and reporters battled not only in print but with fists and guns, sometimes winning their point on the dueling ground. But loyalties and friendships were often fragile and it was not uncommon for a publisher to hire as a reporter or editor someone he had previously criticized harshly.

In this raucous atmosphere, on July 1, 1852, the *Missouri Democrat* was born. After a series of mergers, buy-outs, and changes of ownership, it would become, in 1875, the *St. Louis Globe-Democrat*.

Its founder was Francis (Frank) Blair, an ardent Free Soil proponent who believed that citizens should have the right to determine whether their state would enter the Union as slave or free. He also was an anti-slavery proponent and disciple and one-time friend of Thomas Hart Benton, the Missouri politician noted for his liberal views on the subject. A sculpture of Blair stands on the northeast corner of Forest Park, and a statue of Benton by the illustrious Harriet Hosmer is in Lafayette Park.

Their stand on human rights and dignity, while commendable, was not always based on morality—more often it was based on economics. While they condemned the enslavement of Negroes, fought for emancipation, campaigned against secession and helped elect Abraham Lincoln as president, they also endorsed "colonization," whereby freed slaves would be transported to another country, possibly Liberia, leaving Missouri to the whites.

Despite its name, the *Democrat* was accepted by readers and politicians as a Republican stronghold. (Ironically, its major competitor, the *Missouri Republican,* normally supported the Democrats.)

William McKee, the second owner of the *Democrat,* was sometimes radical, sometimes liberal, sometimes conservative, sometimes middle-of-the-road, but as its publisher for nearly a half-century, he set the editorial philosophy which existed throughout its life: to support Republican and conservative issues in general, but to avoid mere petty partisanship.

It was a lusty, two-fisted journal from its birth, a characteristic which resulted in a number of libel suits, particularly after dueling became illegal, and editors and reporters had to fight with sometimes impulsive and injudicious words instead of guns.

One of the costliest cases in the paper's history involved Sam Cook, president of the Central Missouri Trust Company in Jefferson City. On February 12, 1905, the paper printed an article by Donald C. Fitzmaurice charging that Cook, who had been secretary of state for four years, had sworn that he had contributed money to a campaign fund. Actually, the money had been given by another man, whose identity Cook wanted to hide. The article also charged Cook with selling out legislation in advance in return for political contributions.

The case went to trial and Cook was awarded $75,000 in actual damages and $75,000 in punitive damages. On appeal, the amounts were reduced by the Supreme Court of Missouri to

$25,000 on each, plus interest.

In its own defense, after another lawsuit, the paper editorialized: "There seems to be a sort of mania for suing the *Democrat* for libel. Like the suicide mania, it exists only among the weak and the despairing. It is a favorable indication of the success and enterprise by a newspaper when its enemies attempt to silence it by the gag law of libel."

That was a typical statement by the paper, always ready to do battle against its critics. Early in its history it was a political activist in print and its editors were strong leaders in party politics. But with the years, it became far more concerned with fighting for the betterment of its community.

It has sometimes been isolationist, but normally supportive of foreign policy. When E. Lansing Ray became publisher in 1918, he declared that the *Globe-Democrat* "is an independent newspaper printing the news impartially, supporting what it believes to be right, and opposing what it believes to be wrong, without regard to party politics."

The early publishers brought to St. Louis some pretty high-powered writers, and printed, according to tradition, the work of a president of the United States. Others would ultimately leave to become headliners themselves. Francis Blair became a U.S. Congressman and a Union general in the Civil War. B. Gratz Brown, an early editor, became governor of Missouri.

Henry Morton Stanley, hired in 1867, covered the Indian wars and accompanied Gen. William T. Sherman to the Indian Peace Commission. He later joined the *New York Herald* and was sent by James Gordon Bennett, Jr., to Africa on the famous expedition to find Dr. David Livingstone.

James Redpath, a fiery abolitionist scarcely out of his teens, stayed with the paper briefly before becoming commissioner of emigration for the Haitian Republic, superintendent of education in Charleston, South Carolina, and founder of the Boston Lyceum Bureau which later bore his name.

Theodore Dreiser, later a distinguished author, started work as a local reporter for $20 a week. Joseph B. McCullagh, editor from 1873 until his death on December 30, 1896, has been called "one of the really great editors of American journalism." David R. McAnally Jr., son of the noted editor of the *Christian Advocate*, left the *Globe-Democrat* after two years to become head of the

English department at the University of Missouri. He taught a course in writing which was the forerunner of the university's nationally recognized School of Journalism.

Thomas Hart Benton was elected to both the Senate and the House of Representatives. John Hay, Lincoln's private secretary and later assistant secretary of state, was a *Democrat* correspondent from Washington. Many of his articles are believed to have been written or dictated by Lincoln himself.

Until the mid-twentieth century, the *Globe-Democrat* was run by McKees, Housers, and Rays, their kinfolk and descendants, all of whom became civic leaders as well as newspaper executives. It was, for most of its life, a close-knit, family enterprise.

Charles McKee, William McKee's nephew, rose from reporter to president of the company. Simeon Ray, another nephew, was the newspaper's bookkeeper. Simeon's son, E. Lansing Ray, who started in the business office before he was twenty, became president and publisher and controlled the *Globe* until his retirement because of ill health in 1955. He died shortly thereafter.

The Houser association began when the founder, Frank Blair, hired the chubby-faced German youth, Daniel, as a messenger boy. Blessed with exceptional business sense, Daniel rose through the ranks and became a part owner. His son, Douglas B. Houser, was first vice president until his retirement in 1951. Daniel's grandson, William C. Houser (known as Chad), who had been second vice president since 1935, died in 1950.

The story has been told in great detail by Jim Allee Hart, a former Missouri newspaperman, in *The History of the* St. Louis Globe-Democrat, (University of Missouri Press, 1961.) He wrote:

> All in all, the *Globe-Democrat's* history has been a colorful one. While longevity . . . is no sure and final guarantee of worth, there is a certain dignity in traditions. And, of these, the *Globe-Democrat* has its share. The paper has many and varied claims to distinction—a century in the same family; chief abolition paper in a border State; survivor of Civil War mobbings; friend and champion of Abraham Lincoln; proving ground for such noted writers as James Redpath, Henry Morton Stanley and Theodore Dreiser; survivor of that giant skeleton-in-the closet, the Whisky Ring frauds; backer and friend of Lindbergh; promoter of transportation by water, land and air, crusader for smoke elimination; publicizer of the strange story of Patience Worth.

In his summation, Hart condensed 131 years of journalism history into one paragraph, plucking from the thousands of facts that his research had unearthed the material he thought best illustrated the personality of the *Globe-Democrat* and its leaders.

The Whisky Ring frauds, which Hart called "that giant skeleton-in-the-closet," might have killed the *Globe-Democrat* many years ago. The story broke on May 6, 1875, in a competing newspaper.

William McKee, publisher of the *Globe-Democrat*, was indicted for conspiracy to defraud the government for his connection with this group of revenue officials in St. Louis who planned to use the profits from illicit distilling operation for a political slush fund. He was sentenced to two years in jail and fined $10,000. However, he served only six months. President U. S. Grant then pardoned him and forgave the fine.

"The prediction," wrote Hart, "that if McKee were convicted the *Globe-Democrat* would no longer continue to be an influential journal proved false. The continued success of the paper could be attributed no doubt to [editor] McCullagh's skillful handling of the trial and his ability to give readers a good newspaper."

History has it that McKee served precious little of his sentence in jail. It is recorded that he spent only weekends behind bars. Each week-end, he drove in a highly-polished, stylish carriage to jail and returned to his office Monday morning.

Hart's words regarding the McKee trial coverage were another source of pride for me in the integrity of my newspaper. It did not attempt to protect McKee but handled the news in a straightforward, objective manner.

The more recent coverage of the Patience Worth story, from 1913 to the late 1920s, was equally fascinating to the readers even if far less important. That story began on a July evening in 1913 when Mrs. John Curran and a friend were relaxing with a Ouija board, a fad of the time, with a pointer that reputedly spelled out messages from the spirit world. "Patience Worth" appeared as a spirit guide.

Casper Yost, one of the *Globe's* most illustrious editors, is credited with propelling Patience Worth into national fame. While he neither accepted her spirit messages nor denounced them as a hoax, he apparently was so fascinated with the strange story that he kept it alive for years, and wrote about it in *Patience Worth, A Psychic Mystery*. Not until World War I did people begin to forget

Patience, according to Hart, and by 1928 she "faded entirely from the pages of the *Globe-Democrat*."

I was gratified to see Hart spotlight E. Lansing Ray's tremendous contribution to St. Louis's emergence as a center of air transportation in the early days of aviation. Ray, whom I greatly admired, is remembered especially for a decision which showed the *Globe-Democrat* as a newspaper concerned not only about its immediate community but about the world. He was one of the six sponsors of Lindbergh's epoch-making flight from New York to Paris, where he landed on May 21, 1927, at 10:30 P.M. He had left New York on May 20 at 7:15 A.M. Ray had sufficient interest in it to commit money, as well as enthusiasm. The entire project, including a new plane designed by Lindbergh, cost only $18,000.

The *Post-Dispatch*, incidentally, turned down Lindbergh's quest for sponsorship. His boss, Frank Robertson, had suggested that he go to the afternoon paper to ask for assistance. An editor, according to Lindbergh, declared that the paper "wouldn't think of taking part in such a hazardous flight. We have our reputation to consider. We couldn't possibly be associated with such a venture."

But Ray did support the young, adventurous Lindy. Had I been in his place, I would have done the same thing. The flight was an obvious precursor to the development of a vital part of our economy. The world was trying to achieve this. Without the backing of Ray and other civic leaders, Lindbergh might not have raised the funds for his venture.

The 1920s were exciting years not only in aviation but in every aspect of American life. St. Louis was growing fast. Skyscrapers were changing its skyline and suburbs were transforming its landscape. The stock market was shooting upward turning some investors into instant—and temporary—millionaires. Radio (to the dismay of pessimistic print journalists) had become big business and a new medium for advertising.

The *Globe-Democrat* was keeping pace. By the end of the decade, Lansing Ray had decided that that the paper's growth demanded larger and better quarters. The northeast corner of Twelfth Street (now Tucker) and Franklin—present home of the *Post-Dispatch*—was chosen as the site and the building was completed in 1930.

Moving into its new home, it was soon to face, with the rest of

St. Louis Mercantile Library

St. Louisans awakened on Sunday morning, May 22, 1927, to read of the epochal flight of Charles A. Lindbergh—one of the most dramatic feats in the history of aviation.

the country, the Great Depression. Circulation dropped and staffers were laid off. But the *Globe* was generous in its efforts to relieve the plight of the unemployed throughout St. Louis. It sponsored a wrestling match and a Cardinal-Browns game which raised more than $62,000. It also supported a $4.6 million bond issue as a relief measure.

By the decade's end, the worst of the depression was over, but it would be replaced by world war and its dramatic changes in our American way of life.

And this is when I arrived in St. Louis to begin what would become a lifetime professional career.

- 3 -

THE FRONT PAGE

The Great Depression was ending and although we didn't know it, World War II was soon to begin. I had married Nora Kelly in Chicago. She and I knew only that we were beginning a new chapter of our lives on that winter day in 1939 when we drove through a snowstorm into St. Louis and down Twelfth Street, into the neighborhood that would become my professional home for the next half-century.

I didn't realize that would happen, either. I hadn't come to St. Louis to get into the newspaper business. I had resigned from the *Chicago Examiner* to be an architectural representative for Pratt & Lambert, a paint manufacturing company. But a year later, when an extraordinary teacher and friend, the Rev. Edward Dowling, S.J., suggested I apply to the *Globe-Democrat*, I jumped at the chance. I was hired as a reporter and rewrite man, taking information over the telephone from beat reporters and turning it into stories.

I had always wanted to be either a newspaper man or a lawyer. I had left law school at Loyola University to take the St. Louis job. I had been an editor of the student paper, the *Loyola News*, and loved it.

I don't know how printers' ink got into my bloodstream. I was very close to my parents and grandparents and I was given, in addition to love and support, an exceptional education and high standards of behavior. But no one before me, to my knowledge, had been a journalist. I don't believe my father fully accepted my choice of a newspaper career until late in his life.

I am grateful beyond my ability to express it for the education they provided for me. Without that, I would not have been able to handle the great good fortune which befell me.

My mother, Mae, was the only child of Marguerite Johnston Duncan and Alexander Hood Duncan. My grandmother was said to have been the first non-Indian child born in the area around Humboldt, Iowa. In the 1840s or 1850s, her parents had migrated from Pennsylvania to Humboldt by horse and wagon, among the first three families to settle in Humboldt.

My maternal grandmother, Maggie Johnston, was born in this log cabin at Humboldt, Iowa, perhaps the first non-Indian child born in north-central Iowa.

My grandfather somehow found his way from Canada to Humboldt, where he married my grandmother and became a furniture store owner, a funeral parlor owner, a banker, and a farmer. He was a wise, gentle and compassionate man, and I know that among the things I learned from him, the best was charity.

A few years after my birth in Humboldt on April 12, 1912— two days before the *Titanic* sank—my parents moved to Tulsa,

Okla., where my brother, Bill, was born. My sister, Virginia, and I spent every summer in Humboldt where I worked as a farm-hand and played in the log cabin in which my grandmother was born. She told us about the Sioux Indians who stopped at the cabin for food when they walked along a nearby trail. I am proud that both my grandmother and my mother finished college, for this was an era when few women went past high school, if that far. Grandmother graduated from Humboldt College and Mother from Rockford College in Rockford, Ill.

There was virtually no mechanized farm equipment in my time. Even tractors were rare on those Iowa farms. We used teams of horses to cultivate the fields and pull the grain wagons and hay wagons. We worked in the field pitching bundles of oats at thresh-ing time. The lessons I learned from farm work have lasted throughout my life.

I spent some of my boyhood summers working in my grand-father's funeral home. It was a thrill to drive the ambulance, but pretty sobering to drive the hearse or go with him to pick up the body of a deceased person.

My father, Peter William, was brought to the United States from Germany by his mother, my Grandmother Bauman. He was only seven. A widow, she settled her family in Sheboygan, Wis. I will never cease to be impressed by her courage—a penni-less widow who alone brought nine children to America, steer-age, from Rimbach, Bavaria.

My father, eager for an education, entered a seminary for Ro-man Catholic priests. After graduation at the college level, he left the seminary to go to work. He sold furniture, sometimes travel-ing by horse and buggy. His territory included Iowa and it was at my grandfather's furniture store that he met my mother. They married and my father was Grandfather's business partner for a year or two before moving to Tulsa.

In that rapidly growing city, he opened a store on Main Street, selling fine art objects and home furnishings. I attended Lincoln, Lee, and Horace Mann public schools, but I learned one of the most important lessons of my life outside the classroom.

That lesson was an abiding belief in the dignity of all human beings. It was shaped, I am sure, by one of our nation's worst race riots in 1921 in Tulsa.

My school at that time, Lincoln, stood on the top of a small hill

The Bauman family posed for this studio shot in August 1925. From left: my parents, Mae and Peter Bauman, my grandfather Alexander Hood Duncan, with me (standing), my brother Bill (in front), my grandmother Maggie Duncan, and my sister Virginia.

in central east Tulsa. I remember standing on the school grounds watching as smoke and flames rose into the sky in north Tulsa. I didn't really understand what was happening, but I learned when I got home that whites had conducted a murderous rampage the previous night against the black population, which lived in a small, segregated community north of downtown. White gangs burned the entire area to the ground and indiscriminately shot and killed or wounded perhaps hundreds of black residents. The next day, police rounded up every black person they could find and herded them into a ballpark where they were kept for several days. Public officials could not agree on the number of dead and wounded. Estimates varied from eight to ten to 200. Most believe the 200 figure.

My parents had employed a black couple at our home and when the trouble began, my father hid them in the basement until they could walk on the street without fear.

In 1926 we moved to Chicago where I attended Loyola Academy, a Jesuit high school; Loyola University for liberal arts; and Loyola's law school. At college, I was a member of the track team and my abhorrence of racial prejudice, which had begun in Tulsa, was strengthened when I witnessed the treatment then of black athletes who were not permitted to stay with us, their teammates, at our hotels, or eat in the same dining room. (In a later chapter, I recall how these experiences were translated into editorial policies on the *Globe-Democrat*.)

I had enjoyed working on the student newspaper so much that I thought it would be great to write for a Chicago metropolitan daily. But getting a foot in the door wasn't easy. I applied, but this was the 1930s and every city editor gave me pretty much the same answer. "Why the hell should we employ you? We've got people we laid off three years ago we want to rehire first."

Well, I finally made it. Around 1934, I joined the *Chicago Examiner,* the morning Hearst paper, as a reporter. In those days, very few reporters wrote their own stories. We phoned them in to a rewrite person who would take the information and write the story, occasionally with the reporter's byline. It might have been safer at a desk than out on the firing line.

My city editor was a guy named Harry Romanoff, a short man, very heavy, exceedingly imaginative. He and a man named Harry Reutlinger, city editor of the afternoon Hearst paper, the *American,* are two legends of the newspaper business. They inspired a lot of the action in the play and movie, *The Front Page.*

In the newspaper business, when you walk into the office, you never know whom you will meet or what stories you will cover. As a generalist, I had to be prepared for any breaking news or any assignment from the city desk.

One day, Harry Romanoff sent me out to interview D. K. Stevenson, the former Grand Dragon of the Ku Klux Klan, a prisoner doing life in the Indiana State penitentiary for murdering his secretary while traveling on a train from Indiana to Washington, D.C.

Stevenson had talked to Romanoff on the phone some time

earlier and convinced him he should be interviewed. He said he had invented a new way to generate electricity.

I interviewed Stevenson alone in a small room in the penitentiary. He put a small device about four inches in diameter and five or six inches high on a table between us. There was no screen separating the two of us.

He pulled a small wattage light bulb from his pocket and screwed it into a socket at the top of this columnar device. The bulb lighted and burned steadily.

There was no convenient way to open the base and he said he wouldn't let me take it apart anyway. And he would not let me take the instrument with me. There was no way I could discover the source of the electric current sitting with him in the interview room. Obviously the source could have been, and probably was, a battery. I ended the interview and we did not use the story.

This experience brought back another ugly memory of my boyhood in Tulsa when I watched members of the Ku Klux Klan march through the city streets clad in their trademark white sheets. These demonstrations occurred several times a week and spreading such fear that Catholics—a minority in the Oklahoma population—were often reluctant to admit to their religious faith. I think the sight of these bigoted men helped give me a lifelong sensitivity to mistreatment of minorities throughout our society.

As an adult, I certainly wasn't afraid of William Randolph Hearst, but in that depression-time job which paid less than $20 a week, I could sense the great power that he displayed at his newspaper. He used to come through the office occasionally and the rumor was that after his visit, there would always be people fired. I'm glad to say he never fired me, probably because I wasn't around to be pointed out. I was out on assignment. The Hearst papers' treament of newsmen was one of the precipitators in the formation of the American Newspaper Guild, a reporters' union.

I did have some exciting experiences. One day, a man killed his girlfriend and then himself. Romanoff sent me out to the man's home to get a picture. His wife was there and I told her I was from the coroner's office and needed some pictures to identify the victims. She was showing me an album when the phone rang and I heard her say, "Your man is here right now." It was the damned *Tribune* calling saying *they* were from the coroner's office. I just picked up the album and walked out.

The young reporter in 1935

Another time there was a suicide in a Chicago Loop office building on a Sunday. Police sealed off the building. I called Romanoff and said, "I can't get in. They've locked the building." "Well," he said, "either get in or don't come back."

I made it somehow. That was the city editor's attitude in those days and, believe me, that was some motivation to get a job done.

There was another murder and suicide, and again I was sent to get pictures. I started to jimmy a back porch window of the apartment where I thought the victim had lived, but I found out I was at the wrong damn apartment. A man came to the door. He said, "Oh, I have a key to that other apartment." He let me in and I got the picture.

Fortunately, I never got arrested. It's a wonder I lived through it.

Covering sitdown strikes in the 1930s was pretty hazardous. One was in south Chicago at the Republic Steel Co. in May 1937. That's where I met Harold Gibbons, the labor leader, who later moved to St. Louis and became a good friend. At that time, he was with the CIO Steel Workers, and he was the boss of that strike.

One morning when everything was quiet, he told me that he and the strikers would take over the plant the next day and sit down in it. The police learned about this also. The next day I was standing with the police commander in the middle of a long line of police that crossed a huge field in front of the plant. Out of the distance came a great gang of people, several hundred. They walked up to the police and had an argument and all of a sudden rocks, bricks, and two-by-fours studded with protruding nails started coming through the air from the strikers. The police began to shoot. Piles of the injured were all over the place. I didn't know what to do because I didn't belong to either side and couldn't find safety anywhere. I was right in the middle.

I called Romanoff and he said, "How many were killed and how many were wounded?" I said I didn't know. "Well, dammit," he said, "find out."

Somehow, I did. Don't ask me how. About six were killed and scores were injured.

In north Chicago, Fansteel Metallurgical Co. workers struck and seized the plant in February 1937. The owners tried to get their property back, but the strikers threw bricks and pieces of equipment and everything else they could get their hands on out the windows to hit the police when they tried to get in the four-story building.

The prosecuting attorney had an idea. He rigged up a Trojan horse, a tower on wheels, three or four stories tall, big enough to allow six or eight men on each story. They rolled it up to a series of windows and the police piled out, climbing through the windows into the factory, and arrested the strikers. It took weeks to design and build, but it worked.

Martin Durkin, the secretary of labor for Illinois, who later became secretary of labor in the Nixon administration, had been assigned by the governor to solve the labor trouble. Every day, Durkin would exchange telegrams with the governor.

There were a number of reporters at Durkin's hotel headquarters in north Chicago. He wouldn't tell us what was in the telegrams. So we devised a plan.

We drew straws and we took turns standing at the elevator door. When a Western Union boy came with a wire, we would say we were the labor director's assistant and he would give one of us the telegram. We would read it and then slip it under Durkin's door. When he found out what we were doing, he raised hell, to no avail, and we got our story.

Another strike I covered was the strike of the Chicago Yellow Cab drivers, led, at least in part, by a man named Dominic Abatta. This was following President Roosevelt's successful promotion of the Wagner Act, comprehensive legislation to protect the rights of organized labor.

The cab company management was tough and aggressive. It hired drivers for their idle cabs, which wasn't hard to do in those depression days. The union did its best to prevent daily operation.

For a day or two, news of the strike was sparse. Romanoff chided me and ordered me to dig up a story.

I called Dominic to push him for some news and he asked me to meet him on the corner of Madison and Halstead in an hour. Soon after I got there, a large black limousine pulled up. Dominic asked me to get in and I did, albeit it with some reluctance knowing of the hoodlum operations in Chicago in those days and the criminal influences in the Yellow Cab union. We drove a short distance to an area where a large apartment project was being built. There were a lot of basements for which the walls had been poured but there was no upper structure.

Four or five men got out of the limousine, including Dominic, a photographer, and me. Thereupon one of the strikers got in a Yellow Cab which had been stolen and parked nearby. He drove it into an open basement, got out, poured gasoline over it, and set it on fire. The photographer took a great picture and I had a firsthand account of the initial violence in the strike. Within a few days, strikers began pushing cabs into the Chicago River.

The chief official of the Yellow Cab Company was named Hogan. He was a tough, knowledgeable businessman with a lot of experience running the company. Within a few days of this incident, he negotiated a settlement with the union and normal cab service resumed.

One of the most sensational cases I worked on was the case of Robert Irwin of New York. He suspected that his girlfriend, an artist's model, planned to leave him and became furious. He killed not only Veronica, but also her mother and a roomer in the house. Then he disappeared.

After a week, he showed up in Chicago and called the *Herald Examiner*. Romanoff talked him into surrendering to us. I suspect we paid him a little money, although we didn't do that often. It was Saturday morning and there was a helluva lot of confusion in the office. A young reporter just doesn't walk up to a city editor and ask him what he's doing or what's going on.

Irwin told Romanoff he would be on the steps of the Art Institute on Michigan Ave., wearing a straw hat and carrying a straw suitcase. Romanoff sent Austin O'Malley, an old-time reporter, over to get him and bring him to the paper. O'Malley did so.

When they got there, Romanoff talked to him for several hours, then Romanoff told me I was to be Irwin's caretaker. I was to walk him over to the Morrison Hotel, about three blocks east of the office on Madison and stay in the room with him for a few days.

I said, "What the hell, I can't keep him from running away if he wants to."

He said, "Don't worry. I will have truck drivers there to help you."

In those days a lot of the truck drivers had reputations as hoodlums and several of these big, burly guys walked over with us to the Morrison. I stayed with Irwin in the hotel for about four days. Each day, we got more of his story out of him. We ran the confession in serial fashion, one installment every day.

Meanwhile, the *Daily News* was going insane. They couldn't find Irwin so they could talk to him. Then the *Tribune* induced the police to go to our office and demand that we release Irwin. They were within their rights,

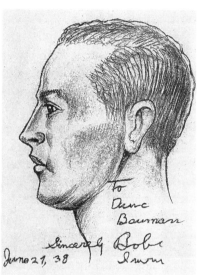

Irwin's sketch of me

of course, but Romanoff said he didn't know anything about him.

In the end, we hired a plane and flew him to New York to surrender him to the police. Actually he was a very pleasant guy. He even drew my picture. I still have it framed in my den.

In those days, the city editor, men like Romanoff, Reutlinger, and Stanley Walker of the *New York World* exerted a lot of power and they were audacious in making decisions to help promote their papers.

Reutlinger became known as the "saviour" of the Dionne quintuplets. That multiple birth in Canada made major headlines in 1934. Reutlinger got in touch with the doctor, Allen Dafoe, and promised to provide needed incubators for the infants if Dafoe would influence the parents to give the Hearst syndicate exclusive coverage. Reutlinger sent the incubators and tied up the parents for Hearst.

The *Globe-Democrat*, of course, was a radically different atmosphere. Not so much yelling or swearing at reporters. It was more like an extended family and we all got along well together. But I suppose I brought a little of my Hearst spirit to St. Louis.

One Christmas, we got word that a dental student had killed his two-month-old baby with an axe. I knew this was a helluva story. So I told Bob Smith, a reporter, to go out and get a picture of the baby. He called and said he couldn't get into the house. I did what I had been taught to do. I told him, "You get in that house, period."

So he climbed through a French door and going in, knocked down the Christmas tree, but he came back with a shoebox full of pictures. We made our selections, then I said, "Take the box back and put the tree back up."

When I started to work at the *Globe,* the riverfront was still undeveloped, downtown was lively and the streets were crowded during the day. Most of the main offices, the banks and theaters, the three big department stores—Famous-Barr, Stix, Baer & Fuller and Scruggs-Vandervoort-Barney, as well as the smaller stores—were concentrated between Broadway and 12th and between Market and Delmar. But we didn't have night-time shopping hours and practically everyone had gone home by the time I got off work in the middle of the night. The streetcars, some yellow and some red, ran all over town twenty-four hours a day. I would board one at three in the morning at Twelfth and Pine to go home. Nora and I lived for a time at the Roosevelt Hotel, then moved to 6208 Rosebury.

I also remember the coal smoke and the dark skies, sometimes at high noon. This was a civic problem that the *Globe* would eventually take the lead in solving.

I had decided I would go back to law school, so I was attending classes at Washington University. I worked from about 6 P.M. to 3 A.M., slept for a few hours, got up to go to class, came home for another two or three hours of sleep, then went to the office.

It was hard to find a place downtown to eat dinner at 8:30 or so. Most places closed early. If we could get away in time, some of us would go to Miss Hulling's Cafeteria or to Pope's on Washington Ave., or maybe to the Bismarck on Twelfth where we could get a dinner for thirty-five cents.

St. Louis couldn't have been more cordial to Nora and me,

two young carpetbaggers. We enjoyed every day of our lives in St. Louis and at the *Globe-Democrat*. Nora had been a statistician at Montgomery Ward in Chicago during our married life there, but she didn't work in St. Louis. Instead, she became active in a number of civic endeavors, including the Daughters of Charity from whose school she had graduated in Chicago, St. Vincent's Hospital, St. Anne's Home, St. Louis Heart Association and St. Mary's Special School.

My life in St. Louis was inestimably enriched by Nora, who patiently and encouragingly stood by me all the way as I moved from reporter to publisher. She accepted without complaint my strange schedule of work and law school and, when I became publisher and had an opportunity to travel and meet distinguished state and national leaders, she happily accompanied me and joined in the proceedings. Nora died February 12, 1990, after fifty-two years of marriage.

Two years later, I married the former Lucy Hencke Hume. Nora and I never had children. When I married Lucy, I got four— Ted, David, Linda, and Douglas, six grandchildren and two great-grandchildren.

Even though these are our retirement years, Lucy, too, takes a great interest in my activities and still clings loyally to the *Globe* where her late husband, Fred, was a city hall reporter. After leaving the paper he was secretary to Mayors Al Kaufmann and Joseph Darst. Their son, David, was the *Globe's* promotion manager.

As I look back over the years, I continue to respect the law as a career. It was exceptionally helpful to combine the law background with my newspaper work. As a graduate of Washington University School of Law, I retain my deep, deep confidence in the law and in the legal profession and have never given up my license to practice.

But I really believe that God was with me when I decided to stay with journalism.

- 4 -

TRANSITION

In the course of our lives, certain events are so shocking that we remember forever where we were or what we were doing when we heard the news. We may forget many details of the event itself, but we can recall immediately the moment we heard it on radio or from a television bulletin or in the newspaper carrier's voice as he loudly peddled an "extra."

I remember as a young man listening to the radio with my father in our home in Wilmette on a Sunday afternoon in 1933 when President Roosevelt announced that all of the nation's banks would be closed on Monday and remain closed until their financial stability was assured. This was in the depth of the depression when depositors were initiating runs on banks to withdraw their money, even the solvent ones. President Roosevelt took the drastic action of closing all banks to save the stable institutions. Not even the most solvent bank can withstand a demand by all of its depositors for all their money at one time, since the most cash that any bank has on hand is only a small percentage of its total assets.

I remember another Sunday afternoon, December 7, 1941, not too many months after I had joined the *Globe-Democrat.* I was listening to the radio as I was preparing to go to work. Suddenly, a bulletin was broadcast. President Roosevelt again was on the air, this time to announce the attack on Pearl Harbor by the Japanese. I hurried to the office where the staff was hustling to prepare a special early edition.

An editorial in that edition read, in part:

> It is a stunning and ghastly act to undertake a major war. Only with the deepest reluctance and realistic foreboding does this country take up arms—yet we will do so with the staunchest confidence, grim and courageous acceptance of duty and an impregnable will for victory.

Of course, we had been long been covering the atrocities of Hitler's warmongering in Europe. As our final edition stated:

"From the time of the proclamation of the Rome-Berlin axis in 1936, the *Globe-Democrat* brought its readers full coverage of the European conflict, often printing 'extras' for such events as the declaration of war by Italy and Greece."

Jim Allee Hart wrote in *A History of the* Globe-Democrat, "By 1939 editorial comment was frequent and partisan. The promises of 'der Fuehrer' were not to be trusted. He was a Nazi madman riding far toward new horizons, and eventually he would be challenged."

Many St. Louisans almost scoffed at the idea that Japan, that faraway land we knew so little about, could think of conquering the United States. Some said it would all be over in a couple of weeks. How foolishly optimistic we were.

Men in the newsroom began to think of enlistment or the draft. I had been taking flying lessons, had my pilot's license and tried twice to enlist in the Army Air Corps. Both times, I was turned down because of a nagging back problem. I flew reporters and photographers on out-of-town assignments occasionally. I still have my license and was flying until a few years before I retired.

Meanwhile, there was a paper to run and we said good-bye to many of our valuable staffers. By this time, I was on the city desk and, as night city editor, I made many of the late decisions about how to play the news. We tried to keep a balance between the good and the bad, and between what was going on in Europe and the Pacific and what was happening at home.

Lansing Ray did not assign staff correspondents to the war zones but some of the staff menbers in the service sent in reports. Larry Schulenberg reported from Iwo Jima, and Justin L. Faherty covered the founding of the United Nations in San Francisco in 1945.

One of the most shocking wartime tragedies occurred right here in St. Louis on another Sunday afternoon, August 1, 1943.

As more than 5,000 watched in horror, a St. Louis-made glider, carrying Mayor William Dee Becker and eight other St. Louis dignitaries and military men crashed on a test flight at Lambert Field. All aboard were killed. Becker's death catapulted Aloys P. Kaufmann, president of the board of aldermen, into the mayor's office. *Globe* photographer Jack Zehrt's dramatic picture of the falling glider with one wing broken off was published throughout the country.

During and just after the war, we faced other major problems at home. In 1944 the "flyboys" in the press room went on a three-day strike and, because the pressmen wouldn't cross the picket line, the paper was not printed for the first time in its history.

The following year, the newspaper's home delivery carriers went on a strike lasting twenty-two days. Ray also faced the financial problem of a sharp rise in the price of paper from $65 a ton to $93 a ton two years later.

With the death of the famed *Globe* managing editor, Joseph McAuliffe, in 1941, Lon M. Burrowes had been promoted to replace him. Burrowes and Louis LaCoss, who won a Pulitzer Prize for a 1951 editorial "The Low Estate of Public Morals," were responsible for editorial policies regarding the war and our national leadership. We supported the war effort with all our editorial power, but we often questioned the actions of Presidents Roosevelt and Truman and, with our conservative and Republican heritage, went after both of them with angry criticism. Our editorials charged that Truman's "give-'em-hell" statements were beneath the dignity of his office and Roosevelt was even accused of being a Communist.

However, when Roosevelt died in 1945, we had words of praise for him and support for his successor, Truman. We called Roosevelt "one of the most unusual and vivid personalities who ever flashed across the troubled horizons of a world which in his time has suffered from the plague of a corroding depression and from the most devastating war since time began." The editorial continued that he had brought into being a new United States "which, approve of him or not, will bear his imprint for ages to come." We also felt that Truman would "see us through" and "would make a go of it."

Three years later, St. Louis achieved fleeting political fame the morning after the presidential race in which Truman, seeking his first full term term, brought about one of the most famous upsets in political history by winning over Republican Tom Dewey, whom the *Globe* supported. The train taking Truman back to Washington from Kansas City stopped in St. Louis. Truman appeared on the back platform of the train waving a copy of the *Chicago Tribune* which carried a banner headline proclaiming that Dewey had been elected. Newspapers all over the country printed copies of Truman's appearance in St. Louis.

August A. ("Gussie") Busch told me that on occasions, not often, and particularly when Truman was a senator, Truman would call Gussie when he came through St. Louis and Gussie would go down to Union Station to see him. He said Truman was never reluctant to accept a token cash contribution from him.

As the war wound down in Europe, rumors came out of Europe for several days that Hitler was about to surrender. Finally about midnight one May night the Associated Press sent out an unqualified bulletin that the surrender would take place the next morning. The last edition of the *Globe* was scheduled to start its press run at 12:45 A.M., in just about forty-five minutes.

W. Ray Loomis, an older man with many years of newspaper experience, was head of the copy desk at that time of night and also the person charged with the final decision about what we would run in the paper. As night city editor, I was in charge of local news.

Loomis showed me the AP copy and asked what I thought we should do. I told him we ought to run a bulletin on page one, with a banner headline across the top of the page in 96-point type, the largest standard type face we had. He didn't agree. He said his experience had taught him never to make a decision of this magnitude and that way one would "never get in trouble."

I insisted we run it and that if we didn't I would protest the decision the next day. He ran the bulletin and, of course, it turned out to be true.

There are serious consequences for a newspaper which prints an erroneous story. No editor wants to be responsible for having done so. One of St. Louis' other papers printed an erroneous story about a Catholic priest arrested for burglary. The public distrusted the paper after that and its circulation and advertising sank to such a low that the paper had to merge with its afternoon rival in order to survive as the *Star-Times.*

The printed story does not disappear into thin air as do radio or TV comments. It remains a tangible property which can forever haunt the error maker.

The *Globe* consistently fought and sought to make our community a better place to live. It prided itself, and was loved by readers for being St. Louis' "local" paper. To me, and I'm sure to other publishers before me, news is what people talk about across the backyard fence

The paper's influence, however, didn't stop at the city or county limits or stay within the blurred boundaries of the so-called "metropolitan" area. The concerns of its publishers grew to address the problems of people wherever they lived, to work for progress across the nation and across the world, to fight against the wrong and support the right, as they perceived the wrong and the right to be.

I was not directly involved in some of those editorial decisions during the years when I was, in turn, reporter, rewrite man, assistant city editor, personnel manager and business manager. But the *Globe-Democrat* was my newspaper home for nearly a half-century and I can take pride in its achievements regardless of when they occurred or who was responsible. The publishers before me set the pattern and pace for my years in that office.

After the war, we picked up on our popular promotions, including the Golden Gloves, Soap Box Derby, Spelling Bee, and the Christmas Choral Pageant. We added more events to our sponsorship list right up until we closed.

Some fifteen or twenty years ago, several men came to my office to propose that the *Globe-Democrat* participate in the establishment of the Senior Olympics. The group included Stanley Cohen, then principal owner of Central Hardware, and Harris Frank, a leader of the Jewish community.

I said we had apprehensions because we didn't want to be responsible for paying damages for claims that the paper was contributing to the deaths of elderly people who overexerted themselves in these athletic events. Otherwise, I thought it was a natural.

They assured me that this wouldn't happen and I said if they could prove that they had adequate insurance and adequate regulations to prevent health risks we would support it. Cohen put up $10,000, the major source of financing in the first year for the Senior Olympics at the JCCA.

The *Globe-Democrat*, I'm proud to say, did support it. Today, it's a national event and hundreds of thousands of dollars are raised annually to give seniors the great opportunity to compete with their peers and display their athletic talents.

More important than supporting promotions such as these, we were a crusading paper. In his homily at a Mass for the members of the media at St. Joseph's Shrine, the Rev. Paul Reinert, S.J., former chancellor of Saint Louis University, called the *Globe-Democrat* the "conscience" of St. Louis.

We campaigned for a new master traffic control plan downtown. If I remember correctly, this was when the "walk" lights were installed, halting automobile traffic at all four sides of a busy intersection to permit pedestrians to cross in any direction, including diagonally.

In the 1950s St. Louis did not have another highway which was as dangerous as Lindbergh Boulevard, especially through the stretch north from Olive Boulevard to Natural Bridge. The *Globe's* managing editor, George A. Killenberg, led a news and editorial campaign to encourage the Missouri Highway Department to install concrete dividers on the road, separating north and south bound traffic.

For years St. Louis media carried stories of drivers and passengers being killed in head-on collisions while using Lindbergh. The Highway Department appeared to be resistant for no obvious reasons. Despite the fact it was a narrow road with many curves, and cars passing each other at high speed in opposite directions with only inches to spare, the authorities offered excuse after excuse.

A few merchants objected because they said the divider would prevent customers from making left turns to their businesses, but they ignored the obvious—that human beings were being killed. We eventually saw those dividers installed and the road widened.

We investigated and exposed corruption in the national and local offices of the Department of Internal Revenue. We campaigned for better runways at Lambert Field and advocated a city ordinance for rat control.

The *Globe* took a brief plunge into radio, although Lansing

Ray believed it was not appropriate for him, as a devoted newspaper man, to promote a competing medium. Earlier, he had bought a one-sixteenth interest in radio station KMOX which he eventually sold.

However, he did become interested in FM because of Lansing, Jr.'s, enthusiasm for that broadcast medium. He obtained approval from the Federal Communications Commission to operate an FM station and built the Globe-Democrat Tower at 12th and Cole streets. KWGD-FM went on the air in 1948 but was not successful and closed the following year.

During the 1930s and 1940s, St. Louis had three major dailies, the *Globe-Democrat*, the *Post-Dispatch* and the *Star-Times*, which, like the *Post,* was an afternoon paper. In June 1951 the *Post* bought the *Star-Times*, increasing its circulation to slightly more than the *Globe-Democrat,* which had for years led in circulation. (The *Globe* did not regain this lead until the early 1980s, when we went ahead of the *Post* in daily circulation by more than 60,000.) The *Globe* hired a number of *Star-Times* people, including the city editor, Aaron Benesch, and Carl Major, one of the outstanding newsmen of the era.

There was also a change in the *Globe* ownership. For more than fifty years, it had been in the names of a number of persons, with Lansing Ray having the controlling interest. About 1951 he bought out the other family's interest and became the sole owner.

Several of the minor shareholders had executive positions with the paper. One evening, while I was at work as night city editor, we received a call that Douglas Houser, vice president, was being held at the Newstead Avenue police station after his arrest for drunken driving. The city editor, Roy Oetter, told me to pick up our colleague and take him home.

I found him at the station. There wasn't any question about his drunken condition. I took him home and went back to work. As I left him at the door of his house, he thanked me for helping him.

My office at the *Globe* was quite close to his. From that night to the day he was bought out by Lansing Ray, probably three or four years later, he never mentioned the incident. But the day he left the paper, he came into my office and apologized at great length for his conduct and expressed his appreciation for my care-taking.

I was on the city desk when a prominent St Louis business-man was arrested for using phony medical prescriptions to buy drugs. We printed that story and I felt we had done what was right.

We didn't go all out to crucify people because they were well known. On a Saturday night in the late 1940s, I was on duty as night city editor when we got a report that a prominent Protes-tant minister, Dr. John McIvor, had been arrested for drunken driving. Oetter sent me out to the Newstead station to see him. He was loud, screaming, disturbing the whole place.

I couldn't get anything out of him that made any sense. There was no question about whether he was intoxicated, and yet he was the moral and spiritual leader of thousands of St. Louisans, a person whose moral conduct was an example to others.

What should we do? The choices, of course, were obvious, one, to print the story and two, to keep it out of the paper. If we did print it, should it be a small item or a major story on page one? I got the name of his doctor who happened to be my doctor as well. I called him and he said, yes, he knew the man could have been drunk, but it was because he had angina for which the doctor had prescribed bourbon and nitroglycerine. Oetter, Lon Burrowes, the managing editor, and I talked about this and we decided we shouldn't demean or hold up to ridicule a man of the church for what was not a calculated crime. So we ran a very small head, recording the incident.

The *Post-Dispatch* ran a full column on page one and jumped inside for another column. The next day it ran a retraction. What we did is what a newspaper should do.

I was especially proud of the *Globe-Democrat* that day. That pride would continue during the years when I was publisher, trying my best to make the right decisions.

Lansing Ray, Jr., who had come home from the war, having been awarded the Legion of Merit for his service with the Army Intelligence Corps, was named assistant publisher and secretary of the Globe-Democrat Publishing Co. However, he died shortly after his return.

Within a few years, his disheartened and elderly father, disap-pointed because family ownership was about to end, began to look for a buyer. In 1955, he found that buyer in S.I. Newhouse.

- 5 -

FIGHTING FOR ST. LOUIS
1955-1967

Before he bought the *Globe* and began visiting St. Louis at least once a month, S. I. Newhouse was something of a mystery to me. I knew him only as the head of a large media empire—eighteen daily newspapers, twenty-eight business journals, and Conde Nast magazines, which included *Vogue, Vanity Fair,* and the *New Yorker.* On one of his visits, he and I were walking through our warehouse when we spotted a penny on the concrete floor. We both leaped for it, but he got it first and held it in his hand at face level toward me and said, "Duncan, that's how I got rich."

Through the years, we developed a mutual respect. Short—just a little over five feet tall—he was unpretentious, and I doubt if the great majority of employees recognized him or even knew when he was on the premises. He was not gregarious and as far as I can remember, never went into the city room, the heart of any newspaper. He usually headed straight for the publisher's office to talk about advertising and circulation, sometimes about state politics, but never, never about news or editorial policy. In the nearly twenty years we worked together not once did he suggest or even hint at an editorial policy or indicate whom we should support in national elections.

Newhouse had a reputation of keeping his word. His first public act was to announce that Ray would continue as publisher as long as he chose to do so. He did not order a single change in the management staff of the paper. After Ray's death in October, 1955, S.I. brought Richard H. Amberg from Syracuse, New York, where he had been publisher of a Newhouse paper, to be the *Globe's* publisher. When our circulation director resigned, Newhouse sent his brother-in-law, Walter Evans, to take that post. And except for a classified ad manager those were the only executive positions he affected.

Newhouse's critics often pontificate that the new owner had little or no interest in maintaining the *Globe-Democrat* as a viable newspaper. Nothing could be more ignorant or untrue. The *Globe* was one of his favorites among his newspapers. He was determined to have a strong presence in St. Louis. If he asked me once, he asked me fifteen times, "Duncan, do you know of any Pulitzer Publishing Company shareholders who want to sell their stock? I want to buy it."

Television began its skyrocket growth immediately after World War II, particularly in St. Louis. The *Post-Dispatch* opened the first television station in the city's history, KSD-TV, Channel 5 in 1946 or 1947.

The joint operation of the *Post-Dispatch* and Channel 5 posed a threat to the *Globe*. Even the dullest human mind can understand what a lure the TV station was to an advertiser who thought if he advertised in the newspaper maybe he would be able to buy a scarce bit of time on KSD-TV.

The *Globe-Democrat's* scramble to get a TV license was lost among the hundreds of applications throughout the country. The paper thought it had friends in the Washington D.C. bureaucracy but, as it turned out, either they were not friends who wanted to help or they simply were unable to help.

In 1952, Stuart Symington, former head of Emerson Electric Co., was elected Missouri's second U.S. Senator, in part because of the *Globe-Democrat's* extensive and vigorous support. The day after the election, C. Arthur Weis, vice-president of the *Globe*, and I visited with Symington at the Statler Hotel in downtown St. Louis. We laid out our TV problem and asked for his help. Within a few months, we had our license.

Newhouse bought Channel 2 as an investment, which was permissible before passage of a federal law prohibiting major daily newspapers in the metropolitan markets from owning TV stations in the same market. When the law went into effect, Newhouse was faced with choosing between the *Globe* and Channel 2, and he decided to keep the paper.

By then, I had succeeded Amberg as publisher and Newhouse discussed this matter with me before making his decision public. He asked if I knew anyone who would be interested in buying the station. I should have been wise enough to raise the money and buy the station myself, but I was constitutionally too much of a newspaperman to even think of running a TV station.

Newhouse was never able to buy the *Post-Dispatch*, but about the time of his death, a major shareholder initiated a revolt that nearly cost the St. Louis Pulitzer family members their historical control of the paper. It was known in the business that there were about twenty Pulitzer descendants dependent on the paper for their living. The dissension arose over Joseph Pulitzer, Jr.'s policy respecting dividend payments which were, in the opinion of the other stockholders—mostly descendants—uncommonly low. After a flurry of corporate infighting the dispute was resolved.

In the first four years of the Newhouse ownership, little was changed. He began his pilgrimages to St. Louis and watched the advertising lineage and circulation with hawk-like vision.

I can tell you from experience that Newhouse poured money into the *Globe-Democrat* to help it succeed. The only time I ever heard him comment with any concern was one day in Washington, D.C., when he said to me, "Duncan, I wish I could make a little money with the *Globe*."

It is of utmost significance to note a defining distinction between the lives of the flamboyant William Randolph Hearst and S. I. Newhouse, whose career spanned the middle and latter part of the twentieth century.

Hearst began his newspaper career at the age of twenty-three in 1887 by becoming the proprietor of his father's *San Francisco Examiner*. He was bolstered by millions of dollars inherited from his father who had struck silver in the western United States. (Incidentally, Hearst's mother, Phoebe Apperson, was a Missourian.) S. I. Newhouse's parents were Jewish immigrants with no means; he started his career working in nondescript newspaper jobs.

Hearst died virtually bankrupt; S.I. died with an estate of $8 billion. Hearst even borrowed money from his mistress, the actress Marion Davies, late in his life to maintain his standard of living.

From the time I began a personal and business relationship with Newhouse in 1955, I resented the denigrating, scornful, and vindictive characterization of him by some of his fellow newspaper owners and especially by union leaders who did not even know him. Each time he came to St. Louis to meet with major department heads at the newspaper, I learned more about him.

One example of his character came to light while I was business manager at the *Globe*. I decided to review the printing contract we had with the *Post-Dispatch*. The contract contained all the conditions involved in the *Post's* responsibilities to print the *Globe-Democrat*. The basis was simple: we paid the *Post* a predetermined sum per page per day to print us. Everything was included in the per page cost. There were a few ancillary conditions, including one in which we agreed to pay the *Post* about $250,000 yearly in reimbursement for a state tax levied on newsprint. On further research I learned that this tax had been removed. It no longer existed.

I told S. I. Newhouse we ought to discontinue paying this sum to the *Post*. He said, "No. I promised to pay it. Please continue." So I continued to pay, much against my conscience.

S. I. Newhouse's character and business principles were a part of the public record after his death, when his two sons, S.I., Jr., and Donald took over the operation. In preparation for the federal estate or inheritance tax, they employed several professionals—a lawyer, an accountant, a banker, and an expert in valuing such estates. This committee recommended to the brothers that the estate file an inheritance tax return of $140 million on an $8 billion estate. The Internal Revenue Service had a different figure. It claimed a tax of $160 million. The estate objected, whereupon the IRS filed charges of misconduct and asked for $190 million, including penalties.

The issue wound up in litigation in tax court. At trial the judge announced that the IRS had an unsubstantiated case with questionable evidence and ordered the case dismissed. The estate paid the IRS its original estimate. I was proud of this vindication of the Newhouse character.

Despite his natural embrace of the system which enabled him to become an enormously wealthy and powerful man, he usually supported the Democratic party. His father had been a socialist, but early in his life, young Newhouse turned his back on that political philosophy in favor of mainstream capitalism. But he didn't push his ideas on others. Through the years, I came to admire him as a remarkably astute businessman. When I learned more of his background—he seldom talked about his personal life—that admiration grew.

Carol Felsenthal quotes Martin L. Duggan, editorial page editor, Ben Magdovitz, advertising director, and other *Globe* executives in her book, *Citizen Newhouse*, (Seven Stories Press, 1998). My name is mentioned several times and she also gives space to Aaron Benesch, our former managing editor and later head of our Washington bureau, and Walter Evans.

I was sorely disappointed in the book. Her appraisal of the family's business practices and her constant and consistently slanted criticism of S.I.—she uses the word "ruthless"—were neither accurate nor fair, and not justified. However, she brings out facts about S.I.'s boyhood and early life that make the reader appreciate his hands-on climb from poverty to prosperity, as well as his ability to build an empire brick by brick and to turn red ink into black.

"Sam, age thirteen, five feet tall, his chubby cheeks giving him the look of a boy half that age. . . became by default the head of the household," Felsenthal writes. His father—chronically ill, lacking ambition, and unable to support the family—moved out of the house. She continues:

> Although an excellent student, he quit school after the eighth grade and that summer he enrolled in a six-week course in typing, shorthand and bookkeeping at the Gaffrey School in Manhattan . . . He soon found work as an office boy with a Bayonne lawyer, police court judge, and machine politician named Hyman Lazarus whose law office was situated above the offices of a weekly newspaper called the *Bayonne Times.*
>
> Sam landed the job by proposing that he work without pay until he proved himself worthy. After four weeks he was making $2 a week for duties that included keeping the office books. He proved so adept a bookkeeper that two years later, when he was sixteen, Judge Lazarus promoted Sam to office manager of the law firm.

Had it not been for an additional chance assignment from his boss, who was part owner of the *Bayonne Times,* to manage the weak newspaper and lift it into profitability, the teenager might have followed Lazarus into a legal career. He studied at the New Jersey Law School at night, graduating in 1916, but he lost his first case, gave his client the $80 in damages he had failed to win for him in court, and left law forever.

By then, the *Bayonne Times* was so profitable that he was earning $30,000 a year. Then, in 1922 came another opportunity which was to dramatically influence his future. He and Judge Lazarus bought fifty-one percent of the *Staten Island Advance* for $98,000 and that newspaper, under the Newhouse management, also became a successful operation. Sam became a full-fledged entrepreneur. When Judge Lazarus died two years later, his youthful partner bought out his share.

He had added another half-dozen or so papers by 1955 when he bought the *Globe-Democrat*. S.I. was an exceptionally family-oriented individual, a quality stemming perhaps from his boyhood when he became the family breadwinner and employed his siblings in his enterprises. He was a strong believer in nepotism.

Sometime in the early 1960s, S.I. said to me, "Dick Amberg wants to fire Walter [Evans]. I can't stand that. Mitzi wouldn't let me come home. I want you to see that Dick does not fire Walter." Mitzi was S.I.s wife and Walter's sister.

When I thought the time was propitious, I told Dick I thought it would be better if he talked with me before firing Evans. He thought a moment, and said, "Since you're so damned fond of Evans, from here on you're his boss and I'm holding you responsible for circulation." I didn't think this was much of a solution but that's the way it was.

Amberg was a man of strong convictions, aggressive and impulsive. During most of his tenure, I was business manager, by his appointment, and Dick and I worked together in good grace. We talked every day about the paper.

In 1959, the ninety-five-day strike by the American Newspaper Guild was catastrophic. After S.I. sold the plant to the *Post-Dispatch* and we moved to the Illinois Terminal Building, we contracted with the *Post* to print the *Globe* and discontinued our Sunday edition.

I was the *Globe-Democrat* negotiator in the 1959 labor dispute which centered on the issues of whether we needed to continue the use of circulation supervisors at all, or how many. Another big issue was that of pensions. At that time, pensions were paid by the newspaper, but at the discretion of the publisher and only to those on the staff whom he chose to receive this benefit. There was no general pension program for the rank and file; not even for all executives.

About a week before the ninety-fifth day, I had a call from Harold Gibbons, then a leader in the St. Louis Teamsters Union and very close to Jimmy Hoffa. After meeting Gibbons in Chicago during the steelworkers' strike against Republic Steel, we had maintained a friendship after both of us moved to St. Louis.

Gibbons told me, "Duncan, my people are sick and tired of this strike, and if you will give me the authority, I think I can settle it for you very quickly."

Things looked pretty bleak at the time so Amberg and I decided to give him the opportunity—with a few admonitions about not giving things away. True to his word, he called a day or so later and said the strike could be settled. We went back into negotiations with the Guild, settled the pension and circulation supervisor issues, and the *Globe-Democrat* resumed publication.

Gibbons never said publicly how he induced the Guild to come to terms, but privately he told me that he had told the Guild strike committee that his membership was "sick and tired" of the strike. His members had supported the Guild by not crossing the picket line but he told the Guild that if it didn't settle within five days, he would authorize his men to come back to work, leaving the Guild out in the cold, since the other unions would follow the Teamsters back to work.

Gibbons also told me quite candidly that if that happened, he planned to organize the news department and other departments under Guild jurisdiction into a Teamster union local. His motives certainly were in his own interests, but he did settle the strike for us.

Years later, Gibbons called me to say his daughter, who had just graduated from college, was rejected for every job when she said on the application that Gibbons was her father. Most business leaders in St. Louis at the time would not get within five miles of Harold Gibbons, much less employ his daughter.

I hired her for our circulation department. She did a fine job for us, was a good employee and gave us no trouble whatsoever. She worked for a year or so, then resigned to marry.

Amberg was a very effective publisher, determined to push the paper forward. He did that very well, leaping with enthusiasm into St. Louis organizations and promoting the progress of the entire metropolitan area. He felt it was essential to the paper that he, as publisher, get involved. His first public service act when he came to St. Louis was to spearhead a campaign for the purchase of a heart-lung machine for Children's Hospital. This was a first for St. Louis, a new device critical to the development of emerging heart surgery techniques.

We all have our little quirks—perhaps they make us more human—and one of Dick's was that he could not stand stop signs. He would not stop for them. He drove through without even slowing down. Everyone in the office knew this so it was no surprise one day when he called me and said he was about to lose his driver's license and asked that I represent him in the Ladue traffic court.

I talked to a couple of officials I knew; he stood trial and was acquitted. As a result, he kept his license. I warned him that he should be an example to others and stop running stop signs. I don't know if he followed my advice.

The Amberg-Newhouse years were to become one of the most exciting and progressive chapters in the long history of the *Globe-Democrat*. We were in a new home—unfortunately much more modest than the building that Newhouse had sold to the *Post-Dispatch*—but we made the best of it and the paper continued to grow and to give much to the community.

There's no doubt that St. Louis is a better city because of the *Globe*. As early as the mid-1950s, the paper was campaigning for rehabilitation of the downtown area and this crusade led ultimately to the building of the Gateway Arch and Busch Memorial Stadium.

The *Globe* had editorialized: "What should be the throbbing, life-generating heart of our city seems afflicted with civic anemia. The district is a victim of blind complacency. Its leaders need to get off dead center, to abandon a shrugging, false conservation that is steadily, obviously eroding the sector."

The Arch is a reality partly because of the *Globe-Democrat's* campaign for federal funds. This story—and that of the *Globe's* campaign for the Poplar Street Bridge—were told in our "final edition."

Dick Amberg, his wife Janet, right, and Mrs. Sid Solomon II were photographed at the Frank Sinatra concert, which the singer dedicated to the Teamsters Union and Dismas House. Sinatra called the concert, staged on Feb. 8, 1967, the greatest of his career.

The history of the Gateway Arch goes back to the depression days of 1933 when Mayor Bernard F. Dickmann formed a civic commission to work for a Federal memorial to the Louisiana Purchase Exposition. Buildings were razed. Eero Saarinen's concept of the Arch was accepted, but nothing more was done during the post World War II and Korean conflict years.

At last, the late Richard Amberg, then *Globe* publisher, said, "Let's get going."

A series by Ray Noonan and Ted Schafers exposed the city's worsening blight and the *Globe-Democrat* hammered daily at Washington for release of promised federal money. When the financial bottleneck was broken on the Potomac, after notable work by Senator Stuart Symington, the Arch on the Mississippi became a reality.

At the same time, the *Globe-Democrat* began a long, continuing campaign for a free bridge linking Missouri and Illinois and on Oct. 8, 1959, published on the editorial page:

"One of the most exciting and stimulating events in recent years is the announcement of Governor Stratton of Illinois that Illinois concurs fully in Missouri's plans for a new Free Bridge over the Mississippi River at Poplar Street and that it will progress into the final stages of planning and preliminary step toward actual realization within the next few months. . . .

"We hope that *The Globe-Democrat* may be pardoned a word of pride in the final realization of the project which has headed our every list for civic improvement for the past three years or more."

But the editorial didn't tell the whole story of Amberg's somewhat unorthodox plan to get the bridge built.

There were only two bridges crossing the Mississippi from Illinois into downtown St. Louis, the Eads and the so-called "free" MacArthur Bridge. Both were of ancient vintage and traffic frequently was snarled at rush hour. Amberg thought it was appropriate that an additional bridge be built to accommodate the burgeoning highway systems that were being constructed, fostered by the Eisenhower administration.

So Dick invited Governor William Stratton of Illinois and Governor Jim Blair of Missouri to a dinner at the Bogey Club, with some fifty or sixty prominent St. Louisans. Each of the governors knew why he was invited and it's a great credit to Dick Amberg that he was able to get them there under the circumstances.

After dinner we assembled in the living room. Dick made a short talk about the need for this bridge and asked the two governors to stand with him at the front of the room. He asked each to pledge that he would work with the other with the powers of their respective states to initiate and build the project. To their credit, they made this pledge and this is how—with the power and persuasion of the *Globe-Democrat*—the Poplar Street Bridge became a reality and, indeed, an asset to the movement of traffic in the St. Louis area.

In addition to his concern for downtown, Amberg also spearheaded a crusade for highway safety and improvement of highways on the city's periphery. The newspaper played a major role in the city's decision to remove dingy structures from Mill Creek Valley so that the area could be opened up to business and industry.

One of the campaigns Amberg organized in the *Globe* was picked up by many others in the state—except bankers. The campaign was to get a statute passed which would require the state to place its money for deposit in banks according to the interest rate that banks would pay the state for that money. State deposits amounted to hundreds of millions of dollars a year after tax collection time, when tax receipts were deposited in banks paying no interest on the deposits. All other deposits bore interest. This was a real bonanza to banks. Dick proposed that banks bid for the money, the bid containing an offer to pay the specific interest rate for a specific period of time on the state's deposit. Banks offering the best rates would receive the state deposit.

The *Globe-Democrat* was successful in that campaign, and banks now bid for state money. As a result of the paper's aggressive editorial campaign, the legislature voted that the money would go to the highest bidders, would go into interest-bearing accounts, and had to be invested in Missouri. It is no longer a matter of political favoritism costing the state millions. In the first year, 1959, the state collected $1.538 million in interest.

In 1959 Ted Schafers and Louis Kohlmeier won a National Headliners award for their series showing how bad rules regarding labor and government bureaucracy were "wrecking" the railroad industry.

In an important aviation story, Schafers disclosed that McDonnell Douglas had built twenty-one Demon fighter planes for the U.S. Navy, but the Navy refused to fly them off the company's ramps at Lambert Field, claiming they were dangerous because of underpowered Westinghouse engines.

The disclosures resulted in House and Senate investigations because $300 million in tax money was involved. Some of the planes were saved by installing General Motors replacement engines, but fourteen were junked for salvage.

"Even though my stories, which won a National Headliners Award for 'outstanding public service by a newspaper,' had made clear that this financial fiasco was not the fault of McDonnell Aircraft Co., James S. McDonnell, the company's founder, was unhappy over the publicity," Schafers wrote in the "Final Edition."

"He told our Washington Bureau chief, Ed O'Brien, 'I don't want to talk to any *Globe-Democrat* reporter again, especially Ted Schafers.' (We later became fast friends.)"

Readers may have forgotten many of the other things the *Globe-Democrat* did to help people, especially those in desperate need of advocates.

A series written by Marguerite Shepard about conditions at state mental hospitals resulted in much-needed improvements in the mental health care system. Citizens were not getting the care they were entitled to. Shepard was one of the most diligent diggers for information, industrious, tireless and dogged. Over a span of two or three years, we ran many, many of her stories on unconscionably deplorable conditions in the mental health facilities of Missouri.

Spurred by these stories, the legislature and governor acted to correct these conditions and ultimately, a mental health director, Paul Ahr, was brought in and did an exemplary job of pulling the state's treatment of the mentally ill out of the mud.

Another series on the lack of service for the mentally ill after state money had been cut off resulted in a new program by the Department of Mental Health to aid those who had been released from institutions with no place to go.

Stories on the plight of retarded children in the state brought about appointment of a legislative committee to study existing facilities and consider more adequate institutional care.

Urban renewal and neighborhood preservation can be traced back to a 1957 *Globe-Democrat* campaign to inform people about a bill long buried in an aldermanic committee. The bill was designed to tighten safety regulations for rooming houses and bring more rooming houses under city inspection. It was opposed by rooming house proprietors.

Because the spread of rooming houses was causing neighborhood blight, the newspaper surveyed neighborhood association officers on the need for a model rooming house law. A series of news articles and editorials on the survey brought about passage of the bill in the board of alderman by an overwhelming vote of twenty-six to one.

The ghost of lawsuits for libel haunts every newspaper publisher and as hard as he and his editors try to make certain of accuracy and protection of individual rights in accordance with the law, there are unfortunate errors that take a well-meaning paper into court. Even if there has been no libel, a person can sue for libel damages if he wants to hire a lawyer and pay the expenses. It is costly to defend a libel suit but that is an imperative. To settle libel suits is an inducement for lawyers to file them in anticipation of a quick settlement.

I also believed that printing a correction when we were wrong and a correction had been requested was a contribution to the integrity of the newspaper. If we admitted our errors, the potential litigator would have to realize that when we refused a retraction or apology we were certain of the correctness of our story and prospects of winning a libel suit were dim.

A world renowned scientist and Nobel Prize winner, Linus Pauling, was one of numerous individuals who were questioned on their political views in a Congressional hearing. When Pauling refused to answer certain questions, the committee voted to seek a contempt citation. Amberg wrote an editorial criticizing Pauling, stating that he had been found guilty of contempt, whereas the committee had only voted to seek the citation.

Pauling sued the paper for $300,000. Like other major newspapers, we carried insurance for libel. The morning we went to trial in the federal court in St. Louis, our attorney, Lon Hocker, received a phone call from our insurance company stating that the firm had negotiated a possible settlement for $25,000 and asking if we could accept it.

I called Newhouse from a phone in the hallway just outside the courtroom and explained this settlement, adding that Hocker and I recommended not accepting it. Once a newspaper has a reputation for settling libel suits, lawyers come out of cracks in the wall to file such suits, hoping to get a quick settlement and make some money. Newhouse agreed we shouldn't settle.

In accordance with custom, the insurance company gave a check payable to the *Globe-Democrat* for $25,000 and we proceeded with the trial at our financial risk. If there were a judgment for Pauling for whatever sum, the newspaper would be liable for the entire amount of the judgment. In effect, the insurance company bought out its obligation to defend the paper in this libel case. But Hocker won the suit.

Pauling got nothing. But neither did the *Globe-Democrat* because Hocker's fee was substantial.

Another lawsuit stemmed from a story we ran about arguments in the board of aldermen, whether the board would appropriate funds to City Hospital to pay for abortions for indigent women. During the debate, a member of the board stated that she had had an abortion and she saw no reason why other women should not be able to have abortions at public expense.

It so happened that there were several women on the board of aldermen and our story named the wrong one as the one who had made the statement. The one whose name we used sued us for libel and offered to settle for $750. Again we refused to settle and went to trial, but we lost. However, on appeal, we won.

In another case, we had employed as a reporter a young man who had studied for the priesthood in a Jesuit seminary. We assumed that as the beneficiary of an exceptionally thorough education he would prove to be a fine person, well-educated, intelligent and of good character. Indeed, he was, but, unfortunately, he made a costly mistake in reporting one case.

Assigned to the Civil Courts Building, he was covering a trial in which a doctor was a defendant in a malpractice suit. The jury brought in a verdict for the doctor. When the reporter turned the copy in to the city desk, somehow he mistakenly attributed victory to the plaintiff against the doctor.

The doctor sued us for $90,000. Even though we established that he had not incurred any damages as a result of the mistake, real or fancied, we lost the case and we paid.

Dick liked to write editorials at home on Sunday afternoons. One was about legislators living in their districts. Mike Kinney was a Missouri senator who lived in Richmond Heights and represented a downtown district. He had been in office over fifty years, serving longer as a state stenator than anyone else in America. Dick wrote an editorial saying every legislator except Kinney should live in his own district. I thought it was outrageous and told him so. He replied that I wasn't the only one who thought so. His wife, Janet, did so too.

I'll say this for Dick. He didn't back off from a fight which was fine with me. A publisher cannot be timid whether dealing with the staff or with others. Admittedly, his impulsiveness resulted in several libel suits, but we agreed that even if we made mistakes, and we certainly weren't trying to crucify anyone, we at least had the courage to speak up.

One editorial by Amberg got us into real trouble, although in the end he was vindicated. A nurse was walking home from a late shift at Lutheran Hospital when a young man grabbed her purse and, in doing so, knocked her to the sidewalk and she was fatally injured.

Dick learned that the young man had several brothers and sisters and that one of the brothers was in the penitentiary for another crime. He wrote an editorial in which he said that women like the mother of the purse snatcher and his brother should be "'prevented from breeding morons and criminals." The mother sued us for libel.

Lon Hocker, our attorney, had been appointed by the court to defend the purse snatcher in his criminal trial so he couldn't act as our counsel on the mother's libel case because of a conflict of interest. Dick employed Richmond C. Coburn, a distinguished St. Louis attorney, to defend the *Globe*.

Coburn asked me to get the academic records from the St. Louis public schools of the brothers and sisters of the purse snatcher. I was successful in doing so, and the records disclosed that the purse snatcher's brothers and sisters were classified as sub-normal by the school system. Coburn presented this to the court and the libel suit was dismissed.

Sometimes the insistence on printing a story backfired. In 1963 the *Globe-Democrat* investigated Circuit Judge Virgil Poelker (no relation to former St. Louis mayor John Poelker) and proved to the satisfaction of the judicial system and Governor John M. Dalton that he should be impeached for misconduct. The legislature was about to take up the issue of impeachment when Poelker notified the governor that rather than go through the agony of impeachment, he would resign.

This was on a Friday and he said he would resign on Monday. The governor told Amberg this and because Dick trusted Dalton and Dalton trusted Poelker, Amberg directed that the story be printed on page one Sunday morning,

It was a long story recounting Poelker's misdeeds. Then on Monday, instead of resigning as he had promised, Poelker told the governor that he was not going to leave office under these conditions.

Left holding the bag, Amberg asked Jack Flach, then our bureau chief in Jefferson City, to find a story that would somehow save the paper's face. Jack worked all morning and couldn't find anything. So we had to run a story Tuesday saying it had been a "misunderstanding."

Fortunately, in this little embarrassing saga, Poelker again reversed himself and in a day or so did submit his resignation.

Another legal battle involved a quarrel with the carriers who, we felt, were charging too much for the paper.

We carried a suggested retail price. In those days, it was ten cents, but we had some carriers who were charging fifteen or twenty cents to deliver the paper to a home. They had all kinds of excuses. Long driveways to walk to the door or porch. Mean dogs snapping at them. We listened to their complaints, but circulation is a vital element in the success of any newspaper.

We were losing circulation. Customers got mad at the carriers and would cancel their subscriptions. It cost us $50 to $100 to get a reader back. I used to answer calls from complaining readers because I thought it was important to try to keep them.

We talked to Hocker. The problem was that we had no control. These carriers weren't our employees; they were independent contractors who bought and sold the routes as they wished. And it was a lucrative business if they had a good area. They could sell a route for as much as $100,000, maybe more.

Hocker said, "Look, let's try this. The antitrust laws in the United States are geared, designed and created to prevent price fixing at a high level, not against keeping prices low."

We did a study and were convinced this was the concept, the intent of the law, and that we were in good shape. We decided that despite this exclusivity we would install a competitive carrier in the territory of Lester Albrecht, who we felt was overcharging his customers. The carrier induced the federal government to file an antitrust suit against the *Globe-Democrat* and we went to trial. We won in federal court in St. Louis, and in the Federal Court of Appeals. Albrecht took our case to the U.S. Supreme Court where I had a wonderful opportunity to be co-counsel with Hocker. Unfortunately, the Supreme Court ruled against us and cost us somewhere around $150,000 or $200,000.

But the decision didn't affect only the *Globe-Democrat*. It hampered the circulation department in every newspaper in the country by reducing a newspaper's ability to sell its product. Lon Hocker was chastened and I thought Amberg would lose his mind. We felt we had lost this case for the whole industry.

However—and it's a shame that Dick didn't live to know this—

just before Christmas 1996, the Supreme Court reversed itself and said the decision had been a terrible mistake. Hocker called me from his retirement home in the East in his glory because he felt he had been the cause of our horrible mistake and was now vindicated.

For all his flamboyant manner and occasional penchant for shooting from the hip, Amberg had a genuinely deep affection for St. Louis and its people. He and I would frequently go to lunch and talk about what should be done at the paper. One day, just out of the blue, he said, "What do you think would happen if I started a boys' club in north St. Louis?" Frankly, I didn't think he had a ghost of a chance.

He was a director of a similar club in south St. Louis. The board chairman had a fit over the idea of a north side club. But J. Arthur ("Cubby") Baer was on the board and said he would help. So Baer and Dick resigned from the south side club and raised $1 million for the north side club.

Dick's idea was to put the club on its feet, then turn it over to the black community. Several outstanding leaders in the local black community, including Frankie Freeman, Donald Suggs, Clem Billingsley, and Judge Theodore McMillan were named to the board.

Dick asked me to find some land but I couldn't locate enough vacant property in one piece. A friend suggested that we call Gussie Busch. Dick didn't want to do that, so he asked a friend to call. Gussie didn't hesitate. He gave us Sportsman's Park on North Grand (which had been renamed Busch Stadium). But when we got around to signing the papers, we found out that Gussie owned all but one little strip, 50' x 100' at Grand and Dodier.

Dick said that was no problem. He would simply call the owner and get it for nothing. But the owner wasn't as generous as Gussie. We had to pay him $37,000. We put the money in St. Louis Union Trust, to be paid out in installments. We had pretty much forgotten about it until Dave Calhoun, president of the trust company, called after Dick had died with the good news that he was sending us, as I recall, $4,000 or $5,000 in interest.

Dick selected the name, Herbert Hoover Boys' Club. Unfortunately, he died right after the dedication. He didn't leave a single record. I set out to reconstruct a list of donors and pledges. The club is still flourishing, still helping improve the lives of young-

Leading St. Louisans were on hand for the groundbreaking for the Herbert Hoover Boys Club on July 8, 1966, at the site of the old Sportsman's Park at Grand and Dodier. At the extreme left is Maj. Gen. Leif J. Sverdrup. Dick Amberg, holding the shovel, is standing next to Nannie Mitchell Turner, owner/publisher of the St. Louis Argus, *the city's leading black newspaper. The arrow in the back points to Bauman, who is standing next to Dan Schlafly, on his right.*

sters and we at the *Globe-Democrat* who had a hand in its founding are very proud of that.

Another organization that can credit its founding to the *Globe* is the Backstoppers. Nick Blassie, former head of the Meatcutters' Union, encouraged Amberg to create the organization. Blassie had attended a meeting in Detroit where he learned about an organization which had for its sole purpose the payment of all of the debts of widows of policemen and firemen killed in the line of duty.

Amberg decided that he and Blassie would start such an orga-

nization in St. Louis. The theory is that a group of people would
pay $100 or $150 a year to belong. Amberg got much of the
membership together. Blassie provided a few members. Upon
the death of a fireman or a policeman, a representative of the
Backstoppers visits the widow and gives her a check for $1,000
to be used in any way she wants.

After the funeral, a Backstopper visits the widow again, com-
piles a list of every debt she has—automobile payments, department store bills, mortgage payments, medical bills. The Backstoppers pay every bill and make mortgage payments as long as
needed or until she remarries. They also provide continuing health
insurance payments and help with education costs for children.

In the first year, several firemen were killed in a fire in a downtown theater. The Backstoppers didn't have enough money to
pay the obligations of these widows so it had to borrow the money
to pay off the bills. Now the Backstoppers have substantial financial resources.

St. Louis has been recognized nationally for years as an exceptionally strong pro-labor city. Translated, this meant that a
large number of labor unions had strong, beneficial contracts
with St. Louis employers.

Anheuser Busch early in its life agreed to labor contracts with
its employees and through the years the working conditions and
wages prescribed in these contracts were outstandingly good for
brewery employees. McDonnell Douglas was organized from
the bottom to the top. Scarcely a major employer did not have
union contracts. The Teamsters were particularly strong in St.
Louis. The *Globe-Democrat* and the *Post-Dispatch* each had at least
ten unions. The Carpenters Union enjoyed a good reputation for
fair dealing.

Some manufacturers occasionally would refuse to locate a new
plant in St. Louis because of the high labor costs brought about
by the militancy of union organization. The cultural institutions
in St. Louis were sometimes a strong enough inducement to overcome the bias against organized labor.

Among these many unions and among the strongest was the
AFL Steamfitters/Pipefitters Local 562. They were at the low
end of the scale in public opinion. I don't think anyone will really
know the extent of the validity, or nonvalidity, of the prevalent

public opinion concerning them. Among those who queried the Fitters' conduct was Dick Amberg.

He gave a lot of personal support and direction to a *Globe-Democrat* campaign to induce the federal government to indict and try several Fitter officers for violating the political action committee (PAC) rules. He never swerved in his goal despite repeated caution by Ted Schafers, the reporter who did most of the work on the stories, that the Fitters were not guilty of misdeeds.

Schafers, who was senior editor when the paper was sold, was named Construction Man of the Year in 1983, in recognition of his "hard-hitting but fair" reporting when he was the newspaper's labor-reporter during those strife-filled, "bad image" years. Here is his point of view:

Construction unions—especially the strongest and most militant—were able to win contracts with builders or employers in St. Louis that exceeded wages or costs obtained by workers living in other cities of comparable size or larger and even members of similar labor unions. Often the difference was not in hourly rates of pay but in costly "work-rules" that resulted in charges of featherbedding practices or jurisdictional disputes that produced a high level of stoppages in the early 1970s on major contraction projects.

These combined to give the city its reputation as a "bad-labor" town to be avoided as a place to move a business or to expand existing manufacturing facilities.

The *Globe-Democrat* hammered away through the 1950s and 1960s until an organization named Pride was formed by all major segments of the construction business— labor and professional services—that reversed this bad image.

What the Pride organizers appreciated was that while the *Globe-Democrat* exposed the bad labor practices and those responsible, it also told the public what the honest and capable union leadership was doing—thus helping to develop meaningful communication between labor and management.

Probably the union most often blamed as a source of St. Louis' bad labor image was Local 562, the Steamfitters—not only because it once enforced some of the mostly costly work rules, but because of its dominance in Democratic politics at local and state levels through its business manager, Lawrence (Larry) Callanan.

In 1965 Dick Amberg, then the newspaper's publisher, became convinced that a political action fund, established by the Steamfitters was being operated illegally at the direction of Callanan.

Larry Callanan

Amberg was given information that collection of union member political "donations" to Local 562 was not voluntary on the part of the membership and he was given the names of some members who would so testify. Al Delugach, Denny Walsh, and I were assigned to the investigation.

Prodded by stories and editorials, the U.S. District Attorney's office became involved. The case was submitted to a federal grand jury and indictments were voted against Local 562, Callanan, John L. Lawler, and George Seaton, who were Callanan's two key assistants. All were convicted in federal court here; all parties received fines and each of the three union officers were sentenced to one-year jail terms. All were declared "guilty of making illegal union political campaign contributions"—the first such conviction under the then existing federal law. The convictions came in September 1968, one year after Amberg had died of a heart attack.

I asked to be relieved of this assignment about midway during the inquiry because I learned the Steamfitters were using a political action program duplicating one used by a Teamster Union in St. Louis and that the Steamfitter-officers had adopted it only after being assured of its legality by a prominent St. Louis labor attorney. Under the circumstances, I felt that not only would it be unfair to prosecute the union and its officers, but also that any conviction resulting would be overturned if appealed to the U.S. Supreme Court.

It took another four years (June 1972) for the U.S. Supreme Court to order dismissal of all charges. But by that time Callanan and Lawler were dead, so they could not savor their victory. Seaton and the union had to wait until February 1974 for their cases to be dismissed in the trial court in St. Louis. The U.S. District Attorney Donald Stohr said in asking court dismissal of all charges against the union and the accused officers:

"The interpretation of the Supreme Court decision will not

support a conviction under the facts of the case."

For his decision, although it was a correct one, Schafers missed out on the Pulitzer Prize and Sigma Delta Chi public service award bestowed on the *Globe* and the other two reporters for having investigated and won convictions in this case.

- 6 -

THE BUCK STOPS HERE

On a Sunday morning, the day before Labor Day in 1967, I received a telephone call that was to open a new chapter in my life as a newspaperman. Janet Amberg was calling from New York to say her husband, Dick, had died unexpectedly early that morning

She asked me to notify Dick's many friends, especially those at their church, Central Presbyterian. I went there that morning, stood in the vestibule after the service and told many of the parishioners about Dick's death.

The funeral was to be held on the following Tuesday. *Globe* owner S.I. Newhouse came for the service. On the way to Lambert Field after the funeral, he asked me. "Do you want to be publisher?" I didn't hesitate. I said, "Yes."

"Well," he replied, "let me think it over and I'll get back to you. Meanwhile, you run the paper."

I later learned that several prominent St. Louisans had written or telephoned Newhouse, urging him to appoint me his publisher. Attorney Morris L. Shenker, George H. Capps, the civic leader who owned Capitol Coal, and builder Joe Vatterott were among them. I also learned that Robert F. Hyland, then a CBS vice-president and head of KMOX Radio, was determined that he would be publisher and had enlisted the support of a number of business leaders in his campaign.

I was delighted at the prospect that I might move into the publisher's office, but it was a bittersweet time. Although we didn't always see eye to eye, Dick had been my friend and had done a lot for me. I had a deep respect for his many contributions to the *Globe-Democrat* and, through the paper, to St. Louis.

In the absence of a final word from Newhouse, I had the responsibility for running the paper without any public announcement or real authority. Initially, some of the staff were a bit resistant to taking orders from me, but I managed somehow. In November 1967 Newhouse called to tell me I would be the publisher.

Community involvement, to me, is an essential role of a newspaper person. I do not believe a publisher can sit in an ivory tower, look out the window and sing praise or anguish over whatever is going on out there without having personal knowledge of the community's activities and needs—not secondhand knowledge or hearsay, but personal experience. I do not believe he can make good decisions and have a significant influence in blotting out the bad and supporting the good otherwise. While he must focus on the small, compact world of the city room, the composing room, the mail room, the press room and on the massive world beyond the threshold as well, at the same time he cannot be ignorant of what is happening in his community.

A newspaper is a public trust and should be operated as such. It is also part of the free enterprise economic system and if a paper cannot maintain sufficient revenue to pay its expenses, it cannot continue to publish. There are no subsidies.

This is an element which makes newspapers so important to the freedom of this country. Only newspapers among the media are totally free. No one except the owner has any real control or influence. This is not true of the electronic media. They are licensed by the federal government and to the extent that threat of license removal is a deterrent to freedom of expression, radio and television are subject to at least potential control.

I maintained that newsroom employees are citizens in every respect with the same privileges and responsibilities as non-newspaper employees are. There is a theory among some newspaper people that reporters are privileged and may decline their responsibilities as citizens to participate in maintaining the social order. I do not believe they can disclaim their responsibilities just because they are newspaper reporters or editors.

Often, from their investigative work about a crime or a civil disorder, newspaper reporters acquire exceptionally pertinent information which law enforcement does not have, but needs. Officials may ask reporters for information. Some decline to answer, claiming their knowledge is privileged. When the *Globe-Democrat* was asked for such help, I always recommended to our staff that they cooperate.

This stand brought about an interesting bout with the *Post-Dispatch* in 1977. Its philosophy on this issue was just the opposite of mine. For a reason unknown to me, the *Post-Dispatch* asked for a file the FBI had developed about me. This file disclosed that I had cooperated, personally and by way of the newspaper, in a few of its investigations. I knew this and, frankly, I was proud to be identified as a cooperative citizen.

The *Post* printed a long page-one story about this file in derogatory terms. I didn't mind the story but I was incensed that the story implied that what I did was improper and a betrayal. Betrayal of what or whom? Criminals?

I then wrote an editorial, "For Hanoi? Or For America?," attacking the philosophy of the *Post* and its publisher, Joseph Pulitzer. I made it as vitriolic and condemnatory of the *Post's* left-wing philosophy as I could. We printed my editorial on page one on Thanksgiving morning and it was signed by me—probably the first signed editorial in the paper's history and one of a very few on page one.

I wondered what Joe Pulitzer's attitude would be the next time we met, and it was not long before I found out. We were guests, with our wives, of Sidney Salomon, Jr., at a Blues hockey game. We arrived first and didn't know the Pulitzers would be there. When Joe arrived, we looked at one another. He walked over to shake hands, which we did, and said, "Duncan, we ought to do more of this."

I wanted our staff members to take part in community activities. This is also contrary to the philosophy of many publishers and editors who believe reporters and editors cannot be completely objective if they are involved. I insisted all *Globe-Democrat* employees serve at the polls or on juries when called upon. We

An Editorial—

FOR HANOI?
OR FOR AMERICA?

The St Louis Globe-Democrat and the St. Louis Post-Dispatch are unmistakably opposed philosophically; i.e. on matters of government, especially fiscal responsibility; on matters of welfare, particularly where immorality is involved, and on other notable issues. Many fine newspapers throughout the nation share the views of The Globe-Democrat.

The Globe-Democrat accepts the inevitability that reasonable persons, and thus, reasonable media organizations, will differ. Difference of opinion is indigenous to a rational world.

Thus, The Globe-Democrat has refrained, as a matter of policy from commenting — favorably or unfavorably — on the conduct or opinions of other members of the media.

In Wednesday's issue, the St. Louis Post-Dispatch published a cheap shot, a biased and slanted item about The St. Louis Globe-Democrat. In its normally hypocritical manner, the Post-Dispatch presented material about The Globe Democrat as a news story, when in fact it was an editorial in a bogeyman's costume. Had the Post-Dispatch had the journalistic character and professionalism to publish its Federal Bureau of Investigation story as an editorial, The Globe-Democrat would have respected the afternoon paper's prerogative to express its opinion, and we would not have commented about it.

The Post-Dispatch editorialized story said The Globe-Democrat in recent years had published material about student dissidents, especially in St. Louis County at Lindbergh High School. The Post-Dispatch story said the student dissident stories were "planted" by the FBI and implied they were the result of "conspiratorial" ties between The Globe-Democrat and the FBI. The story blatantly implied a nefarious alliance between The Globe-Democrat and the FBI for unworthy purposes.

It is most certainly true that The Globe-Democrat has published news stories in the past about dissident student activities; in the St. Louis area, in the Midwest and throughout the United States and the world. To the best of my knowledge and recollection, these stories originated in the normal manner incident to any news story: from an interested reader who notified the city editor, a parent, a student, a witness or scores of other sources.

For the Post-Dispatch news story to state that the FBI arranged stories in The GlobeDemocrat through contacts with the publisher of The Globe-Democrat is a villainous lie typical of the depraved thinking of a Communist "Big Lie" technique — designed to undermine the fabric of a country. It is true that I personally knew J. Edgar Hoover, the long-time, respected director of the FBI, and enjoyed an hour or more visit with him in Washington only a few days before his death in May of 1972. It is a privilege to identify Clarence M. Kelley, present FBI director and former chief of police of Kansas City, as a friend. Neither Mr. Hoover nor Mr. Kelley at any time provided me any information relative to any news stories, past or present.

Mr. Hoover and Mr. Kelley have never at any time communicated news material to, or made any request of Martin L. Duggan, editor of the editorial page of The Globe-Democrat, or George A. Killenberg, managing editor of The Globe-Democrat.

We are at a loss to account for the FBI memoranda, unless the explanation is that some overzealous agent sought to advance himself by taking credit for what The Globe-Democrat produced in its normal pursuits.

In the normal course of community, social, and business activities and news work, we have known a succession of FBI agents in charge in the St. Louis office. At no time has any of these men of impeccable character and ability ever "planted" a story in The Globe-Democrat by way of my office or that of Mr. Duggan or Mr. Killenberg. Quite the contrary, the St. Louis office of the FBI has consistently maintained a frequently frustrating reluctance to release news material to The Globe-Democrat.

The Post-Dispatch story, to the contrary, emits a barnyard stench which is a measure of a good deal of that paper's pretense at news coverage: Rot.

This is an appropriate occasion to offer a statement expanding on The Globe-Democrat's news and editorial policy, expressed daily in our masthead. The Globe-Democrat's purpose is to serve the interests of our community, state and nation. The Globe-Democrat's intention is to be supportive, generally, of community institutions. It is not, as it appears to be with the other daily in St. Louis, nitpickingly destructive, denigrating and demeaning by repeated irresponsibility and informed criticism. We believe in the United States of America.

We believe in the integrity and the future of the United States, including the integrity and objectives of the FBI. During the late 1960s and early 1970s, when universities were being bombed and burned, and in some cases innocent citizens murdered; when banks were being bombed and burned; when a hall in Congress was bombed; when peaceful, personal access to national political conventions was being denied to orderly Americans, The Globe-Democrat believed and still believes that it was the duty of the FBI to apprehend those threatening the internal security of the nation.

The Globe-Democrat played a constructive role during this period, this newspaper is proud of its participation and contribution.

The Globe-Democrat cherishes its role as a supporter of the American system. The Globe-Democrat suggests that the frequently slanted news coverage in the Post-Dispatch, most especially its recent 10-part Page One Dudman series paying tribute to North Vietnam's oppressive and dehumanizing leadership out of Hanoi, is a shameful disservice to St. Louis and America.

We prefer pro-Americanism.

Duncan Bauman
Publisher
St. Louis Globe-Democrat
November 24, 1977

I met with FBI director J. Edgar Hoover in his office on April 7, 1972, shortly before his death.

paid them the difference between what they earned on election day duty or poll duty and their regular salary.

However, this means they and I had to walk a fine line between the need to keep certain matters confidential and a newsman's natural desire to break a story first. For myself, I can say that never did I return from a board or committee meeting to give the city room a report on the subject matter just so we could beat the competition. Once the reporter got the news, I was able to confirm its accuracy.

With my appointment as publisher, the opportunities for community service flowed across my desk like a Mississippi flood.

Among the more than fifty volunteer posts I held during my years at the paper were: president of the Health and Welfare Council; vice president of the United Way; secretary of the Board of Election Commissioners; director of the BJC Health System; president of Catholic Charities; vice chairman or secretary of the Missouri Baptist Hospital Board of Trustees; member of the National Board of Junior Achievement, Inc.; president of the Convention and Visitors Bureau; president of Herbert Hoover Boys Club; president of the Newman Chapel Lay Advisory Board; member, board of trustees of the National Jewish Hospital and Research Center.

I was also a director of the Municipal Theatre Association and of the Saint Louis Symphony Society; member of the advisory board, Young Men's Christian Association; member of the Lay Advisory Committee, St. Louis Medical Society; president of the St. Vincent's Hospital Lay Advisory Board; director of the Missouri Chamber of Commerce; member, Capital Fund Review board of the St. Louis Metropolitan Chamber of Commerce; president, Child Center of Our Lady of Grace; member, board of directors, Dismas House; president, Newspaper Personnel Relations Association, and chairman of the REJIS Commission.

I refer to these not in self-aggrandizement but to illustrate the broad scope of community betterment through agencies I have been privileged to serve. I was deeply honored and pleased to be selected as St. Louis' Man of the Year in 1983. An interviewer described me as a "respected St. Louis mover and shaker and policy maker" and wrote that "local observers call him one of the most powerful men in St. Louis."

Well, I don't know about that, but I do know that a newspaper publisher has a rare opportunity to shape his community—not by promoting his own personal and philosophical agenda but by promoting high ethical and moral standards, supporting what is good and uncovering the wrongs that poison society and derail social and civic progress. If he does not choose the high road and take advantage of that opportunity, he is not doing his job.

At the *Globe-Democrat,* the buck stopped at my desk. I could not prevent a reporter from making a mistake. I could reprimand or even fire that individual if the mistake were serious, but in the last analysis, the responsibility for the newspaper's quality and truthfulness had to be mine.

I was fourteenth in a line of publishers—some were also owners—in the *Globe-Democrat's* history. Each brought to the job his own journalistic and leadership skills and his own method of operation. Each worked in a different atmosphere, each faced new problems as America moved from an agrarian into an industrial and high-tech society and St. Louis developed into a major Midwest metropolis.

None of us worked alone. A succession of team players through the years supported the publisher and built the *Globe-Democrat* as a powerful, ethical presence in the nation. However, the publisher is the ultimate decision-maker. I believe a newspaper's quality is relative to the courage and willingness of its owner and the publisher to be responsible leaders.

The task of a publisher should be not only to run the newspaper and take a particular stance on the editorial page, but also to help the community and its residents, many of whom may never even look at a newspaper or become aware of problems outside the four walls of their home.

My job took me into the newsroom, into editorial conferences, into labor disputes, into personnel decisions and, beyond the newspaper, into the community, into the state and the nation.

We used to have an editorial meeting almost every morning at ten. We would go over the night's news and talk about editorials. Most of them I read before publication, some I wrote myself.

I think the one I got the biggest kick out of writing was only two words long. There was a professor at Washington University, Barry Commoner, whose philosophy was too left-wing for me to swallow. I had been privy to Dr. William H. Danforth's decision to leave the practice of medicine and become chancellor of the university, so I felt very close to him and felt I could talk with him frankly.

I asked him one day when the hell he was going to get rid of Commoner, being fully aware of tenure, the academic world's equivalent of unionism. I had had calls from people asking me the same question. Russ Savage, general manager of Sears and head of the Boy Scouts, called one day to say he was concerned about Washington University and could not in good conscience continue his contributions because of its ultraliberal educational atmosphere. Danforth was pretty cautious and rarely said anything without careful thought. He told me it would take "some time" to resolve the issue.

When Commoner did leave a year or two later (he was not discharged), I wrote an editorial headed "Commoner Leaves Washington University." The editorial read: "Good riddance."

George H. Killenberg, our executive editor, made most decisions about the play of stories and the make-up of page one day in and day out, and I respected that because he was a great newspaperman and I usually agreed with him. However, I had the final say.

When our astronauts landed on the moon on a Sunday afternoon, I happened to be at a social gathering and called George to say I wanted virtually nothing on page one except a huge blue image of the moon. Amour Krupnik, an artist and head of our computer functions, also wanted only the moon.

George kept calling me back to make sure that was what he was to do. Finally, I told him after the fourth or fifth call, "Dammit, George, that's the way it's going to be."

I think it was certainly one of the most dramatic front pages in the history of the paper and received national attention.

In my view, the publisher has the responsibility for determining the policies which the paper will espouse editorially, the parameters of the news content, the range of news coverage and language which will be used, advertising content which will or will not be permitted. He is responsible every day after publication for what has appeared in his paper.

Some American publishers in recent years have chosen to disclaim responsibility, shifting that to anonymous editors. This is wrong, in my judgment, and has led significantly to the recent trend to seek and print news of salacious and titillating content which is not in the public interest. I believe that the newspaper has a duty to uphold public morals and responsible social conduct.

Our editorial page and news content reflected this philosophy

One of the great front pages in the history of daily journalism, published this way on my direct orders.

every day, to the best of my ability. Martin L. Duggan, our editorial page editor, and a staff of three writers knew from our many discussions what our editorial policy was. We had frequent meetings to discuss policy or, in some cases, how to handle a particular subject. If we could not reach a happy consensus, I made the decision.

I recall one incident. When it became known that Fidel Castro was releasing hundreds of Cubans to flee to America, Martin thought it might be appropriate to applaud Castro for this gesture. I was out of town on business and Martin called me about the concept. I recommended that since we didn't know the whole story we hold off for a few days. As it turned out, we learned that Castro was also freeing hundreds of criminals from his prisons and dumping them on America. The United States was even forced to establish secure holding facilities for these criminals at substantial cost to the taxpayers.

We were pleased that we had not fallen for Castro's deceit.

From their crude beginnings centuries ago as letters from one man to his neighbors, friends, and to the general public, American newspapers have played a major role in shaping the opinions and actions of their readers, and determining the fate of political candidates at the same time. Through endorsements and editorials for or against proposed legislation or civic actions, the *Globe-Democrat* carried on that tradition.

Whether print journalism's influence has waned or grown since the days of Horace Greeley and his admonition to "Go west, young man," I cannot say, but that should not relieve publishers of their obligation and opportunity to lead. It has been said that an endorsement by the *Globe-Democrat* was worth at least 75,000 votes in a statewide election.

We printed a list of our endorsements on page one on election day. Voters took them to the polls and many have said that what they miss most in the paper's absence is that sample ballot.

Most voters are not familiar with every single candidate and every single issue on the ballot. We made our recommendations based on the cumulative knowledge of the staff. We never claimed infallibility for the ballot; we just offered our best information.

Normally, because of our conservative bent, we supported conservative candidates and those usually were Republicans. But in many cases we supported Democrats, including Senator Stuart Symington and Governor Warren E. Hearnes, who despite his party affiliation was more conservative than many running on the Republican platform.

Such decisions were not always easy. When Jack Danforth, a Republican, ran for the U.S. Senate against Stuart Symington for the first time, we endorsed Symington, much to Danforth's dismay. In keeping with our policy, I met with him personally and told him we were not going to endorse him.

I know he was horrendously disappointed, but a few days after the election (which he lost) he called to say that he thought I might be criticized by our mutual friends for my role in the election. He wanted to tell me–so that I would be able to tell my critics–that he did not blame me and that he looked forward to working with me in the future.

During all of my nearly fifty years at the *Globe-Democrat* and the countless number of contentious relationships with political figures I never saw any other such demonstration of character as Jack Danforth displayed with this phone call. He had just gone through the rigors and travail of a race for the U.S. Senate and lost, and he called to express concern for *me*, not himself.

I was most happy in his future campaigns to give him our endorsement and he proved to be one of the exemplary leaders in the U.S. Senate. In fact, he became known as as the conscience of the Senate, a man to whom his colleagues turned for counsel on controversial moral issues.

Within weeks of becoming publisher, I pledged our political endorsement to a longtime friend running for St. Louis alderman, long before the filing deadline for the office. A far superior person also filed for the same office before the deadline.

I would liked to have endorsed the second, but I had given my word to my friend and I stayed with him. I learned a useful lesson: Never endorse a political candidate before the deadline for filing for office had passed. Incidentally, our candidate lost.

We were frustrated that we could not make responsible endorsements on the issue of retention of judges. Almost no other elected or appointed official has the power so drastically to affect the lives of citizens for good or ill as Missouri Circuit Court judges, Courts of Appeal or Supreme Court judges. Voters are asked to vote to either retain judges in office or reject them. In the case of other officials, voters usually can make rational judgments based on what the media tells them about the conduct of those officials. But it's rare that the media publishes enough about a judge to give the public a good basis for a judgment.

The media itself knows little. It has some advantage in having daily knowledge of judges' work but no tally is kept. Such a tally would be expensive to maintain and almost impossible to keep on a reasoned or equitable basis.

Under the Missouri court plan, which is used in urban areas, a group of citizens in specific geographic and court jurisdictional areas asks for nominations of individuals to be appointed to the bench when there is an opening. The panel, consisting of ordinary citizens, lawyers, and judges, sorts out the nominations and submits three names to the governor who appoints one of the three. The sitting judges are subject to retention votes at regular intervals, varying with the court: circuit, appellate, or supreme.

The media doesn't have access to a factual report on judges' competency and I doubt if such a report even exists. Members of the bar do have a bar association vote on retention, apart from the public vote, but due to lawyers' obvious bias, their vote is not wholly reliable.

So how does the public become informed? The answer is that it doesn't. Therefore, the public vote on such crucial public servants is a farce and borders on deceit.

The *Globe-Democrat* created forms for evaluating judges similar to those we used to obtain information from other elected officials for our endorsement. We sent them out prior to an election and the response was vehement, sad, demeaning, arrogant, and insulting. The judiciary told us loudly and in large numbers to back off, that the record of judicial competence was "none of your business."

What the judiciary was really saying was that it was none of the *public's* business what the judicial record showed.

We sought advice from the Missouri Supreme Court and received none. So we dropped the idea, as good as we thought it was.

Many states have turned to a nonpartisan court plan similar to Missouri's because it is better than the elective system. Having judges run for election creates the same conflict of interest for judges as for any elected official because of the need for financial contributions. In some urban areas, it might cost millions of dollars to win a judicial seat. One of my classmates in law school told me that before we had the nonpartisan court plan he borrowed the limit on his life insurance to pay for his campaign. That is wrong.

Perhaps in the future a program will be available to the public to inform them on judicial qualifications.

When I became publisher, I made some changes which might have been called radical. I forbade the use of the "N" word anywhere in the paper, even in quotations. The order was tested when Ben Magdovitz, our advertising director, came storming into my office with a full-page ad promoting a movie that had the forbidden word in the title. A newspaper requires advertising revenue to exist and this ad would have brought in about $3,000 a day. Ben said, "All right, you're so damn smart. What are you going to do about this?"

For a moment I didn't know what to say. In desperation, I suggested he call the producer and ask him to change the title. Ben was incredulous and doubtful if this could happen. But at my insistence he did call—and sure enough, the producer changed the name. We ran the ads and collected the money.

The *Globe-Democrat* was among the first of major newspapers in the United States—along with the *Post-Dispatch*—to eliminate the use of the words "Negro" and "white" in classified advertising columns and news stories. During my forty-five years with the *Globe,* the newspaper was erroneously regarded by most of the black community and some white liberals as anti-black. This was an ignorant and prejudiced point of view. My personal commitment to racial justice was deep and consistent.

Sometime after becoming publisher, I became concerned because there was such a substantial volume of massage parlor advertising in St. Louis newspapers. It was evident that many of these ads were for massage parlors which were fronts for prostitution.

I called Ben to my office and advised him that henceforth there would be no massage parlor advertising run in the *Globe-Democrat.* Ben protested that this would be a substantial revenue loss. I conceded that but felt that the standards of the paper were worth more than this income. He also protested that some of the massage parlors were legitimate and it wouldn't be fair to cast those enterprises in the same bag as those who were fronts for prostitution. I also conceded that and told him that if he could pledge to me that the ones he was running were legitimate, we'd certainly use them. He said that would be too difficult and agreed to cut them all out. I felt so strongly about the issue that I called Glenn Christopher, the *P-D* vice-chairman and general manager, told him what my philosophy was and asked if the *Post* would be willing to participate. He refused and the *Post* continued to run the ads, a couple of columns a day and much more on Sunday.

About two or three years later, Glenn called to say he was happy to advise me that the *Post* was going to cut out the advertising. One of the ads had carried a wrong phone number, that of two respectable elderly women in south St. Louis. They had received numerous crude calls and threatened to sue the paper. The advertising was eliminated and the dispute with the women was settled.

I was taught some principles as a boy and I believed in them and saw to it, to the extent that I could, that the paper operated that way. An institution either has principles or it doesn't.

I made other changes. I decided we would not use the term, "Ms," which infuriated some women of the staff. Earlier, I had suggested to Dick Amberg that we not use movie star Elizabeth Taylor's name. I felt she was a disgrace and didn't belong in our paper. Dick agreed that henceforth we would use her name only in a significant story.

Another change I ordered embarrassed and angered some of our readers–but I'm sure it saved many lives. We published the names of persons arrested, suspected of driving under the influence of alcohol.

American law defines an automobile in the hands of a drunken driver as a lethal weapon. I was aware of the abuse of our legal system by drunken drivers who have the means to employ skillful attorneys to defend them when charged with driving while intoxicated and worse when they have an accident and injure or kill another human being.

When drunken drivers kill another human being and manage to avoid serious punishment, it is a flagrant violation of human relations.

I believe that public embarrassment or being ostracized by one's peers is a significant form of punishment. In fact, for some people it's the absolute worst form of punishment. I thought it might help to reduce the number of drunk drivers on the street if the *Globe-Democrat* published the names of persons arrested and charged with driving while intoxicated.

Believe me, this worked. There was a visible reduction in such arrests. Interestingly, the biggest reduction was among the citizens most capable of knowing better and knowing what they were doing was wrong—among the better educated and more socially visible.

The paper was besieged by calls from people who asked us not to use their names. The callers ranged from some of our community's most prominent citizens to the most lowly. To my knowledge, and I'm very proud of this, no one at the *Globe-Democrat* ever caused a name to be deleted from the list.

While I don't believe any employee at the *Globe* ever killed a story because somebody appealed to us not to print it—I know I did not—I did refuse to print one story which I concluded before publication was untrue.

We had an excellent investigative reporter by the name of Denny Walsh. He had a dogged determination and worked diligently until he got his story. Sometimes he developed a personal agenda in his work, and he reflected it in his stories from time to time.

Denny had developed a series of stories detailing organized crime in St. Louis which were designed in part to show that Mayor Alfonso Cervantes was affiliated with the Mafia. First of all, according to the best information I had from knowledgeable sources, there was no Mafia in St. Louis, as distinguished from organized crime. The term Mafia is frequently used in the media to describe organized crime, but it is a misnomer.

I had asked George Killenberg to show me Denny's stories before they ran. Then I made maybe thirty phone calls to verify some of the material. At one point Walsh specifically identified a social gathering as a Mafia party. He said Cervantes attended and acted as a bartender.

I satisfied myself that this story was not true. Most of what the story reported was true, but not the Cervantes incident. I asked that this be corrected, whereupon Walsh flew into a rage, vilified me, and resigned. We printed the series, but not the Cervantes item. Later Denny sold the series to a national magazine which ran the whole thing. Cervantes sued Denny and the magazine for libel.

Cervantes lost the case, not because Denny was right, but because it is virtually impossible to libel a politician. To me it was not a question of libel but a question of character; whether we were going to vilify a man for something I was satisfied was not true.

I think that's the duty of the publisher. A publisher should hold himself responsible for what's printed and he should see that what's printed is responsible. I'm proud that I did that. I resent the cowardice and irresponsibility of some publishers. I heard one of these publishers blame his staff instead of taking the responsibility. It doesn't make a damn bit of difference who prepares, writes and edits the story, the publisher is responsible. For him to say, "I didn't have anything to do with it; my staff did it," is a cop-out.

The St. Louis Newspaper Publishers' Association was an organization maintained by three newspapers—the St. Louis *Star-Times, Post-Dispatch* and *Globe-Democrat.* Its purpose was to represent the three papers in a coordinated way in labor relations and in public affairs. When the *Star-Times* sold itself to the *Post-Dispatch* in 1951 and went out of business, the remaining two papers maintained the association.

The association employed a full-time executive and a secretary, whose office was at the *Post-Dispatch,* unfortuately so, I felt. During my tenure the executive was Munro Roberts, a former international vice president of the Mailers' Union and an attorney. I, along with Ed Evers, the *Globe-Democrat* mechanical superintendent, represented our paper. When Evers died, I became the *Globe's* sole representative.

The association was also a buffer against either newspaper sandbagging the other in the matter of charitable gifts. For years charitable gifts were made by way of the association, sixty percent of a gift was designated from the *Post-Dispatch,* forty percent from the *Globe-Democrat.* Shortly after becoming publisher, I changed that to a fifty-fifty arrangement.

Subsequently, while I never disagreed with a suggestion from the *Post* to make a donation, the *Post* quite frequently declined to participate in a gift which I suggested. Then I eliminated the joint giving altogether and the *Globe-Democrat* made its own annual gifts, which were substantial.

The main purpose of the association was to be an entity which would serve the common interests of the papers in an equitable manner, without favor to either member. One role was to negotiate labor contracts for the papers. The exception to the union contract representation was the St. Louis Newspaper Guild, which represented news, editorial, circulation, classified advertising and circulation department employees, with a few exemptions, like myself, the editorial page editor, the managing editor, the advertising director, the circulation director and their office staffs.

Labor union problems at both St. Louis dailies grievously hampered production and resulted in excessive costs. We had to constantly address the concerns of ten different unions.

Language in the Typographers Union contract, which covered printers, provided for five departments in the composing room and prevented us from transferring an idle printer from one department to another during a production crisis. At deadline time, if we had an urgent need for another man in news makeup we could not transfer an idle printer from advertising makeup to news makeup, even if the advertising makeup man was patently not busy or needed in advertising makeup. If the urgency threatened to delay publication and it was imperative to have more manpower we had to employ a substitute printer from the union hall while our employee stood idle. It required more than two years of negotiation with the Typographers Union, and probably twenty meetings, to get the union's permission for us to install new equipment to set the daily financial market reports. It had required ten to twelve printers to set the market tables each day. We could set the markets with three printers with the new equipment.

At one meeting where we continued to be stalled on this issue, Roberts got up from his chair and bellowed that the *Post-Dispatch* would never demean the printers by asking for such a concession. He walked out of the room and I adjourned the meeting. After a few more meetings the printers agreed to the use of the new equipment by the *Globe-Democrat*, but not by the *Post-Dispatch*.

Two years later, in negotiations for a new Typo contract, Roberts asked for the same concession for the *Post*. The printers were furious and reminded Roberts of his conduct two years earlier.

Ultimately the printers capitulated.

Of all the unions in our place, the printers were the only union which had irresponsible leadership. It was not uncommon for them to lie or to misrepresent the meaning of parts of their contract during the period of its existence.

The Paperhandlers' Union was continuously contentious and difficult. The engravers were gentlemanly in their relationship with the paper. The Teamsters could be depended upon to follow the terms of their contract responsibly.

On one occasion the president of the Pressmen's Union interceded in my behalf when two unruly pressmen were threatening me with bodily harm. He warned them to stop their threats or he would pound them both into the asphalt they were standing on. His name was Joe Ox and I'm grateful to him for his respect.

Our pressroom was a featherbedded calamity. Our presses were relatively new, high-speed Goss presses which were manufactured to give us more than 50,000 papers per hour each. They were designed and manufactured to be run by six or seven men per press. The union contract required us to use up to twenty-two men per press for a sixty-four-page edition when we used four colors, and slightly less when we used only one color or black and white only. We were frequently overmanned by as many as fifteen men per press. If we were running three presses, which we often did, we were overmanned by as many as forty-five men each night. That represented a lot of cost.

A ludicrous example of manning was part of the Electricians' contract. If it was necessary to change a light bulb in my office—or anywhere in the building for that matter—even in a desk lamp, two electricians were required. The two would solemnly show up, one carrying a ladder, change the bulb and leave.

As I outlined in the first chapter, dock hands were notorious featherbedders. After the papers were printed they were delivered to the mail room where they were bundled and labeled and then sent down to the dock for loading into the delivery trucks. When a subsidiary plant was built in Maryland Heights to facilitate delivery of the papers, it was built without a dock. We used newly created equipment to deliver the papers directly into the trucks. We used Teamster union dock hands to load trucks at the Twelfth Street plant, but we did not need dock hands at the new plant. The Teamsters refused to allow us to operate without dock hands at the new plant, so we had dock hands on the payroll but not working in Maryland Heights.

Years ago, in the late 1950s, we saw a way to reduce the work load for employees in the paper storage room and simultaneously make their work safer. We had room in a subbasement to store a sixty-day supply of newsprint, virtually guaranteeing us newsprint in the event of a newspaper mill strike or a railroad strike. A roll of newsprint weighs more than 2,000 pounds, is about seven feet long and three and one-half to four feet in diameter. Newsprint was delivered to us by railroad, on a railroad spur alongside and level with doors into our subbasement. The track was underneath what is now Tucker Boulevard, formerly Twelfth Street.

Paper handler employees would unload boxcars using wooden prods with one end being a metal shiv. They manhandled these heavy rolls out of the car, into the paper storage room which was the length and width of our building. Then they stacked the rolls horizontally, two and three high, by hand.

We thought it would be better for all if we used forklift trucks with heavy-duty steel ribs to protect the driver should a roll fall from the stack. Instead of manhandling the rolls across a huge space and manhandling the stacking, the forklift would do the work.

The union said no, repeatedly. It took us three years to get the union's permission to install the forklifts.

In labor negotiations I frequently, urgently, and seriously warned the unions that practices like these would drive one St. Louis newspaper out of business, causing the loss of hundreds and hundreds of jobs instead of only a few. Their derisive decision was to protect a few at the cost of many.

During the course of a Teamster strike at both dailies, I met alone with Joe Pulitzer in the Duck Room at the Racquet Club. We discussed how to handle this strike. In the discussion, I told Joe that the *Post-Dispatch's* practice of settling strikes by giving unions virtually what they wanted without any struggle and the resultant increase in the cost of publishing would ultimately result in one of the two newspapers being destroyed. I urged him to be more vigorous in his defense of management.

Whereupon Joe said, "Duncan, the *Post-Dispatch* is pro-labor. We're going to do our best to help the unions. We're going to

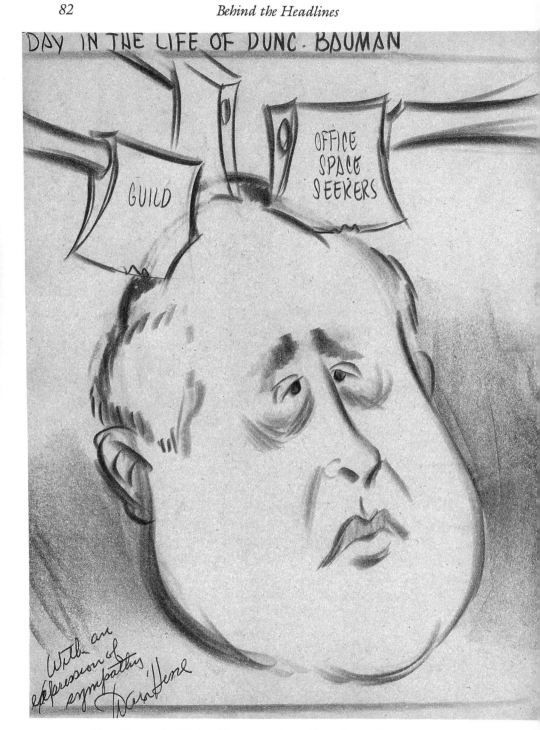

Don Hesse, the Globe-Democrat's *stellar editorial cartoonist, drew this panel for me. It shows some of the headaches of being a publisher, but none of the joys.*

continue to do this until such time as that philosophy threatens the existence of the *Post*."

What should have been considered standard, and was by the *Globe-Democrat,* was what was best for the continuation of the papers, for the preservation of this vital community function, not what was best for the *Post's* political philosophy.

The electricians struck the papers on a Saturday morning. I was the labor negotiator for the *Globe* and Munro Roberts for the *Post*. He and I had spent countless hours, day and night, for months negotiating this issue. About 4:30 in morning, the union negotiators came back into the room where we'd been meeting and told us they wouldn't accept our offer. They promised to strike the papers at 5 A. M., and they did.

I'd been up maybe twenty four or thirty-six hours by that time. We had a meeting with the *Post* in a few hours in a corner parlor room at the Jefferson Hotel. Joe Pulitzer, Amberg and I and a few others were present. Pulitzer walked up and down the room waving his arms and in strident language protested that the unions would have to learn that the *Post-Dispatch* could not be a "bottomless pit of money." That was his phrase: "'The *Post* is not a bottomless pit of money."

We adjourned the meeting, with the understanding that neither of the two papers would settle precipitously, that we would try to take a position that would encourage the electricians to realize that we had to settle at a decent rate.

I went home to bed. About four o'clock Saturday afternoon, I got a phone call that Joe had offered the union virtually what it asked for and had unilaterally settled the strike. The *Post* was going back into publication Saturday evening for its Sunday edition.

The *Globe-Democrat* and the *Post-Dispatch* negotiated jointly with the respective committees representing the mechanical unions, but each paper signed its own contract. *Globe* contracts and *Post* contracts were not always identical. Each newspaper negotiated alone its separate contract with the St. Louis Newspaper Guild. The content of each paper's Guild contract varied materially.

For years the weekly suburban *Journals* in the St. Louis area were a powerful force in advertising and newspaper readership. Among the most influential were the *Southside Journal* and the

West County Journal owned by Frank Bick. Bick took over the operation and ownership of these papers from his father and ran them with much of the conservative philosophy of the *Globe-Democrat*.

The Suburban *Journals* found a way to be devastatingly competitive to dailies. In the area of the cost of producing the newspaper the *Journals* had an overwhelming advantage. So far as I knew they did not have union contracts and the consequent wage costs and restrictive working conditions. Their advertisers were able to buy advertising in a paper which was distributed solely within the advertiser's business area. Until the *Globe* developed its zone sections—North, South, East and West—a *Globe* advertiser paid for our entire circulation but in the case of a neighborhood merchant, he needed only a portion of it. Even our zone sections were not as specifically distributed as the *Journals*.

The major disadvantage the *Journals* suffered was that they were distributed free and thrown on lawns whether the readers wanted them or not. Some readers resented the intrusion and threw them in the trash; others picked them up and used the ads. Thus *Journal* publishers were never able, with accuracy, to define the exact number of readers the advertiser was buying. *Globe* and *Post* subscribers were definable within a few hundred each day.

The *Journals* were measurably formidable competition for advertising dollars, causing a serious revenue loss to the dailies. Fortunately, news readership was a different matter. There the dailies clearly dominated.

When the *Globe-Democrat* pursued a solution to a serious crime it frequently offered a significant reward for information leading to the solution of the crime. It was not uncommon for Frank Bick to call and say, "Now, privately, I'll put $10,000 in the pot for the reward. I don't want any identification or recognition for it, but I'll help."

Bick's suburban *Journal* also was the only paper in St. Louis up to that time which publicly attacked the *Post-Dispatch*. On May Day, 1946, the *Post* flew the Russian flag alongside the American flag over its main entrance on 12th Street. Bick ran a long, page-one highly critical editorial with a photo. This attracted national attention.

Newspapers have traditionally been regarded as a home for "characters." Unquestionably reporter Ralph Wagner was one.

For many years he covered the East Side, meaning East St. Louis, Granite City, Wood River, Alton, and other towns in that geographic area. His territory was home to the hoodlum element, gambling and prostitution in the 1920s, 1930s and early 1940s. He knew, and was expected to know what was going on over there and who was running what. He did. He looked, talked and acted like one would expect a person to look who lived and worked in the environment he did.

Until after World War II newspaper reporting was almost exclusively a man's world. Early after the war we hired Marguerite Shepard, probably only the second or third woman general news reporter in the history of the paper. She had been a schoolteacher in Evansville, Ind., and had a short stint on the Evansville paper when she came to the *Globe*. She was the most persistent reporter on our staff. She never let a news source off the hook until she got the answers to which she thought she was entitled, and she could always be counted on to get the story to which she had been assigned. It might have taken awhile, but she got her story—and it was always well-written, thorough, and accurate.

Jack Flach, a Belleville native, started early in life on the *Globe-Democrat*. He became our political editor and was one of the best, if not the best, on our staff at getting exclusive stories, most frequently in the political arena but sometimes outside his

Jack Flach

bailiwick. His work developed more results for the community than any other single person on our staff, and for that matter, probably more than most reporters of other papers. He succeeded in having judges and a sheriff removed from office. On top of this, he had an uncanny talent of being able to retain his news sources, even though he frequently offered stories derogatory to the source.

Ted Schafers was another personality everyone remembers, and properly so. He was a native St. Louisan who began his career at the *Globe-Democrat* as a copy boy in the newsroom, the equivalent of a messenger boy. He ended his career as business editor and assumed the chore of rebuilding and preserving St.

Joseph's Church, now St. Joseph's Shrine. Early on he covered the Circuit Courts beat, the source of daily stories out of the criminal division. A major number of exclusive political stories were originated through his work.

Ted developed one exclusive story after the other on the Greenlease kidnapping case. He contributed countless other exclusive stories to our paper, and, as with Flach, he was able to retain news sources, even though we printed unfavorable material about them.

Another personality on the staff was Joe Moran, responsible for coverage of the St. Louis Police Department. When Joe came to the paper he had been a telephone boy in the police department, meaning that he answered phones in a police station. He never had any other assignment during his entire life but police headquarters. His night counterpart was Barney Evans, also a unique personality. Barney ultimately retired to a town in southeast Missouri where he pursued his interest in painting.

Walter Orthwein is also remembered fondly. He was a member of the widely respected Orthwein family, which was related to the Busch family. Walter was a large man physically, and had a personality that made its mark. He was a bit of a practical joker. Once he decided to confound his wife, so he carved monkey's feet out of art gum erasers, dipped them in ink, and printed them on the kitchen ceiling in his home so it would look as though a monkey had scampered across the ceiling.

Walter had a career-long ambition to stop customers of the First National Bank in St. Louis on Locust Street down-

Popular Globe *feature writer Beulah Schacht mugs for the audience as she dangles from a parachute harness during a Gridiron dinner.*

town from parking on the street while they had business with the bank. The area where customers parked was legally a no-parking zone. Police more frequently than not ignored brief parking in the spaces to accommodate the bank. Walter didn't like that.

Our company nurse, Virginia Shearer, was a "character" as well. After many years and much help to countless employees Virginia retired. She moved to a small community in Arkansas to live with a son. After a few years of retirement our accounting department advised me that she had not cashed her retirement checks for many months. I had a reporter work to find her. We used all the normal means but could never locate her. Her checks continued to remain uncashed. We finally stopped her checks after a two-year search for her.

For many years St. Louis suffered from the experience of the All-Star baseball game of July 12, 1966. It was extremely hot and humid–the temperature on the field was in the low 100s. Sweltering reporters from across the nation wrote negative stories about the city. This reputation haunted us for years despite concerted efforts to show the country St. Louis had great attributes and the weather was not always miserable.

When a reporter from *Town & Country* interviewed me one day for a story on St. Louis, I could tell from his questions that he had his mind set on a negative piece. By happenstance at that time I knew the publisher of *Town & Country*, a slick, well-done and attractive magazine published by the Hearst Corporation. I called him and protested what I assumed would be another criticism of St. Louis. He astounded me by asking if I could refer him to a writer who would do a good job for the magazine. I recommended LucyAnn Mueller, then a reporter for us and a superior newspaper woman. He pulled the assigned reporter off the story and hired LucyAnn for the special project. She worked up the story and it turned out great.

During the time I was personnel manager for the *Globe-Democrat* a young woman who had just graduated from the University of Michigan sought a job at the paper. She seemed to be an ideal candidate for us. Lon Burrowes liked her, and she was employed as a reporter.

She was Harriett Friedman, who later met one of our newsmen, Jim Woods, and married him. She had an interest in politics. By way of experience in University City, she became lieu-

The Globe-Democrat *staff in 1983 before the paper closed. GDB is at center in the front row.*

tenant governor of Missouri and was exceptionally effective. She gained national acceptance and served in numerous positions serving the interest of women. Jim had left us for the *Post-Dispatch* but Harriett remained with us until she took on political life full-time. I am proud of the leader she became.

Sometime in the 1970s it became necessary for me to appoint a new managing editor. As most large daily newspapers are organized (except for those who deceptively try to fool employees into believing that job titles are as good as a raise in salary), there are not many major department head positions on a paper: only publisher, editor, editor of the editorial page, managing editor, circulation director, advertising director, and mechanical superintendent.

The appointment of a managing editor was significant for many reasons. Traditionally in the industry, men had always held that title. We had a woman city editor. She decided each day what local news would be covered, what place it would hold in the paper's makeup, and who would be assigned to cover specific stories.

This was Sue Ann Wood. Both our news staff and management had a continuing high regard for her talent and her work. She had been a superb reporter and writer, one on whom we could always depend for being able to get the story to which she had been assigned, and for having consistently good judgment of what the important news was each day. Local news in our judgment at the *Globe-Democrat* was the essential ingredient of our

Sandy Britton, left, and Catherine Mahen kept my office running smoothly.

paper.

I broke with tradition and appointed her managing editor and never regretted it. She was the second woman in the history of American journalism to serve as managing editor of a major American daily newspaper. A native Missourian, she came to the *Globe-Democrat* from the *St. Petersburg Times*.

When I announced the planned closing of the *Globe* in 1983, Sue Ann was one of those chosen by the *Post-Dispatch* to come on its staff.

Since I left the newspaper in 1984–I refused to call it "retirement"–I have been asked, "Aren't you now out of the loop?"

To a great extent, I am. I no longer have the authority to write editorials or order changes or support in print political candidates and worthwhile civic projects.

I have stayed active in as many organizations as I can. But I must concede that I do regret being "out of the loop." I have never lost my insatiable desire to be productive.

- 7 -

THE CITY, THE COUNTY, THE STATE

For over sixty years, St. Louis and Missouri have been my home. I would not trade the great Midwest with its friendliness and its unpretentious community spirit for all the glittering sophistication of New York or California, nor even for the growing sun country of the Southwest.

I am especially fortunate to have been in the newspaper business which has given me the opportunity to know our political, cultural, educational and religious leaders. The *Globe-Democrat* played a major role in community and state affairs, and I reaped the reward.

The power structure in St. Louis is honorable and productive but more than that, the people at the top actually work for the city. I don't know of any other city where individuals give so much of themselves as they do here. Civic leaders are personally involved. They don't assign an assistant to do their work.

Civic Progress is the organization which takes on major civic projects. It approves or disapproves proposals that come before it. Sometimes members say, "Not only do we approve, but we want to participate in getting it done." If something will cost, say $5 million, Civic Progress may say, "Okay, the public should put up $4 million. We'll put up $1 million."

At that moment, that day, members commit themselves to $1

million. Each member goes back to his office, writes a check for his share and sends it in.

Traditionally, there are less than thirty members of Civic Progress, all CEOs of major corporations. When I was a part of the organization, there were twenty-seven members. Not all members make equal payments when there is an assessment. There is a long-standing formula whereby members contribute to the extent of their financial position. For example (and this is *not* the literal formula), the five most affluent members may contribute one-tenth each of the total assessment; others, five percent, others three percent, and so forth, until the goal is met. This is also the type of formula which members use in determining for themselves what part of a campaign for funds they will give to an accepted community-wide campaign by a legitimate St. Louis organization or agency.

I understand a person who does not have the financial means or influence to be an active member might instead offer significant knowledge or special qualifications. But to get things done, there has to be the ability to provide a share of an assessment.

I believe that it would be hard to find a similarly effective, productive, and loyal group as Civic Progress anywhere else. It has been a major contributor to civic peace through its committee on race relations. It also has a committee on education, whose sole purpose is to find ways to improve public education, and a committee on health care, working to improve the accessibility of health care to all.

If it weren't for the good will, integrity, and decency of the people who have power, this city would not be nearly where it is today. In all my years in the management of the *Globe-Democrat* and as a reporter, I have never known any one of these powerful leaders ever to have done the wrong thing for the city or to have gained anything personally.

Things don't get done unless someone who has economic power, leadership power, and political power gets behind it. That's the secret of Civic Progress.

St. Louisans have long had a genuine, active interest in keeping downtown St. Louis, the metropolitan area's core, alive and have done what they could to reverse the blight that has plagued it. An early demonstration of the concern and a determination to do something began shortly after World War II ended, more than fifty years ago.

A group of citizens determined to build a new baseball stadium, a hotel and several parking garages. The fruition of their efforts was realized in the middle 1960s when Civic Center Redevelopment Corporation (CCRC) began work on the project. Busch Stadium was first used in May 1966.

CCRC was a voluntary group of St. Louisans, citizens and businesses, who contributed money to finance the project, which was located in the southeast quadrant of downtown. Ostensibly the contributors bought stock or debentures issued by CCRC.

Many of those who participated financially considered their investment a contribution. They never really thought they would receive a financial return or even get their money back. Many gave their stock or debentures to charitable organizations in St. Louis and charged the donation to charity on their income tax returns.

One such participant called me one day and asked if I could name a social agency who would accept, as a gift his CCRC stock or debentures. I suggested the Herbert Hoover Boys Club and he followed up on the suggestion.

The planned construction was completed, with Jim Hickok, chairman of First National Bank, then president of CCRC. Much public attention was drawn to the work, especially the hotel (Stouffers) and the Busch Stadium, where the Cardinals moved when they left Sportsman's Park on the north side.

At that time, Stouffer's had the largest room in the city for banquets, topping the historical front runner, the Chase Park Plaza. For instance, more than 1,300 people attended a dinner in the Stouffer ballroom to honor John Joseph Cardinal Carberry on his return from Rome, where he had just been made a Cardinal. For years the place to hold a large banquet was Stouffers.

The CCRC board of directors was stunned and surprised one day when Anheuser-Busch made a public offer for the CCRC securities. The offer provided for the purchase of the 202,685 shares of CCRC stock at book value ($65.08 per share as shown in the 12/31/80 annual report) and $1.00 for each of the 20,018,982 debentures. The offer thus aggregated $33,209,722.

The board's immediate reaction was that it could not make a responsible decision on the offer because it was not aware of the fair value of the CCRC properties. Charles J. Dougherty, then chairman of the Union Electric Company was president of CCRC.

The CCRC board promptly contracted with Goldman, Sachs

& Companies to undertake a study and to advise the board as to what CCRC might expect to realize in a sale of its properties. When the Goldman, Sachs report to CCRC concluded that the Anheuser Busch offer amounted to less than the fair market value CCRC directed Goldman Sachs to seek a buyer, a "white knight," who would offer a higher price.

This effort by Goldman Sachs resulted in a number of interested inquiries from the U.S. and Canada. One of the more memorable was David Murdock, a well known financier from California, who flew to St. Louis for inspections and conferences and then made an offer of $50 million for all the CCRC stock and debentures.

The *Globe-Democrat* published an editorial commending Dougherty for his work and suggesting that the offer be accepted.

Charlie was incensed. He came to my office and heatedly castigated me for the *Globe's* bad judgment, all the time insisting he could get a better offer but not if we continued to recommend the first offer. We expressed hope that he would do better.

Well, he did a lot better.

However, it was the offer of Apex Oil Company (Samuel R. Goldstein and Tony Novelly) of $125 for each share of stock and $1.35 for each debenture (aggregating $52,361,251) which was a principal factor in pegging the price that Anheuser-Busch ultimately paid: $126.52 for each share of stock and $1.37 for each debenture, aggregating $53,069,712.

Dougherty, an ex-U.S. Marine in World War II, had stood his ground and earned an unbelievable benefit for the city. The loyal St. Louisans, individually and corporately, who believed in their city and wanted to help, got their money back with a profit.

But the unanticipated by-product which was exceptionally beneficial to the city was the financial windfall for many social agencies who had been given Civic Center stock and debentures by owners who considered them worthless. It was an unbelievable benefit which had never happened before and probably will never happen again.

The Girls Scouts received more than a $1 million, the Boy Scouts even more, and the Herbert Hoover Boys Club was given more than $700,000. These monies, resulting from Charlie Dougherty's good work, gave many outstanding social agencies a firm financial footing which they never would have had without it.

For many years, prior to World War II when portions of the slum buildings along Market Street between Eighteenth Street and Twelfth Street were cleared, St. Louis officials and city planners envisioned a landscaped mall a block or so wide running from the riverfront west to Eighteenth Street. The initial work west of Twelfth Street (now Tucker) was encouraging, but the efforts to develop the area east of Tucker was marked by two steps forward and one step backward.

At a point in the late 1970s most of the work had been completed except for a building or two which still remained to be removed. At least one of the properties needing to be removed was owned by a real estate developer by the name of Donn Lipton. Not only was he reluctant to sell his property to the mall committee but he also had plans for what the future mall development should look like. He and the committee simply could not get together.

About that time I was a member of the board of Downtown in St. Louis, Inc., a self-appointed membership agency dedicated to the interests of downtown St. Louis. Two members, Richard Ford, then president of First National Bank, and Robert Hyland, then head of KMOX Radio, were working diligently to complete the mall. Frequently they would come to a directors' meeting to report a step forward, only to come back a month later to report the anticipated movement had not taken place. One of the disappointments was that Mayor Jim Conway would pledge to help with a concept and then back off.

It occurred to me that the *Globe-Democrat* might be able to be of help if Donn Lipton was a real stumbling block. I called one of Lipton's good friends, Lee Kling, prominent St. Louis businessman and Democratic party leader and asked him if he would meet with Lipton and me about the mall. Kling agreed and Lipton agreed.

At our meeting Lipton explained why he had not been able to resolve a deal with the mall committee. Lipton said that he felt he could not trust H. Edwin Trusheim, chairman of General America Life Insurance Co. and chairman of the mall committee. Both Kling and I assured him that he could trust Trusheim and we asked him, if we got some assurance to that effect, would he enter serious negotiations regarding his building? He said he would. We got those assurances for him, and the misunderstanding was cleared up.

Negotiations resumed and Lipton was able to find a resolution which satisfied him. His building and the old Western Union building with its hundreds of miles of wiring disappeared, and the mall was about as complete as it's going to be for a while—until a movement is successful in removing that artistic monstrosity, the Serra sculpture at 11th and Market.

Two prominent St. Louisans came to the *Globe* one day to ask us to make a contribution to the proposed Serra sculpture. I refused.

Several months later, Si Newhouse, S.I.'s son, a collector of modern art, called me and said, "' I understand you are not going to make a contribution to the Serra sculpture."

I said, "That's right."

He asked, "Would you mind if I made a contribution?" I said that was all right with me, if he used his own money and not *Globe-Democrat* money. He promised it would come out of his own pocket. It did.

After it was built, two widely known art supporters in St. Louis stopped me one day at the Noonday Club. They said they understood I didn't like the Serra sculpture.

I said, "That's right. Most people don't."

One said, "if you will support me I will organize a campaign to move it." I agreed we would do that.

Shortly afterward, I announced our plan to close the *Globe-Democrat,* or we would have gotten rid of it. It's so damn ugly and meaningless. What the hell does a bunch of steel plates mean? I think it is simply inexcusable as a piece of art. Art is something that is supposed to be pretty and attractive and pleasing to the eye. How does that definition fit the Serra sculpture? We missed our chance to get rid of it.

A half-century ago, convention facilities for the city were pretty much limited to Kiel Auditorium. When convention business was finally seen for the economic boost it gave a city, plans were begun for a much larger, more attractive center, and the designated location was on Delmar, east of 12th Street (now Tucker Blvd.).

As the one-time president of the Convention and Visitors Bureau, I acquired some knowledge of the value and importance of conventions to any city. Delegates and their families at that time spent somewhere around $100 to $150 per day per person. I'm sure that figure has increased dramatically as St. Louis continues to offer more attractions.

Gen. Leif J. Sverdrup, founder of what was then Sverdrup & Parcel, an engineering company, successfully bid for the construction contract for the new convention center. This would require a great deal of money, of course, and the public defeated a bond issue to provide it.

It was decided to resubmit the bond issue for public approval. The feeling was that Mayor Al Cervantes' participation in the first election had been a detriment because at that time his popularity was declining. A group of prominent St. Louisans asked him to stay in the background for the second campaign, which he loyally agreed to do.

It was also decided that it would be important to enlist the support of northside voters. Philip F. Lichtenstein, a banker in South St. Louis, was appointed to seek the approval and cooperation of the black ministers and they agreed to help. There was another intensive campaign and this time the bond issue passed and the money became available—a tribute to the willingness of many St. Louisans to work together.

In the course of the planning, a controversial issue arose which needed the approval of the board of aldermen. Sverdrup called me one day to say that this issue was pending before the board and he thought it was crucial that it be passed. He asked if the *Globe* could help. I called Red Villa, a long-time highly respected alderman, and he said he would be happy to get together some votes. The aldermen did pass the issue and we wound up with an attractive new convention facility.

Out of respect for the mayor it was named Cervantes Center. It's a proud addition to downtown and a mecca for convention-eers who enjoy the hospitality and the attractions of St. Louis.

Alphonso Cervantes was a popular political figure, first as an alderman and then as a two-term mayor. He was exceptionally enthusiastic and imaginative and had superb public support for many years. A try for a third term brought him down because of unfortunate misconceptions about his integrity, rumors that were absolutely untrue.

Following the New York World's Fair in 1964-65, Cervantes was determined to bring two of the Fair's popular attractions to

St. Louis. Both of them had ties to his Spanish ancestry—the *Santa Maria*, a replica of one of Columbus' ships, and the Spanish Pavilion. Both were to haunt him in his campaign for a third term.

The cost of bringing the *Santa Maria* here was estimated at $300,000. Cervantes raised the money from friends, each of whom gave about $30,000, anticipating it would be returned from ticket sales for visitors to the ship docked on the riverfront. It turned out to be a popular attraction but not too long after it was brought here, disaster struck. A storm on June 28, 1969, broke the ship from its moorings. It drifted across the river, struck some pilings and sank. It could not be raised and restored.

The Spanish Pavilion was a different story. Cervantes estimated it would cost $3 million to bring the beautiful Spanish building here and reconstruct it. He envisioned a center for meetings with good restaurants. Others, including General Sverdrup, estimated the cost at $7 million.

Cervantes raised the initial funds without much difficulty from civic-minded individuals and corporations, including the *Globe-Democrat.* Construction began and the cost skyrocketed. Cervantes appealed to civic leaders to help raise the additional money. One was Sanford Zimmerman, then chairman of Famous-Barr, our major advertising account.

I had declined to give additional money toward the $7 million, feeling that Cervantes should have been more accurate in his estimates. The *Globe* had already given money to meet the first cost projection. Then we abruptly relented and gave two more $5,000 gifts for the pavilion. The reason I relented was that Cervantes had Zimmerman call me and ask for a gift. With that call, I didn't hesitate. It was the ultimate in pressure. The Spanish Pavilion became a reality, an asset and an impressive bit of architecture. It is now the lobby and first floor area of the downtown Marriott Hotel.

Cervantes was a diligent and devoted citizen of St. Louis who had made his own way in the world, becoming very successful, and was conscious of the vicissitudes of living. He was a very genuine individual, but he had the misfortune along the way to have incidents develop which caused mistrust on the part of the public, so instead of winding up as a man having served a city so well with a good reputation, he wound up with somewhat of a blight cast over his administration which wasn't justified at all.

Somewhere along the line the construction of an airport at Waterloo, Ill., fifteen to twenty miles east of St. Louis, to replace Lambert as the city's principal airport became an issue. There was both significant support, led by Cervantes, and strong opposition.

Early on, Sverdrup & Parcel told the *Globe-Democrat* that Lambert could be enhanced to serve St. Louis well into the twenty-first century. Later the engineering company took a different stance and urged the construction at Waterloo. Wallace (Buck) Persons, longtime head of Emerson Electric, was appointed by Governor Christopher S. Bond to head a citizens committee to oppose moving Lambert. Persons worked harder and more successfully than anyone can relate and he was successful. The Waterloo concept was finally dropped.

During the course of the debate Cervantes' critics contended that Cervantes and his friend, Tony Sansone, had secret investments in the Waterloo area from which they would profit following construction of St. Louis' airport there. The *Globe-Democrat* spent hundreds of hours of reporters' time investigating the rumor. We were totally convinced that neither Cervantes nor Sansone had a single, minute investment from which they would profit. The public wasn't convinced.

During his second term as mayor, Cervantes suddenly changed the rules about the sale of beer at Lambert Airport. For years, Anheuser-Busch had had exclusive rights. Suddenly, without fanfare, Falstaff appeared on the shelves.

This infuriated Gussie Busch, who told Cervantes he would never serve in public office again. Cervantes was determined to run for a third term, however, despite Gussie's opposition.

When the next campaign came around, I had in mind urging one of three young aldermen—Dick Gephardt, John Roach or Milton Svetanics—to run for mayor in the Democratic primary. I talked to Gephardt, but he said he was interested in going to Congress and becoming speaker of the House of Representatives!

I asked Gussie if he would support any of the three but he declined, saying he wanted John Poelker, just retired as city comptroller, and asked that the three of us meet at his home at Grant's Farm on a Sunday afternoon. At that meeting, Poelker declined to run, pointing out that his wife, Ruth, was ill, and she had asked him not to seek public office again. But Gussie persisted and told John he would guarantee him a $300,000 campaign fund and a job at the brewery for life if he lost.

The next Sunday John returned to Grant's Farm for a second meeting with Gussie and me and said he would run.

Early in his campaign to win his third term nomination in the Democratic primary against Poelker, Mayor Cervantes and his wife, Carmen, came to see me. They asked what we thought of his chances to win the primary. Would the *Globe-Democrat* support him? We told him we did not think he could win the primary because the public thought (wrongly) that he had used public money to bring the *Santa Maria* here; that the public thought (wrongly) that he did not handle the move and reconstruction of the Spanish Pavilion prudently, despite its benefits; and that the public (wrongly again) was convinced that he planned to profit from moving the airport to Waterloo. Further, we told him that the *Globe-Democrat* would not support him, as we had in the past, and that we planned to support John Poelker.

Carmen could not hold back tears and the two of them left in obvious despair. Cervantes did run for the third term, but Poelker won the primary and went on to become mayor. Cervantes went back to his insurance business.

During the campaign, Poelker asked me to see if Benny Goins, a strong, young black leader who had been elected license collector in 1968 and was opposed to the William Clay organization, could be persuaded to support his bid for mayor instead of Cervantes. I talked to Goins and he agreed.

Shortly before the primary election date, Goins came to my office and told me that a man representing himself as a Cervantes supporter had placed $30,000 on Goins' dining room table and said it was his if he would agree to switch his support to Cervantes. Goins said he had just bought his house, which he was very proud of, and that he really needed the money. He asked me what he should do. I pointed out that he had pledged his support to Poelker and should honor that pledge.

Even though I'm sure he needed the money, he promised me that he would reject the offer, and he did.

Years went by and out of the blue Goins was indicted by a federal grand jury for taking a bribe in a political matter. It was small, around $1,500. He was tried, convicted and served a year or two in the federal penitentiary. I didn't believe then, and I don't believe now, that if Benny Goins rejected a $30,000 bribe and kept his word, that he would take a pipsqueak bribe.

I spent a couple of years trying to get a presidential pardon for Goins but did not succeed. I managed to get the pardon most of the way through the Department of Justice but could never get it onto President Bush's desk. I have reason to believe that it would have been signed. It was so important to Goins because when he was convicted he lost the right to vote or hold public office.

It was shameful to witness the way his former friends deserted him when he was released from prison He couldn't get a job until, fortunately, Sorkis Webbe, Sr., then an influential Democratic leader, found work for him at the Gateway Hotel, the old Statler.

When Aloys P. Kaufmann, one of the city's few Republican mayors, left office, he took a position as president of the chamber of commerce. Several years later, the chamber elected to retire him. He came to see me in my office and told me that the chamber's retirement benefits were inadequate, that he simply couldn't live on its financial offer. As I recall, it was somewhere in the very low five figures per year.

I said I would try to persuade the chamber to take better care of him. I thought one way to do it would be for the *Globe-Democrat* and the *Post-Dispatch*, in recognition of his years of service to the community, to offer to supplement his retirement income.

I talked with *Post* officials who shocked me by agreeing with me that we should pay the former mayor a supplemental income that would allow him to live at least in a modest manner. I then told the chamber that was what we were going to do if the chamber was unwilling to match the needs of the mayor. Shortly after that, the chamber did offer him a retirement income which he accepted and the newspapers were never called upon to supplement his retirement benefits.

It was a bit disconcerting to learn after his death that he left an estate in the high six figures.

In 1965, on the last day for a candidate to file for mayor on the Republican ticket, no one had filed. There was a Democratic candidate but there was no Republican.

Wayne L. Millsap was a vigorous young Republican protago-

nist, an attorney who had run for president of the board of aldermen and had been active in every election in behalf of Republicans. He lived in the city and practiced law in the city, starting
his law career with the Lon Hocker firm after graduating from
Saint Louis University Law School. Millsap decided that the Republicans should not be embarrassed by not having a candidate.
The election should not go to the Democrats by default.

He rounded up a man by the name of Maurice Zumwalt, who
was the head of a replacement door manufacturing company in
the city, and induced him to run for mayor.

Millsap took Zumwalt off to see Al Kaufmann late in the afternoon and Kaufmann, too, urged him to run. Zumwalt agreed
and they showed up at the Election Board at about 8:00 in the
evening. The filings closed at 8:30. Zumwalt filed, ran for mayor
as best he could, but was defeated by the dominance of the Democrats.

It is to be noted that the biggest single supporter for Zumwalt
was Howard Young, father of Cy Young of American Zinc Smelt-
ing. Howard walked into Zumwalt's office one day and gave him
$5,000 in cash, the biggest single contribution in the campaign
and representing most of the money that Zumwalt had to spend
in that election.

Jim Conway, a St. Louis businessman and southside city resident, had been a member of the Missouri state legislature when
he announced he planned to run for mayor of St. Louis following
John Poelker. When he appealed to Gussie Busch for financial
support, Gussie asked me to meet with him and Conway in his
brewery office.

For some time Conway had worn a Santa-Claus-type beard
that made him most identifiable. Gussie listened to Conway's
pitch for a while and then said, "Shave off that beard and I'll help
you." I knew Gussie meant business because he had expressed
distaste many times over the beards some of his Cardinal baseball players wore.

Conway protested that the beard was a mark of distinction for
him in public life and besides, he said, "My wife likes it." Gussie's
response was to tell him he would not support him if he kept the
beard.

The next afternoon Conway shaved his beard and Gussie supported him. He won.

At this writing, I notice that the beard is back.

When alderman Vincent Schoemehl entered the Democratic primary for mayor of St. Louis he, like most candidates for political office, visited the *Globe-Democrat* to seek our endorsement. Our group, including Martin Duggan, editorial page editor and myself, queried Schoemehl on many issues.

One question related to his position on reopening Homer Phillips Hospital. Homer Phillips Hospital was dedicated and put to use in 1937 by the city to deliver health care to black citizens of St. Louis. Black medical school graduates from all over America came to Homer Phillips to serve their internships. The hospital came to be the source of immense pride to the black community.

As revenue for the city declined and the costs of operation steadily grew, city officials looked for places to save money. By this time black patients were being served at City Hospital in addition to Homer Phillips. Mayor Conway took the perilous road of closing Homer Phillips. This caused consternation, disappointment, and vigorous opposition from the black community. (Incidentally, a black classmate of mine, a fellow athlete at Loyola University named Lucius Davis, graduated from medical school and took his internship at Homer Phillips.)

Thus the issue of the closing of Homer Phillips was intense in the primary race between Conway and Schoemehl. Schoemehl had promised voters that he would reopen Homer Phillips. One of our questions to Schoemehl was, "Where will you find the money to reopen and operate Homer Phillips?" He said that he would answer us off the record. We accepted this.

Schoemehl then said, "I do not intend to reopen Homer Phillips."

As mayor, he did not reopen Homer Phillips, but to his credit he did not forget the obligation of the community to provide health care for the poor. He persuaded Gene McNary, St. Louis County executive, that it was in their mutual interest to set up a facility, jointly financed by the city and the county, to provide health care for the poor. This became Regional.

The *Globe-Democrat* played a major role in the political development of Mayor Freeman Bosley. I had known and admired his father, an alderman, for years. I became friends through the years with the Roberts men, Steve, first, and then Michael. I admired their presence on the scene. When the *Globe-Democrat* soured on Joe Roddy, the longtime St. Louis Circuit Clerk, young Bosley was coming into the picture. The Roberts men introduced me to him during a lunch at the Missouri Athletic Club. I was impressed with him, his presence and his education.

So, when the question of whom the *Globe-Democrat* would endorse in the Democratic primary race for Circuit Clerk we decided to endorse Freeman, Jr. He beat Roddy and went on to win in the general election. Joe Roddy was terribly disappointed in the *Globe-Democrat.* We think we were the deciding factor for Bosley because of our strength in south St. Louis, where young Bosley got a number of votes. Subsequently we also endorsed Junior for his second term. We were not in business when he ran for mayor.

It's also worthy to note, for historical reasons, that the *Globe-Democrat* endorsed Carl Officer, when he ran the first time for mayor of East St. Louis. He became the city's first black mayor. I had known his parents, who ran a funeral home in East St. Louis. His mother, Myrtle Officer, was a *Globe-Democrat* Woman of Achievement. I understand that Carl Officer is now working in the family funeral home business, which his grandparents founded, and has a location in St. Louis.

In 1956 while I was personnel manager of the *Globe,* Governor James T. Blair appointed me to the City of St. Louis Election Board. I had known Governor Blair for several years but had not even hinted to him about an appointment. I believe my appointment was instigated by John Hahn, a popular political writer for the *Globe* who was close to Blair, since Hahn asked me casually one time if I would accept a nomination to the election board.

Amberg approved the idea of my appointment so I accepted. It turned out to be a valuable and very educational experience, affording me a practical, firsthand knowledge of working politics. My service on the board never conflicted with my duties at the paper, nor did my duties at the paper ever conflict with board responsibilities.

When the governor offered the appointment, I asked if he had specific objectives he'd like our board to address. He said he had only one. He hoped we would buy voting machines. The funds had been appropriated for several years, but prior boards had not been able to agree to buy them.

I am everlastingly grateful for the character and integrity of my fellow board members. The board chairman was Michael L. Galli, a product of the Italian Hill area of St. Louis and a self-made, successful real estate man long interested in Democratic politics. He advised me, kept me from making a fool of myself, and we became lifelong good friends. The other Democrat was Dr. Daniel Nack, a chiropractor. My fellow Republican was Eugene Wienke, a banker. By law the board consists of two Democrats and two Republicans. The chairman represents the party of the governor (Blair was a Democrat), and the secretary represents the other party, so I became the secretary.

Following the governor's suggestion, the board set about to buy voting machines. We solicited bids from three manufacturers and bought the machines from the lowest bidder early in our first year in office. We spent somewhere between two and three million to buy the machines.

Obviously, we needed a building in which to house and maintain them. They were about the size of a medium-sized upright piano and very heavy. We found a new warehouse building, all on one floor, next door to the Rallo Construction Co., adjacent to Southwest High School at Arsenal and Kingshighway and bought the building.

Next we needed a trucker to haul the machines to polling places, about 600 of them, before election day and return them to the warehouse after election day. We advertised for bids, knowing from research that in other cities the rates for hauling varied from $17 to $22 a trip, out and in, totaling just over $40 at the top. Special trucks with mechanical lifts were required because the machines were so heavy men could not handle them.

Four or five local haulers submitted bids. The lowest bidder, which we were compelled to accept by law, was the Slay Transportation Co. The bid was for $7.50 per machine per trip, making it $15 round trip. This was astonishingly low and the board was concerned that Slay would find he couldn't provide the service after he had been at it for a while. We called him to a meeting and told him about our concerns. He said he wanted the job and refused to withdraw his bid, so he got it. He performed flawlessly during our term in office.

Like many Lebanese in the city, Slay became interested in politics and was a significant factor in Democratic party activities in both city and state. He also was always willing to lend a hand to worthy charities. His special interest was the Southside Boys Club which he served as president.

I was very pleased with Slay's conscientious and efficient service, but I must admit that a board experience with some other St. Louis citizens was disillusioning

After a short time on the board Wienke and I learned that a substantial number of Republican judges and clerks could not read or write. We thought such a deficiency should disqualify a precinct judge or clerk, so we discharged them. To our consternation we found it almost impossible to replace them. Citizens did not want to work in the polling places. To fill the vacancies we subpoenaed St. Louis residents from every list we could find—the Missouri Athletic Club, the Noonday Club, the Racquet Club, and so forth—until we filled the roster. That experience taught us what a disenchanting number of citizens, including a number of prominent ones, were disgusting hypocrites, the first to scream about dishonest elections while refusing to serve in the polling places.

Unfortunately many Americans think cynically and distrustfully about their government and belittle it, whether it's federal, state or local. The effectiveness and values of our government are dependent upon citizen involvement and it's distressing, and sometimes frightening, to think of the long term consequences of citizen indifference and apathy. Such precious rights as voting, serving on juries and working in the polls on election days are examples. Good government results from participation and better government from more participation, never from less.

Missouri has the distinction of having a state senator serve continuously and longer than any other state in America—Mike Kinney, who served in the Missouri Senate for over fifty years. He represented a downtown St. Louis district and, curiously, lived in Richmond Heights in violation of residency requirements. Kinney sent us a batch of names of people to be employed at the election board, which was a patronage office. Wienke and I did not employ them. When Galli and I went to Jefferson City to get a wage increase for our employees we did not get it. Kinney refused to allow the increase.

Later Kinney sent us another group of his constituents for employment. We hired them. A few months later we repeated our request for a wage increase. We got it.

During our term from 1956 through 1960 Galli and I personally canvassed voter registrations when we found several registrations from a single address, or for other obvious reasons. In one election we found about forty persons registered from one storefront address on Olive Street near Jefferson. We personally struck all these illegal registrations from the rolls. On each election day he and I spent the day visiting precincts to show our faces. If we were concerned about potential disturbances at precincts where we knew there had been acrimonious campaigning, we asked for and got special police escorts.

Our board felt we delivered responsible administration of elections in St. Louis during our tenure and we believe there was a minimum of fraudulent voting.

One of Governor Blair's projects while in office was to establish a permanent organization which had for its sole purpose the honoring of Missouri citizens who had contributed in a significant way to the improvement and development of the state of Missouri. To this end he originated the Academy of Missouri Squires.

The Squires tradition continues to this day. The membership is limited to 100 persons. New members are initiated only when a vacancy in the list occurs, generally by the death of a member, occasionally by resignation.

New members are invited to become a Missouri Squire after nomination by a member, or anyone acquainted with the Squires. Applications are reviewed by a nominating committee, which sends its selections to the governor, the Chief Squire, who extends an invitation.

Members are inducted at a luncheon hosted by the governor in the governor's mansion, which is the Squires annual meeting in the fall. Members are given a cane bearing the member's name and date of membership and a pin insignia.

Sometime after leaving the governor's office, while practicing law in Jefferson City, Governor Blair arrived home late one afternoon, put his car in the garage, which was part of the house, and went inside. The next morning the governor and his wife were found dead of asphyxiation. There was absolutely no evidence of anything except a tragic error. Apparently the governor left the engine of his car running and fumes entered the house by way of its ventilation system.

Unbelievably, Charles F. Spoehrer, a much sought-after management labor attorney, and his wife, Jane, suffered the identical fate. Charles and Jane played bridge at our house on a Saturday evening. Both were in excellent spirits during the evening. There was not even the most remote hint of any mental or physical problem. They left about 11 P.M. Apparently Charles drove his car into his garage under his home in Olivette, and he and Jane walked upstairs to their living quarters. The next morning both he and Jane were found in their beds asphyxiated. Again no evidence whatsoever of any unusual circumstances. Fumes from his car engine permeated the house through the ventilation system.

Warren E. Hearnes served two four-year terms as Missouri's governor. During one of his races for governor, Hearnes and I discussed his chances of winning the primary. I told him it appeared he would not win enough wards in St. Louis to carry the city. He asked for a piece of paper, wrote on it the wards he would carry, sealed it in an envelope and left it with me to open after the election. He had predicted every ward he would carry. He won the majority of the St. Louis vote and the primary.

As his second term was ending, I asked a staff member to research legislation which Hearnes had successfully passed. This disclosed that he had engineered through the legislature more than thirty major bills. When a civil disturbance over desegregation issues seemed imminent in Kansas City, he dispatched the National Guard. There was no riot. I wrote an editorial commending his high level of leadership, among the best of all our governors.

During the last few months of Hearnes' term, a federal grand jury in Kansas City under the direction of Bert C. Hurn, a U.S. Attorney, began an inquiry into Hearnes' handling of political money and related activities. The assistant U.S. Attorney who actually did the grand jury work was Paul Anthony White.

Information leaked to the media about grand jury testimony received wide publicity. The result was the virtual destruction of the career of a decent, capable, effective public servant. Warren Hearnes was not charged with any misdeed by the grand jury, but he was unsuccessful in subsequent efforts to continue his public career.

There was a repellent sort of irony in this case. The prosecutor, White, not long after the Hearnes investigation, was charged with molesting young boys and then convicted. Later, he was tried and convicted of an IRS offense and faced charges of having issued a number of bad checks.

This same Kansas City grand jury at the same time and again under White's leadership indicted a highly respected St. Louis banker, Don Lasater, chairman of Mercantile Bank, on charges regarding political donations from other bank officials prior to his appointment as CEO and chairman.

Two of Mercantile's directors, Ed Clark, then president of Southwestern Bell, and Maurice (Dude) Chambers, then head of International Shoe Co., strongly defended Lasater at board sessions and persuaded the board to allow Lasater to remain in his position.

Before the grand jury ended its term the indictment against Lasater was withdrawn. Had it not been for the loyalty of two powerful civic leaders, Lasater might have suffered the same loss of prestige as did Warren Hearnes.

For many years, the *Globe-Democrat* enjoyed a relationship of mutual respect with members of the Dowd family in St. Louis. It began with the father of the family, Edward P. Dowd, once the night chief of police, who could always be counted on to help the press when it was seeking late-breaking news at night from the St. Louis Police Department.

Two of his sons, Edward and Robert, became successful lawyers. Both enjoyed politics and worked effectively at it. Ed became president of the Police Board. Robert became a circuit judge and then was on the Missouri Court of Appeals. Both had children and there are now four or five Dowds from the third generation practicing law in St Louis.

Ed served as circuit attorney of St. Louis, an elective post. He earned a great reputation in the prosecutor's office both for his legal skills and for his high level public service. In 1972, he announced he would run for governor of Missouri on the Democratic ticket. The *Globe-Democrat* had generally supported both Ed and Bob in their political activities. Ed now asked for our support in his race for governor, and most of our news management staff wanted to endorse him.

We knew, however, that Ed had accepted a substantial political donation from the Steamfitters Union. Under Amberg's direction we had not been supportive of the Fitters.

Ed and I met in the lobby of the Chase Hotel to discuss his endorsement. I told him that we could not endorse him if he kept the union donation. He protested that the donation would not affect his administration as governor. I reminded him of the political strength of the Fitters and told him I didn't think he could escape their influence even if he tried. I told him if he would return the contribution and make the return public, we would endorse him. He declined and we did not give him our support.

Unfortunately–for him–he lost.

Shortly after Christopher S. Bond began his first term as governor of Missouri in 1973 he announced that he would discontinue the practice of giving selected prominent citizens low numbered license plates for their automobiles. Historically the governor personally assigned plates numbered below 100. A selected few other elected state officials assigned the remaining numbers up to 10,000.

Many Missourians took great pride in the license numbers they had for their cars. Usually the number represented a significant one to the holder–a home street address, a wedding date, a birthday date, and similar occasions. Stan Musial had number 3000, symbolizing his record of 3,000 hits. Maj. Gen. Leif Sverdrup had a special number which was dear to him My predecessor, Dick Amberg, had number 9, which his widow still carries. I had number 2222.

This was the best I could do, in keeping with *Globe-Democrat* tradition. When automobiles were first licensed E. Lansing Ray, then publisher, had number 22, representing his home address. When he died, another *Globe-Democrat* executive latched on to number 22. Still another had number 222. So the best I could manage was 2222. Bond cut all this out.

The reaction was outrage. Maj. Gen. Leif Sverdrup, one of Governor Bond's strongest supporters and money raisers, told the governor he would no longer help him with contributions. Stan Musial lost his 3000 and complained. Mrs. Sylvia Souers, the widow of Admiral Sidney Souers, had number 625 which she resented losing. In terms of serious state government issues the number issue was scarcely a life or death matter, but it was very, very troublesome to the governor.

Within a short period of time Governor Bond found a great solution. The system of assigning the plates would be reinstated but the recipients would be required to pay a special fee of $25 annually to have the number. This worked.

At a St. Louis Gridiron Dinner after the practice was resumed, Bond, who traditionally attended the event, presented me at the dinner with a special license plate, not an official one, with my nickname on it—"Dunc." The gag got a big hand. The *Globe-Democrat* had been strongly critical of the governor for fouling up the special plate system.

Louie Buckowitz was one of St. Louis's widest-known, active and effective Democratic political leaders. He ruled the 10th ward, a genial, serious, and most likable man. His wife, Georgia, was also active in politics, serving as St. Louis Park Commissioner and at one time operating a Missouri state fee office in downtown St. Louis in the Mansion House.

Georgia was a member of a United Way committee of which I was chairman. My secretary did not realize that at the time the Noonday Club did not admit women and I neglected to check the list of guests for a committee meeting. Georgia appeared and the head waiter told her she could not be admitted. I heard her outside the meeting commenting loudly, "I was invited to this meeting and I'm going in."

I spoke to the management and she was admitted. The Noonday Club later changed its policy to admit women as guests and, subsequently, as members.

When Highway I-55 was being planned, it was to run through Louie's ward. A substantial number of the residents did not want the highway, so Louie opposed the construction and for a long time it was stalled. Finally, Louie made a deal with Dick Amberg which I was not privy to, and approved the project and the highway was finished.

At the time of Kit Bond's election to his first term as governor, Georgia was operating her Missouri fee office in the Mansion House. A state fee office sells license plates and certain other licenses. The operator charges a premium for the service and remits to the state somewhat less than what is collected. Histori-

cally, these offices have been given to effective political supporters of the governor. Georgia had gotten her office from Governor Hearnes, and now she was about to lose it under the Republican Bond administration.

Louie told me that if Bond would allow Georgia to keep her
office, he would guarantee the governor six votes in the Missouri
House of Representatives any time the governor needed them. I
told this to Bond and asked him to keep Georgia in her fee office,
but Bond refused.

Early in Bond's term, he pushed a reorganization of a number
of administrative officers in several state agencies. This required
approval by the legislature. Bond called to ask if I could help
him with some votes. I reminded him of the votes he declined
from Buckowitz. Bond, I'm sure, was embarrassed by the reminder
but he did succeed in getting legislative approval for his reforms.

Close to the end of Bond's first term, I happened to be a guest
at a luncheon in the governor's mansion in Jefferson City. Bond
took me aside and said he was confident of reelection—he was
running against Democrat Joe Teasdale—but he was worried about
the chances that William ("Full Time") Phelps could be reelected
lieutenant governor. He asked if the *Globe-Democrat* could supply
some extra emphasis on behalf of Phelps.

I agreed and the *Globe* pushed hard for Phelps. When the bal-
lots were counted, Phelps had won, as we hoped. But Kit Bond
had lost to Teasdale in a dramatic upset.

Joe Teasdale, a Kansas City lawyer, began his race for governor of Missouri in an unique fashion, walking across the state to
meet voters. Once in office, he continued to make some unusual
decisions.

As with many political figures, it was not uncommon for him
to visit the *Globe-Democrat* to discuss issues and problems. On
one visit, I asked if he intended to be present in a day or two for
a luncheon at the Noonday Club in St. Louis with Prince Charles
of England. He said he had declined the invitation but asked if
we thought he should attend.

I told him it was his duty, that as governor, he represented the
people of Missouri and it would be exceptionally discourteous
and arrogant not to attend.

Teasdale then said he would attend the luncheon for Prince
Charles if he could be re-invited. I called Harold E. Thayer, chair-

man of Mallinckrodt Chemical Co., one of the luncheon chairmen, and he said he would send another invitation immediately.

The protocol for meetings with British royalty is, to say the least, a bit demanding and formal. One requirement is that all guests be present before the royal personage appears. I had also been invited and was astonished that Teasdale wasn't on hand when Prince Charles arrived. Finally, Teasdale got there—after the end of the reception and tardy for lunch.

A few months after the election, he had received an invitation along with other governors, to visit the Ford Motor Co. in Detroit. He also had declined this and we criticized him in an editorial commenting that he owed it to the people to represent them at the Ford meeting to lobby for continued Ford interest in Missouri, such as the Ford assembly plant in Hazelwood.

Late in his term of office, I was in Jefferson City to attend the funeral for Howard Cook, chairman of the Central Missouri Trust Co., a Jefferson City bank. The Cook family owned the bank which was one of the most powerful political influences in the state.

I had an appointment to see the governor, and he asked why I was in Jefferson City. When I said I was to attend Howard Cook's funeral he asked, "Who is Howard Cook?"

I could hardly answer. His ignorance of the name of the family and its political power was incredible. I explained the history of the Cook family's participation in Missouri life. He then called in Brendan Ryan, a St. Louis attorney who was working temporarily as Teasdale's chief advisor. He said, "Duncan thinks I should go to the Cook funeral. Do you agree?"

"Absolutely." said Ryan.

So Teasdale did attend. He got there very late.

When John Ashcroft, who had served two terms as attorney general, first ran for governor of Missouri, he was challenged in the Republican primary by Gene McNary, longtime St. Louis County Executive. Ashcroft came to St. Louis early in his campaign and asked us to introduce him to as many St. Louisans as we chose to. He felt he was little known here and needed some respected support. Among those to whom we introduced him were John Jordan, then managing partner in Price Waterhouse, and Harold Thayer of Mallinckrodt.

Thayer developed a strong money-raising relationship with Ashcroft. McNary was broadly known and supported in St. Louis, especially by those who made political contributions. One of his chief money raisers was Howard (Cy) Young. Both Thayer and Young were members of the Bogey Club. Members meet for lunch every Saturday of the year, so there is always interesting conversation before the meal. A strong rivalry developed between Thayer and Young to attract Bogey membership support for their respective candidates. Occasionally, the contest became a bit heated and discussions a bit tense.

Ashcroft went on to win the primary and the election. After two terms, he was elected to the U.S. Senate. He had been mentioned as a potential Republican candidate for the presidential nomination, but announced that he would remain in the Senate.

For many years the federal district court in St. Louis was regarded by those who had knowledge of the federal court system as one of the best, if not the best, in the entire United States. It kept its docket current and its efficiency was admired all over the country.

Years ago the commissioner of Internal Revenue, the man who is responsible for the collection of our federal income taxes, called and told me he admired the work of our federal court so much that he wanted to meet the judges who sat on the court. He asked if I would introduce him to the judges if he came to St. Louis from Washington. I told him I would arrange the meeting. He came out and had lunch with our judges to find out how they ran such an outstanding court.

The judges at that time were all direct products of our political system. Each one had supported candidates who won, had solicited votes, had talked issues with voters, and had provided transportation for voters to their polling places on election day. In other words, they had been politicians. But they wound up creating the most admired federal court bench in the United States. Isn't that the way we want our government to be, responsive to citizen need?

The members of that court included John K. Regan from St. Louis; Roy W. Harper, James Meredith, and H. Kenneth Wangelin, all from southeast Missouri. Usually individuals come to the attention of political leadership for nomination for the federal bench by way of political activity in their home environment.

Roy Harper had earned an enviable reputation throughout the Missouri political world for producing election results for candidates to whom he pledged his support. One of these was Harry S Truman, who was a U.S. Senator from Missouri before he was president of the United States. Nomination for a federal judgeship usually comes first from a state's U.S. Senator to the president, who submits the nomination to the Senate for confirmation.

President Truman nominated Roy Harper. The Senate twice rejected Harper's nomination, or allowed it to die unacted upon. Only on the third try was Harper approved. Politics from start to finish, but it produced one of America's finest judges. Harper heard a case in which a shareholder in a publicly held company sued to recover damages from directors of the company who had not been as responsible as they should have been in overseeing the company's operation. Harper ruled that a director of a company had a duty to know what was going on in the company whether or not he'd been told. This caused consternation among a lot of Americans who served on company boards. It also applied to directors of charitable institutions.

Jim Meredith earned his recognition as the campaign manager of Missouri's longtime Democratic U.S. Senator, Stuart W. Symington, and it was Symington who paved the road for Meredith.

In the course of things it turned out that Meredith, a southeast Missouri native, where segregation was as intense and deep rooted as any area in the United States, was the federal judge who heard the school desegregation case in St. Louis and established one of the first school busing examples in America—a judge reared in furnace of segregation who established one of the first enforced integration programs in our country! That's politics.

Jack Regan was steeped in Democratic politics in south St. Louis. He starred in the world of ward politics, from getting votes to running precincts and wards. His service on the bench was in the same high result, high integrity arena as his companions.

Kenny Wangelin never lost his country personality and approach to life. No one appearing before him could mistake his origins or convictions. He represented the people on the bench. He told me on a number of occasions that he kept a revolver under his bench for protection and I believe him.

These men were inspirational examples of leadership growing out of politics.

Circuit Judge Ted McMillian, a black man, aspired to be a member of the Missouri Court of Appeals. I asked Governor Hearnes to appoint him and he asked if he could be excused from the first appointment available and give the second opening to McMillian. I agreed and in due time McMillian was named to the Court of Appeals. Later, the distinguished jurist became a member of the federal Court of Appeals for the Eastern District of Missouri.

Not all judges are as distinguished. Southeast Missourians felt a bit more comfortable when they learned that Circuit Judge Lloyd Briggs would leave the bench.

Jack Flach, the *Globe's* political editor played a role in the judge's departure on March 21, 1980. Briggs was an inveterate supporter of Democratic candidates in his southeast Missouri territory and Democratic candidates for statewide office and was thusly rewarded. He was known as Teasdale's main man in southeast Missouri. Political contributions flowed to Teasdale through Briggs, who was a dominant figure in Scott County politics, a part of the famous Bootheel of Missouri where votes were produced and delivered for candidates on order.

Briggs importuned Teasdale for appointment to the Circuit Court bench, a significant upward move in status. Teasdale made the appointment early in his term. Not a few months into his appointment complaints about Briggs' judicial conduct began to reappear. Jack was tipped off by a member of the Missouri Supreme Court's disciplinary committee that the committee was looking into the complaints.

The *Globe-Democrat* sent Flach and other reporters down to the Bootheel to see what facts could be developed about Briggs' conduct. The paper's investigators established a number of questionable acts by Briggs, including raising political funds for Teasdale while a member of the bench, ignoring admissable evidence, and conduct toward women defendants.

In 1980 Briggs was charged by the committee with numerous counts of misconduct. This was upheld by the Missouri Supreme Court and he was removed from his position. In 1985 Briggs pleaded guilty to tax evasion associated with illegal drug trafficking.

During the term of Governor Hearnes, John Doherty, one of St. Louis' best-known chiefs of detectives, wanted to be chief of police. A good friend of mine, Ed Walsh, was a member of the police board at that time. He was the purchasing member of the board, a dedicated individual and a man of substantial personal wealth. He had no ax to grind in terms of influencing any favors for business or anyone else. He was simply a good citizen. He lent a great deal of stability and respect to the board.

Governor Hearnes called me one day and said that he wanted Eugene Camp to be the chief. Hearnes wanted to know if I'd talk to Walsh about the appointment. Walsh favored Doherty.

Doherty had earned a colorful reputation in the police department. He was notorious for physically assaulting criminals when they declined to do his bidding. The *Globe* had run a substantial story about a fist fight that Doherty had with a couple of hoodlums downtown on Lucas around 9th Street. Doherty himself told me that on one occasion he heard that a couple of hoodlums from Detroit were moving into St. Louis. He went to the airport, met them and told them to leave town, and if he ever saw them in St. Louis, he'd see to it that they suffered physically. According to Doherty, they left town the same day, and he never saw them again. Doherty was a principled man, an old-time policeman who would have been a very strong chief.

Walsh and I met one day at the Racquet Club to talk over the problem. Walsh told me in no uncertain terms that he was supporting Doherty and he would continue to support Doherty, not Camp.

I reported that to the governor, who was upset about this. He wanted Walsh to know that if he didn't change his position the governor wanted Walsh's resignation from the police board. I told Walsh this. Walsh said he would resign. He did and Eugene Camp was appointed chief of police.

I met with Doherty in the lobby of the Missouri Athletic Club and told him what was going on. He was a very disappointed man. I felt very sad about it, but to John Doherty's everlasting credit, he continued to serve loyally under Camp and remained a friend throughout the years until he died. He was a fine man.

Shortly after that Hearnes' term as governor expired and Governor Bond came into office. Bond asked me about what I thought about Walsh. I told him about Walsh's character and his fine service. Bond then reappointed Walsh to the police board.

When Gene Camp retired as chief of police, I undertook a personal campaign to have Bill Brown, a lieutenant colonel in the department, the rank just below chief, named to the top position.

Brown had been a street policemen. He had an exemplary career as an officer and had many friends in the department and in the political and civic world. Deeply religious, he occasionally spent his spare time working with retarded and mentally ill children at Our Lady of Grace facility.

Homer Sayad, then chairman of the Police Board, had ideas for qualifying officers to be chief by using a test for academic knowledge, different from tests employed by preceding boards. Sayad didn't think an outstanding record of production, as well as experience and leadership, was good enough. He preferred a sophisticated testing technique and advice from purists in psychological consulting.

I ultimately achieved a pledge from three of the five police commissioners, including Mayor Schoemehl, to vote for Brown as chief. Schoemehl personally assured Brown and me he would vote for Brown. Joe Morrissey, who favored another candidate, said he would back off and support Brown if I would promise to support Joe's candidate the next time around. I agreed to do so.

But it was to no avail. The board rejected Brown.

However, shortly after the decision was made, Brown became ill with what was believed to be a severe case of influenza. When his high fever didn't abate, Jewish Hospital proposed a severe intrusion into his brain to cure him.

Brown's family physician, Dr. Everett R. Lerwick of Missouri Baptist Hospital, disagreed with the diagnosis and asked that Brown be released to him. The hospital would not agree to do so until Lerwick threatened to "carry him out on my back."

After a less serious brain operation, Brown recovered and it was revealed that his medical problem had been encephalitis, not influenza.

Despite severe memory problems, he is physically well and happily retired from the police department. Had he been named chief, there would have been controversy over his ability to serve and he would ultimately have had to retire.

For many years Robert Young, a Democrat, represented the

west and north county district in the House of Representatives in Washington. From the *Globe-Democrat's* perspective we thought he did an exceptionally effective and commendable job representing his district. He was elected because of the heavy blue collar vote from north county and despite the opposition from business interests who disliked his early history as a member of the Fitters Union. Before going to Congress he had been a long-time memberof the Missouri legislature as a representative and senator with a good record.

While he was in the Missouri Senate he came to me one day with a problem and asked if I'd help. He explained that he was pushing legislation to help the new University of Missouri branch in Normandy buy a piece of ground from the Daughters of Charity who had large holdings of land across Natural Bridge south of the university. But, he said, Governor Bond did not approve of this legislation.

At the same time Governor Bond was interested in rehabilitating the aging Wainwright Building in downtown St. Louis, both to provide state office space in St. Louis and preserve a historic property. Young said he was opposing Bond's plan for the Wainwright Building but he said if Bond would change and support his University of Missouri project he would change and support Bond's Wainwright program. He asked me if I would speak to the governor.

I explained the deadlock to Governor Bond and he agreed to the deal. The results have been good for everyone.

Bob continued to work for his community even after retirement. He told us that Vince Schoemehl, St. Louis' former mayor, employed him as a lobbyist to try to sell his former cohorts in Congress in Washington on appropriating money to build the new Thomas F. Eagleton Federal Building. Money did come and the building is almost completed. We're sure Bob's work helped.

Bob was one of the Missouri legislators whom the *Globe-Democrat* honored with its legislative award. His proudest moment, he told me, was having his father and mother watch him receive the award.

The *Globe-Democrat* was blessed with a superb news staff. Members of the staff were dedicated to their work, rarely complained, and always did an outstanding job of developing stories. This dedication created problems once in a great while.

A young, talented, and attractive young reporter, Tim O'Neil, was assigned to St. Louis County. One of his duties was to cover the office of the county executive. Tim had a record of being accurate and reliable. We never had a complaint about inaccuracies in his stories and he was not known to miss stories or play second fiddle to the competition.

The county executive, Gene McNary, surprised me by telling me that he felt that O'Neil was unfair to him and he wanted him removed from the county assignment. George Killenberg, our managing editor, and I both talked with O'Neil at length and we were convinced that the real basis for Gene's complaint was that O'Neil was holding McNary's feet to the fire. In the meantime Gene had several of his supporters whom he knew were good friends of mine call me. Not the least among them was Howard L. Young, indeed a good friend and one of Gene's best money raisers. He asked that we move O'Neil.

I had a luncheon meeting with Gene again and he finally admitted that his request had been motivated largely by the discomfort O'Neil was causing him by his persistent questioning on public issues. I told him this was exactly what we expected O'Neil to be doing and was the best reason for leaving him in assignment. We did not move O'Neil. Gene immediately began to answer McNeil's questions again.

Moving him would have been a devastating blow to reporter and newsroom morale. What reporter would persist in getting a story if he thought his efforts would cause him to be disciplined? We'd never get the good news stories with that kind of fear in the newsroom.

In his race for a second or third term as U.S. Senator, John C. Danforth ran against Harriett Woods, former Missouri lieutenant governor and former *Globe-Democrat* reporter. Jack ran his usual race and he and his supporters were confident of his re-election until the *Globe* published a poll about two weeks before the election showing Harriett closing the gap, as compared with two earlier polls. This startled the Danforth team and shocked them into immediate action. Senator Danforth called me at home on a Sunday afternoon and asked if the *Globe-Democrat* could provide additional support. We did so.

Wayne L. Millsap, a St. Louis attorney and inveterate Republican political activist, George H. Capps, a top Danforth money raiser, and a number of other effective Danforth loyalists met overnight and developed a strategy to enhance Danforth's voter appeal. Danforth was told about the potential for defeat and concentrated his time in Missouri.

Jack went on to win, but by a small margin. Had he not gotten busy to energize his campaign he might have lost.

In recent years at a birthday party dinner for Wayne, Jack and his wife, Sally, were present. Jack was one of the many who toasted Wayne, and in his remarks said, "It's a dead certainty that I would not have had the political career I've had were it not for Wayne Millsap."

After Wayne failed to win an aldermanic position in his early life, he remained an intense and participatory party worker throughout his life and counseled many aspirants to success, including former Governor Bond, now Missouri's U.S Senator.

Wayne first brought Kit Bond to my office in the late 1960s, when he ran unsuccessfully for Congress from the Hannibal district. His support for Jack Danforth goes back to that time when Danforth was induced to run for attorney general of Missouri. His election to that office marked a resurgence of election of Republicans to state offices in Missouri.

Another behind-the-scenes Republican Party stalwart is Howard Ohlendorf. He is widely known for his persistent money-raising efforts and for his personal participation. He ran twice for Congress, unwisely perhaps, against Leonor Sullivan, the very popular Congresswoman from south St. Louis, and of course he lost.

A native St. Louisan who lost his parents at an early age, Howard was raised by relatives and had to cut his education short. He married a St. Louis girl named Irma—he claimed she was the key to his life—and they had eight children: Mark, Marilyn, Margaret, Elizabeth, Paul, Ruth, Gail, and Nancy.

Early in life Howard started working for an orthodontics supply company. He later bought it and it now bears the family name and is run by his son Mark. He made his company a success, quantitatively and qualitatively. He and Irma have traveled to virtually every country in the world. If they missed one, I don't know which one it was.

As Howard prospered, he bought land here and there. Some of that land he has given to the city and the county for parks. He donated the ground for the dinosaur park in St. Louis County. A park in the southwest city is named for Howard and Irma. Just recently he paid for the improvement of a great fountain in Tilles Park in St. Louis County.

Many St. Louisans remember Forest Park Highlands, the amusement park on Oakland Avenue between Kingshighway and Hampton. The Highlands had a wonderful merry-go-round which disappeared when the park closed. In the 1970s or 1980s Howard began a search for it and found many of the wooden animals that were used as seats. He had them refinished to perfection and they're now part of the restored carousel in St. Louis County's Faust Park. He has made other significant contributions to the enhancement of Faust Park.

Howard followed the Lutheran faith; his late wife, Irma, was a Catholic. All of the Ohlendorf children were raised in the Catholic faith and Howard became chairman of the men's club at Irma's parish. No one excelled Howard as a participatory citizen.

Lawrence Roos was one of the most highly respected political office holders we've had in the St. Louis area in the last fifty or sixty years. He was St. Louis County Supervisor for four terms with overwhelming support. He chose to run for governor and was nominated on the Republican ticket. He was defeated by a shocking margin. Given that Missouri has traditionally been a Democratic state and Republican governors have been scarce, I believe Roos was also an example of underlying prejudice because he is Jewish. I don't believe we've ever had a Jewish governor. We've had only one Catholic governor I'm aware of –Joe Teasdale–and his election was a fluke.

In 1976 Jim Thompson, a Republican, formerly U.S. Attorney in Chicago who rigorously prosecuted a number of Democratic politicians and sent them to the penitentiary, was elected governor of Illinois.

The *Globe-Democrat* hosted a dinner for Thompson, whom we had supported, at the St. Louis Club. About 125 prominent St. Louisans attended.

Thompson gave a modest report on political life and his election, and then opened the meeting to questions. One of the questions asked of Thompson was, how do you think the city of Chicago will fare with Mayor Daley gone? Richard J. Daley was a back-of-the-yards Irishman who was the authoritarian, assertive Democratic leader of the city, reelected a number of times, well thought of nationally in Democratic circles. He was mayor during the 1968 Democratic National Convention in Chicago when Vietnam protestors rioted.

Thompson gave a surprising but honest and accurate answer. He said Chicago would suffer desperately with Daley gone because Daley was the type of politician who could be depended upon to keep his word. When Daley gave his word to a citizen that certain results would occur, the mayor could be relied upon to fulfill his share of the deal, whatever was required. Thompson pointed this out and said he didn't think that whoever succeeded Daley would have the same talent for getting things done in Chicago. It was an interesting answer by a Republican who prosecuted Democrats, about a Democrat.

In mid-1984 Governor John Ashcroft sent Dick Rice, then Director of the Missouri Department of Public Safety, to see me with the request that I head a fund drive to build a memorial to all war veterans in Missouri irrespective of the war they served in from the beginning of our country. I was exceptionally reluctant to be responsible for a money-raising campaign, being aware of the elements involved in a successful effort.

Rice explained the governor's aspirations. Ashcroft felt that the lack of any evidence of the public's appreciation for war veterans in Jefferson City was inappropriate and that there ought to be a memorial. He acknowledged a prior effort had failed. His plan was to build the memorial adjacent to the capitol building.

The failure of a prior campaign was a significant issue in my decision. That campaign had taken place only a couple of years previously. The memory by donors of having made an earlier gift would hamper my effort, since the donors would not want to give twice to the same effort. But with the governor's and Rice's pressure I accepted.

The goal was to raise as much as possible from the public of a total of about $2,500,000. The governor pledged that the Missouri legislature would make up the deficit.

We organized the campaign and were honored that the veterans' organizations were enthusiastically supportive. Representatives of all the major veterans groups were present at our initial meeting in Jefferson City. James Whitfield of the Veteran's Commission coordinated the fund-raising among the various veterans groups. Rice provided me with an office and secretarial assistance in his office space in the capitol.

The American Legion was a major player. It ran stories about the campaign and appealed for funds in every issue of its statewide monthly publication. The Legion raised a notable amount.

I went back to the major donors in St. Louis, starting with Anheuser Busch and Emerson Electric. Anheuser Busch has a sales department dedicated to selling its beer to military installations. The manager of that department was most understanding and also extremely helpful. Despite the brewery's earlier gift of $50,000, he agreed to ask his company for a second gift of $50,000. The brewery agreed to the second gift, which was a huge start.

Then I had breakfast one morning with Chuck Knight, chairman of Emerson Electric, in a company private dining room. When Knight asked what I wanted, I told him and he said yes. He gave a second $50,000. Not a single first giver refused to make a second gift in the original amount.

Don Lasater, chairman of Mercantile Bank, agreed to help.

The Veterans Memorial in Jefferson City

He raised a lot of money, too, and the legislature allocated sufficient funds to make up the balance. The memorial was built on a site immediately across the street north of the capitol building. It was designed by the Leo A. Daly firm and built by Booker Associates of St. Louis, at the personal direction of Roger Peterson, then chairman of the company. The final cost was $1,734,711. It was dedicated November 11, 1991, with ceremonies attended by Governor Ashcroft and scores of military dignitaries.

Some experiences in life stand out over others in valuable learning gained from them and the cherished friendships which develop. One of these experiences for me was my appointment as Missouri chairman of the Employer Committee for the Support of the Guard and Reserve.

Early in the 1970s, I was visited in my office by three general officers of the U.S. Department of Defense. They asked me to take on the chairmanship and I readily accepted. Through the years I had enforced a policy at the *Globe-Democrat* of strong support for the military defense and the responsibilities of the Guard and Reserve appointment certainly fitted my policies and those of the paper.

Following World War II the United States began to downsize its standing force–the number of military personnel on active duty at the same time. America instituted the volunteer serviceman concept in place of the draft. Salaries of armed service men and women increased sharply to meet the realities of maintaining a volunteer force versus maintenance by draft. Thus the nation's cost for a standing force rose like a rocket.

A further product of this policy was an increasing reliance by the military leadership on the National Guard and Reserve troops. Very quickly, the dependence on such a Reserve force rose to sixty percent in many units and as high as 100 percent in a few specialized units.

Military commanders quickly sensed the value of low personnel turnover. This saved money and created a better force because of personnel experience. To cope in one way with personnel turnover the military created the Employer Committee for the Support of the Guard and Reserve (ESGR).

An employer support committee was formed in each state. The state chairman was usually a citizen with some measure of public identity. Committee members were citizens and representatives from each of the major military units stationed in that state.

Since National Guard troops were made up of individuals who had full time civilian jobs, and served in the Guard in their spare time, their ability to be effective and happy members of the service was dependent in significant measure on a good relationship with their employers because of the need for time off from work. The same was true of Reserve force members.

As in all human relations, strain and debate frequently arose. Differences often arose with Guard and Reserve members, threatening the member's economic security. To preserve the security of themselves and their families, many would resign from military service.

The duty of our committee was to obtain information on bad employer-employee relations and to resolve differences so that the men and women would remain in service and still maintain a good relationship in their civilian jobs.

I think our Missouri committee did a commendable job. Its members included many wonderfully generous, knowledgeable and effective citizen members. The inactive military was stupendous in its support. Maj. Gen. William Branson was the first to offer help. The adjutant general of Missouri was supportive on every occasion.

Our committee's success would not have been possible without the superb and untiring assistance of Maj. Gen. Charles DuBois (Ret.) a World War II ace. He was the heart of our committee.

For me, the lessons I learned about friendship and support were overwhelming and never to be forgotten.

The Missouri ESGR would have been stultified had it not been for Col. Kenneth Schrerer of the Missouri Air Guard 131st Fighter Wing Col. Schrerer and his office organized our meetings, kept track of our work assignments, and provided everything we needed.

Fortunately, St. Louis had and has numerous civic-minded corporations. If I needed funds for a function, such as being host for national meetings, these businessmen responded generously. Our two national meetings here were notable in the program's history.

Most Missouri employers maintained equitable policies affecting relationships with employers who served their country as National Guard and Reserve members. I cannot remember a single employer who was contacted by the committee to settle an employee dispute who did not settle the issue fairly and set up rules to avoid such problems in the future.

Note should be made of a small Missouri employer with a total or five or six employees, every one of whom was a Guard or Reserve member. He was proud, and so were his employees, that none of them had ever had a problem with the owner over this duty. The committee gave him the Pro Patria award, the highest honor the committee could award.

I was inspired and encouraged by the evidence of friendship and loyalty which pervaded the service units. I was greatly impressed by the character of the general officers group.

Maj. Gen. William Work is an example. Born in a southern Illinois country town, he was so poor he shined shoes on the street when he was eight or ten to help his family's finances. His life was a demonstration of what America is about, that from his humble beginning he became a high-ranking officer. He was a joy to know, a feeling I know was shared by hundreds of his troops.

Ted Wetterau, retired chairman of Wetterau, Inc., in St. Louis succeeded me after more than ten years, as chairman of the state committee.

So many local companies are being swallowed by giant corporations today. The structure of leadership in the city is changing, and I wonder what the impact will be on St. Louis in the twenty-first century.

Civic leaders get results by inspiring others to act, or by example, or by muscle in the form of IOUs: they give and they ask for something in return. Success of a project to aid or improve the community usually is headed by a corporate individual, someone who is easily identified and respected, or by an equally well-known and respected local citizen.

I hate to use examples, because I know we're missing hundreds of others, but a few who come to mind are Dave Calhoun, Jim Hickok, Buck Persons, Chuck Knight, Gussie Busch, Harold Thayer, Ted Jones, Harry Harrington, Don Brandin, Andy Craig, Buster May, Ben Wells, George Capps, J. S. McDonnell, Dude Chambers, Charles Allen Thomas, Zane Barnes, plus scores of others. Many of these people didn't want the responsibility of leading a community endeavor but they accepted that task as a duty.

It's obvious that it takes a while for a person who moves to St. Louis to recognize the same community needs and obligations that a local person recognizes, and sometimes there is a deterioration of beneficial interest in playing corporate "musical chairs."

The departure of the Southwestern Bell headquarters was an immense loss to the community—a loss of both leadership and financial contributions. The same is true of Boatmen's Bank which, after acquiring First National, sold itself to NationsBank, and in turn NationsBank sold itself to Bank of America. There may be continued financial contributions, but there isn't the local leadership there used to be.

Still, new leaders emerge and new projects get attention. For instance, in the effort to bring professional football back to St. Louis, Jerry Clinton, a highly successful businessman who had started life as a poor boy living in the projects, was one of several individuals dedicated to obtaining a team for the city. Others were James Orthwein, Fran Murray, and the great Chicago Bears player, Walter Payton.

Orthwein and Clinton had a controlling interest in the association; Murray had a minor interest. Clinton and Orthwein agreed that if Murray got out each would have an equal opportunity to buy Murray's share. Murray did get out and Orthwein bought his share, Clinton says, without notice to Clinton. For many months, Clinton toyed with the idea of a lawsuit against Orthwein. Nothing came of this but Clinton and Orthwein were estranged.

The first step in obtaining a team was building a suitable stadium. After the agreement to build the stadium, negotiations to bring a team to St. Louis continued without Clinton's inclusion. Clinton says that had he been a member of the group which made the first presentation to the National Football League, St. Louis would have had a team much earlier.

By this time Clinton had invested some $7 million of his own money in the effort. When the St. Louis promotional group got to the point of needing an agreement to use the new domed stadium, problems developed. Clinton controlled the stadium. He wanted, and deserved, to get all or most of his money back. This requirement on Clinton's part was unjustifiably criticized until the deal was made to reimburse him.

The remarkable fact is that Clinton had been able to create a coalition of disparate groups and individuals to provide the money to build a mult-million dollar stadium. Alone—and that's the operative word—he convinced a Democratic state legislature with a Republican governor, a Republican-controlled county council, a Republican County Executive and a Democrat-controlled city board of aldermen with a Democratic mayor to be responsible for building a domed stadium and paying for its construction on an equal basis.

It's almost impossible for the city to get funds to rehabilitate the fire department. It's frustrating to try to get the city and the county to agree even on a route for the expansion of its light rail system MetroLink, let alone pay for it. That's why Jerry Clinton's achievement is so remarkable. The dumbest—or smartest—human being in the city or county or state would not have bet a single penny that the three governments would agree to this.

It's a good bet that there would not be a domed stadium and there would not be a professional football franchise back in St. Louis without the singular, unprecedented and tireless efforts of Jerry Clinton, the boy from the projects.

- 8 -

MR. BAUMAN GOES TO WASHINGTON

The White House and Capitol Hill were nearly 1,000 miles from the *Globe-Democrat* city room, but we had the obligation to cover, interpret, and comment upon national news, as well as local and regional.

The *Globe* gave me the opportunity to keep in touch with the men and women who were creating that news. I got to know several presidents and, of course, the majority of the men and women who served eastern Missouri and southern Illinois in the Senate and House of Representatives.

I have often been asked, in view of the newspaper's watchdog stance regarding holders of public office, if a politician can be honest.

Absolutely. We have wonderful examples. Jack Danforth was impeccably honest. This is not to say that a politician doesn't moderate differences of opinions between himself and others or within his own group.

Bob Dole referred to that in his 1996 campaign for the presidency. The only way a politician can be successful is to produce results for his constituents. He can't do that by being a loner. He has to work with others to get things done. In the Senate or House you don't stand up and say I'm the only one who is going this way and you must follow me. It doesn't work that way. He has to trade and give and take to get what he wants like the others do to get what they want.

As Dole said, as long as one doesn't compromise principles or integrity or honesty, mediation or conciliation is not bad. I was very pleased that Dole made that point.

I was very impressed by Pat Buchanan's bid for the presidential nomination in 1996. One of the benefits of his campaign was that it caused the political leadership and much of the public to realize more of what is going on in America. His voice called attention to economic and social problems that were not being heard and I hoped that would bring about some solutions that would not have been achieved otherwise. I am convinced that his campaign was beneficial for America,

Among the presidents who served between 1967 and 1984, I was closer to Richard Nixon and Ronald Reagan than the others. I was invited to the White House by all but Jimmy Carter. I was never impressed by his humble country boy image. I always felt that he demeaned the presidency because he chose to carry his own bags—he wasn't upholding the perception of power, which is so important.

The protocol for a formal White House dinner is truly impressive. Guests arrive at the south door, which I refer to as the basement door. Inside it's hardly like a basement. It's exactly what one would expect the White House to be, beautiful. On one's right is the China Room, where sets of china from earlier administrations are on display.

After showing one's invitation at the door, the guests are ushered a short distance to the foot of the stairway leading to the main floor. There a dress-uniformed member of the military—

I was a frequent guest at the White House. Here I'm with President Gerald Ford.

army, navy, marine corps, or air force—gives the lady his arm and all walk upstairs to the East Room where the president and the first lady receive.

It never failed to impress me how well staged the reception line is. The line starts with an aide, to whom you give your names; the aide passes your names on to the president; next to him is the first lady. By the time a guest reaches the president, he is ready with a personal word or two. I think Nixon was the best at this.

The guests are served a drink and mingle for a short time in the East Room. If one chooses, he may walk through the other rooms between the East Room and the West Room. When dinner is served, the crowd moves through the main hall to the West Room to be served. The setting is as elegant and impressive as it ought to be. Seating is by placecard and often there is a notable administration official at your table.

There are the usual formal toasts of welcome, dinner and, on occasion, a short talk. Perhaps the most distinguished dinner we attended was one given for the shah of Iran before he was deposed.

On rare occasions, following the White House dinner in the West Room, there will be dancing in the main floor entrance foyer, always to the music of a Marine Corps Band. An unforgettable event.

I learned never to take a taxicab to a White House dinner. I used a limousine instead. Taxis are not allowed to wait for their passengers on the White House grounds. Limousines are. There are no telephones in the White House which a guest may use to call for a ride. It's really a bit embarrassing to walk down the long White House driveway in white tie and tails with your wife on your arm and the limousines passing you by!

It will never cease to be a thrill for me to have a room on the southeast corner of the Hay-Adams Hotel on an upper floor and look out at night to the south and see the White House lighted brilliantly on the outside with the American flag proudly flying.

I thought Nixon was one of the brightest people we've had in office. Of course, I didn't have daily contact with him and was not privy to many things that were going on. When I visited with him in his office or at a dinner, he was always very cordial and thoughtful, and made me feel I was the focal point of the occasion.

His adventures in China were way ahead of his time. His experiences in Russia were very worthwhile. I regret terribly that he had bad advice, but Watergate was blown out of proportion by the media. The issue was between two political factions; it had nothing to do with society's values. The burglars were seeking information. The crime occurred when they went through a locked door and consequently when Nixon, like Clinton, lied. That's when we discontinued our support for him.

One of the most memorable experiences we had was after the U.S. astronauts landed on the moon. President Nixon gave a state dinner in honor of their achievement at the Century Plaza Hotel in Los Angeles shortly after the men returned to earth. Mindful of the part McDonnell Douglas Aircraft Co. had played in the successful landing, Nixon invited the chairman and founder of the company, J. S. McDonnell, and his wife, Priscilla. His invitation provided for guests and through his everlasting kindness "Mr. Mac" invited Nora and me.

Our table was directly in front of the head table. We were not ten feet from the astronauts and the president. Other guests at our table were the ambassador from Ghana to the United States and his wife and Jacques Cousteau, the undersea explorer, and his wife.

After the dinner, as we all expressed appreciation to our hosts, Nora noticed that an exquisite memento, a silver toned plaque about five by eight inches commemorating the dinner and a gift of President Nixon, was missing from her place at the table. She looked around and saw Rosalind Russell holding two plaques. Nora approached her about this, whereupon the movie and stage star asked, feigning innocence, "Oh, is this yours?'" Nora replied that it certainly was and Russell said, "I didn't think you'd want it so I took it." She then handed it to Nora.

President Nixon called me at the *Globe* one day to ask if it would be possible to persuade Gussie Busch, a Democrat, to support his reelection. I called Gussie and he agreed that he would go along with the president's request. To emphasize his support, he gave a dinner in the big house at Grant's Farm and invited prominent St. Louis area Democrats, including major labor union leaders. About sixty attended.

As a special attraction, he induced John Connally, former secretary of the treasury, governor of Texas, and one-time Democrat, to speak. Connally was extremely persuasive and convincing. Here, as at other meetings I had attended, he completely captivated the audience. The dinner concluded without a negative or angry response. Of course with this audience, there were few overt offers of support. I believe that many of the leaders privately supported Nixon, but could not do so publicly. The Teamsters, incidentally, did come out in favor of Nixon.

One Nixon invitation was to a prayer breakfast in the East Room. Billy Graham was the minister.

On another occasion, I was invited to a meeting which followed the government's announcement that it was making the first loan in history to a private corporation.

I felt a little out of my customary environment as I sat in the cabinet room in the presence of President Nixon and again John Connally, along with ten or twelve business tycoons from major corporations.

The men were universally, vocally, and emphatically opposed to the loan. But after Connally spoke for about thirty minutes there was not a dissenting voice in the room.

At such a men-only affair, the president would give each guest a memento, such as a golf ball with the White House seal or a pair of cuff links. Each man also went home with the memento for his wife, perhaps a compact, again bearing the White House seal.

Several years after he had left public life, I invited Nixon to come to St. Louis for an event, as I remember, at the Herbert Hoover Boys Club. I expected to hear from some sixth-level functionary, but was astonished to receive a letter from Nixon himself, regretting that he couldn't accept. It was a most cordial letter in which he recalled some of the events we had attended together, and thanking me for the *Globe-Democrat's* support during his presidency.

One of the benefits of being in the newspaper business was the opportunity to assign myself to cover the national political conventions. The experiences I had at these conventions and the friendships I made there with political leaders benefited my ability to make decisions at the paper. Beginning in 1968, I attended all of the party conclaves until the paper closed.

From some discussion among ourselves at the newspaper, we

came upon the idea that it might be helpful to our ability to cover the news if many of us to got to know more of our elected officials personally and for them to know us. By us I mean the members of the *Globe-Democrat* staff who covered government and political news.

Since a number of us regularly attended the national conventions every four years, we thought it might be a good idea to host a dinner at each, Republican and Democratic, for all of the official Missouri delegates and the official southern Illinois delegates, plus other local political notables who might be attending.

It turned out to be one of the best activities the *Globe-Democrat* took on. There is an unending memory of the dinners by many delegates, some of whom, even fifteen years later, tell me again what a wonderful experience our convention dinner was.

When the conventions were held in New York, we took over a restaurant for the Republican affair, which was a luncheon. A TV reporter unwittingly became intrusive at that lunch and we had to ask that the reporter defer her interviews until afterward. The dinners and luncheons were social affairs to benefit the *Globe-Democrat* and we tried to keep them that way.

Our New York Democratic dinner was at the Windows Restaurant atop of the World Trade Center at the south end of Manhattan, a never-to-be-forgotten event. To make the occasion even better, the man in charge of our dinner was a transplanted St. Louisan.

The two conventions in 1968—Republican in Miami and Democratic in Chicago—were especially memorable for the violence generated by Vietnam War protesters.

Nora and I were driving from our hotel in Miami Beach to the Miami Convention Center with Gen. Leif Sverdrup when we were stopped on Biscayne Boulevard. Protestors on both sides of our car rocked it back and forth in an effort to turn it over. I told Nora that if it didn't stop, I would drive on and run over them. Fortunately, they stepped away and we drove off.

At the Convention Center we were again blocked by a bunch of demonstrators and the situation was obviously tense. There were no threats, but they just stood in front of us, interfering with our progress. General Sverdrup, who was then in his middle seventies, a World War II hero who served as MacArthur's chief engineer in the Southwest Pacific, said that nobody of that ilk— and he used some pretty strong language—was going to stop him.

He got out of the car, swung at two or three of them, pushed his way through the crowd, and walked into the stadium.

Lucyann Mueller Boston, then our society editor and a great reporter, was in Florida to help cover the convention. She was in a bus with other reporters when demonstrators stopped the bus, poured gasoline on it, punctured the tires, sprayed the disembarking passengers with spray paint and set fire to the vehicle. Lucyann came into the Convention Center in tears, but to her lasting credit, she worked the whole evening in a spray-painted dress.

That was the atmosphere in which Richard Nixon was nominated. Based on the knowledge he had of the demonstrators' misconduct, he had reason to wonder where the country was headed.

That same summer of 1968 was the year of the notorious Democratic convention in Chicago where great numbers of people protested and police became disorganized. It was a sight never to be forgotten. The incidents were symptomatic of the times.

Somehow I met a young man in Chicago who I presumed to be part of the protest movement. For some reason, he trusted me and invited me to attend a meeting of the protesters, a day or two prior to the convention. There I learned the plans they were going to carry out.

I decided not to print the material in advance. I was so taken aback by their plans that I didn't believe they would really happen, but every one of the major incidents that I had heard about actually occurred during that turmoil.

Sidney Salomon, Jr., a St. Louisan, was then one of the most influential and powerful Democrats in America. He was then, or had been, chairman of the finance committee of the Democratic National Committee. Salomon had invited Nora and me to dinner at the Standard Club, the premier Jewish club in downtown Chicago, along with four or six more people including Stuart Symington, then U.S. Senator from Missouri.

Senator Abraham Ribicoff, a U.S. Senator from Connecticut, had also been invited. All of the other guests were at the table when Ribicoff arrived. When Sidney introduced Nora and me, the senator looked at me and said, "What in the hell are you doing here? You don't belong here. You should get out." Sidney and his wife and the other guests were embarrassed but we all stayed for dinner.

Ribicoff had been scheduled to be a principal speaker at the convention session that night. Some of his remarks were critical and derogatory of Chicago because of the protesters and of the security being provided by the Chicago police. Mayor Richard Daley, the longtime Chicago mayor and leader of the Illinois convention delegation, was motivated by Ribicoff's nasty and demeaning remarks during the convention to rise to his feet from his floor seat and disrupt Ribicoff's speech with an angry reponse. This resulted in substantial national press attention, heightening the angry environment.

Mobs of protesters and dissenters roamed Chicago's streets at night, especially on Michigan Avenue between Randolph Street and the Hilton Hotel on Michigan Avenue at the south end of

Greeting Vice-President Hubert H. Humphrey in 1968, when he ran for the presidency. Aloys P. Kaufmann, St. Louis's last Republican mayor, is in the center.

the business district. Many of the clashes between police and the protesters occurred as police tried to maintain security for convention guests and other citizens. It was here that Hamilton Thornton, the editorial page editor of the *Globe-Democrat*, a somewhat aging and dignified individual, was sprayed with skunk scent as he tried to get back into the Hilton after a night convention session.

Literally thousands of protesters swarmed the Chicago streets for the week. Many slept outdoors, especially in the parks. Lincoln Park, just north of the business district, was overwhelmed with protesters who made the park their home. Many others were in Grant Park, the area between the business district and the lake. It had to be seen to be believed.

After being nominated for president on the Democratic ticket

I met with future president Ronald Reagan in St. Louis in 1968.

at the 1972 national convention in Miami, George McGovern named Missouri Senator Thomas F. Eagleton as his running mate. Nora and I were at the convention, staying at the Ivanhoe, a hotel owned by St. Louisans Stan Musial and Biggie Garagnani, a major Democratic contributor. Tom and his wife, Barbara, also were staying there.

Tom thought it would be proper and significant if Governor Warren Hearnes of Missouri gave one of the seconding speeches. He suggested this to McGovern who turned him down flat. Perhaps, that was because Hearnes, although a Democrat, was one of the most conservative political figures in the state, more so than many Republicans. McGovern, of course, represented the epitome of liberalism.

After the convention McGovern returned to his home in South Dakota, and Tom and Barbara went to Hawaii for a brief vacation. Within a few days after the nomination, a Detroit newspaper reported what most of us in the Missouri media knew—but not the general public—that Eagleton had had health difficulties.

Much to his credit and with great character, Tom had overcome both and had gone on to become one of the best, brightest and most effective senators in Missouri history. But when the story broke in a Detroit newspaper, some in the press clamored for his removal from the ticket.

Tom later told me that almost every day he called McGovern from Hawaii and discussed the matter. McGovern urged him to overlook the criticism and stay with him and assured him that together they would win the White House. Then he discovered that McGovern had been allowing members of his entourage to tip the press off to other stories which would further damage Eagleton, all while he was reassuring Tom of his support.

After ten days, Tom had had enough. He informed McGovern that he would not remain on the ticket as vice-president. McGovern then chose Sargent Shriver, John Kennedy's brother-in-law, and they were soundly trounced in the November election.

Despite his political philosophy (which I didn't always share), Tom has total integrity and is a brilliant guy. He was a hard working senator and never did anything except his duty. We were very fortunate to have both him and Danforth in the Senate. When Danforth went to Washington, Eagleton taught him the ropes, even though they were of different parties. They became close friends.

Eagleton left Congress, he told me, because money-raising became such an onerous and unpleasant task. He didn't want to embarrass himself by having to beg for money. Tom's secret ambition, most of us thought, was to be the nation's baseball commissioner.

Jack Danforth got out of politics because he felt he didn't want to put up with the problems there anymore. He wanted to devote his life to different pursuits, and his family is very important to him.

The American people lost a valuable pillar in the U.S. Senate when Jack retired. Many senators regarded him as the conscience of that body. If other senators had a problem with an issue, morally or spiritually, they frequently talked to Danforth, a lawyer and an Episcopal priest, about it. And they would generally agree with his opinion.

Many people criticized Danforth for his loyalty to Clarence Thomas. Thomas, with Danforth's support, was nominated to the Supreme Court by President George Bush. When Danforth was Missouri attorney general, Thomas worked for him, and through the years they maintained their friendship. Danforth had enormous respect for Thomas and I do, too. I think any human being who survives the injustices which the white people inflicted on black people and achieves distinction, regardless of the hardships, deserves an immense amount of credit. Thomas' life shows a great fortitude and ability to withstand those vicissitudes.

Thomas has done a good job on the Court. He's a good lawyer with a conservative philosophy. The Court needed a black to replace Thurgood Marshall; it needed a conservative for obvious reasons.

I have been asked if perhaps Danforth made a deal with President Bush, that Thomas' appointment to the Court was something of a payoff. In politics you have to accept the fact that anything is possible. But I know Bush—he used to come to our office when he was vice-president. I also know Danforth well. I do not believe there was any deal whatsoever.

The *Globe-Democrat* played a significant role in the political life of Danforth, as it did for many political figures. Most active community people knew that the paper's policies were conservative. I was conservative and the paper was generally considered to be a supporter of conservative candidates.

In the late 1960s or early 1970s, there was quite a drought in this part of the United States. It was so severe in the area around St. Louis that many of the Illinois farmers ran out of water. They had to resort to hauling water in tank trucks and even in buckets for their stock and personal use. Many farmers had to drill new wells, some as deep as seven and eight hundred feet, a few as deep as 1,000 feet.

It is evident, incidentally, that according to studies at the University of Missouri-Rolla (then Missouri School of Mines) the water table in the United States is being reduced alarmingly, and that ultimately, perhaps in the lifetime of the younger people today, water is going to be a very scarce resource.

A group of people proposed that the Meramec River be dammed southwest of St. Louis and a large reservoir created, which would be available for both recreation and irrigation. Enthusiasm for the dam gained momentum and widespread support. Then an immense controversy blew up and opponents became quite vocal. Obviously, the folks who were going to lose their land didn't want it, but the federal government bought a lot of land in preparation for this dam.

Eagleton and Danforth became interested in the project and both announced opposition to it. They worked in the Senate to defeat the funding for it. I had a meeting with Danforth on a Sunday afternoon in the living room of George Capps' home in Huntleigh Woods. For several hours we discussed the validity of the project.

Danforth offered numerous reasons for his opposition, such as costs, lack of utility, and numerous other reasonable arguments. In the end he said, "A lot of people like to canoe on the Meramec." This is true. Congress defeated the project.

John Ashcroft is a little in the Danforth mold. I think he will represent that sound moral and spiritual base exceedingly well. Although he was mentioned prominently as a candidate for the 2000 Republican presidential nomination, I believe he was wise to turn that down in favor of continued service in the Senate. He hasn't yet had enough experience in international affairs. And, of course he doesn't have the imprimaturs either.

During my career, several members of the House of Representatives from this area have been notable.

Leonor Sullivan, a Democrat, was as close to an ideal as a citizen would want. She followed her late husband into Congress, serving the south side of St. Louis and adjoining St. Louis County prior to the election of Dick Gephardt.

She was a gentle, kind, easy-to-meet and very bright individual. Her achievements were many; best remembered was her conception of and successful passage of the food stamp program. In later years she was immensely disappointed in the abuses of the program and tried to enact corrective legislation,

Her successor, the Democrat Gephardt, a southside St. Louis alderman, had told me when he first made his decision to run for Congress that he wanted to be speaker of the House. Had it not been for the Republican sweep in 1996 and had the Democrats remained in control, it is likely that he would have been elected to that prestigious post. He still has presidential aspirations and certainly is the recognized spokesman for House Democrats today.

Bill Clay and the *Globe-Democrat* never got along, from his days as an alderman. When he was on the board of aldermen, I visited him to discuss what the paper thought was an issue which should interest him. As a reporter I asked him several questions which he answered by ordering me out of his office with the words, "I'll never do anything while I am in public office to help a white man." He has kept his word.

Clay, a Democrat, is an exceptionally sharp-minded, knowledgeable, uniquely skilled political leader. He was and is capable of being one of the House's most forceful and productive leaders. His tunnel vision of his obligation to serve his constituents has thwarted this. Challengers to his House seat, even capable Democrats, have not been able to dent his popularity. He and the *Globe* differed on the majority of issues. It is difficult to pinpoint a single measure during his years of service which has been of value to the general public and for which he deserves credit for its passage.

Tom Curtis, a House member for years representing the central and west county area, was the darling of the Republicans. He was a vain but knowledgeable Congressman who blinded his constituents with his exhausting harangues on the merits of legislation. He was broadly admired as Mr. Clean and Mr. Knowledge.

The experience of many constituents was that Curtis rarely did a specific service following a specific request. The *Globe* once suggested that he refer what the paper considered to be an unethical act by a fellow Congressman to the House ethics committee. He was totally and discouragingly ineffective. There were numerous other occasions when the *Globe* thought he should "stand up and be counted." He let us down.

Sidney Salomon, our host when Abraham Ribicoff was so rude to Nora and me, was a man of whom all St. Louis should be proud. A civic leader, with a deep interest in government and the community, he bought the St. Louis Blues hockey team to keep them in St. Louis and then bought the Arena and refurbished the old structure, even installing new seats. After some years of the team's indifferent success, he sold the Blues and retired to Florida.

Privy to many government confidential matters, he once told me how Harry Truman became the vice-presidential candidate, a post which would catapult him into the presidency.

A St. Louisan, Robert Hannegan, was chairman of the Democratic National Committee during President Roosevelt's last race for the White House. Missourians were interested in having Truman, then a U.S. Senator, be the vice-presidential candidate and asked Hannegan to see Roosevelt and get his pledge to name Truman as his running mate. He did and Roosevelt agreed. Fearful that Roosevelt might not keep his word, Truman supporters sent Hannegan back to the White House to get the pledge in writing, which FDR gave him.

However, after Roosevelt had been nominated at the convention, word got out that he was planning to name another running mate. Hannegan was sent to see him, with written pledge in hand, and the president agreed to stand by it.

Salomon also told me of a bitter and mean state primary contest in which he had endorsed one of the candidates for governor in the Democratic primary. He received a telephone call threatening him with death if he did not abandon his endorsement. He stood his ground, informing the authorities of the call. His candidate won and nothing more was heard from the caller.

One of St. Louis' most prestigious, valuable and significant citizens was probably one of the least known. The contradiction was startling.

A southern gentleman in appearance, conduct and personality, retired Admiral Sidney M. Souers was persuaded to come to St. Louis from a successful business career in Louisiana to take over the operation of a failing life insurance company, Central States, located on Washington Avenue, just east of Grand.

By the early 1940s, Souers had become a close friend of Harry Truman. As president, Truman asked Souers to come to Washington to help him administer the sometimes frightening duties of charting America's role through the end of World War II and in the postwar world. Souers took a leave of absence from what had then become General American Life Insurance Co. and did very successfully whatever Truman asked him to do.

One of his most important assignments was to organize the Central Intelligence Agency. Later, Truman asked him to form the National Security Council, an advisory body in the White House.

Despite these major contributions to our nation's welfare and future, Souers was unfailingly a quiet, unassuming man with courtly manners who was the epitome of everyone's grandfather. He became a major philanthropist, whose gifts were little heralded. His major interest was in medical research and his charity was continued after his death by his widow, Sylvia. Saint Louis University Medical School is a major beneficiary of their estate.

Jack Dwyer, an old-time Irish politician, was the Democratic power in St. Louis during the 1950s and 1960s. He was chairman of the city Democratic committee and the number one man in the Northside 4th ward. He learned that John F. Kennedy had sent two representatives to St. Louis to help in his 1960 presidential campaign, and he advised Mayor Raymond Tucker to "get those two bastards out of town."

He added, "We can't win if if they're here, but we'll win it if they're not."

Tucker convinced the two men to leave and Dwyer carried the city for Kennedy by a huge majority.

Eddie Rickenbacker was a famous race driver and the leading American World War I fighter pilot, an ace. He returned to active duty as a pilot in World War II, was shot down in the Pacific, and floated around for twenty-two days before he was rescued.

On November 22, 1963, he was in St. Louis to speak to businessmen at a luncheon at the Jefferson Hotel. Dick Amberg was at the head table; I was in the audience just in front.

Rickenbacker's speech was a vitriolic excoriation of President John F. Kennedy, vindictive and vicious. In the middle of the talk, Dick received a note from the *Globe* newsroom informing him that President Kennedy had been shot. I could see him deliver the note to the toastmaster who in turn, gave it to Rickenbacker. Rickenbacker obviously read the note, then continued his speech without any diminution of his vicious attack on the president.

A few minutes later, Dick got a second message, that the president was dying. The same action followed: Dick to the toastmaster; the toastmaster to Rickenbacker, and still, no interruption of the speech. A third note informed them all that the president had died.

By the time Rickenbacker had finished, news of the assassination had apparently circulated through the audience and the room was about three-quarters empty.

Some years later, Nora and I were guests at the White House for a dinner. Rickenbacker was also a guest. I could not hold my tongue. I introduced myself and told him I was going to ask him a question and he didn't need to answer.

I asked him if he remembered the talk in St. Louis, and he said he did. Then I asked, "Why in the hell didn't you quit speaking when you got the notes that the president had been shot and then had died?" He looked at me for a minute and very quietly said, "That was the worst mistake I ever made in my whole life."

Robert Kennedy, attorney general of the United States and John's brother, was known by some political leaders to have wielded great power with an iron fist. I had lunch occasionally with Ed Long, U.S. Senator, a prominent Missouri Democrat. Dick Amberg despised Long for some reason, but I liked him. At one of these luncheons Long told me he was absolutely terrified of Robert Kennedy because of his ruthless, vengeful use of his power. He worked vigorously to reduce the power of organized crime and most everyone agreed he was a tireless opponent.

For a U.S. Senator to say that he, in one of the most respected and powerful positions in political life in America, was terrified of Bobby Kennedy says a lot.

George Bush was greatly criticized for moving us into the Persian Gulf war, but there was no question in my mind that the irresponsible leadership of Iraq had to be disciplined and a means found to assure the world that Iraq did not have chemical, bacteriological or nuclear weapons because of the irresponsibility of its government. I question whether bombing alone would have achieved that end. It could have changed the course of history.

China was opposed to bombing, Russia was opposed. For Bush to put together a coalition supportive of U. S. action was an astounding feat. Suppose after the bombing the public clamor over civilian deaths and unnecessary damage grew to such an extent that the Arab world coalesced in a power opposed to America. That would have been a disaster.

First of all, economically, this country cannot survive more than a few weeks without the oil we get from the Middle East. Suppose that an anti-American coalition decided not to sell us any oil. Suppose that Russia influenced other countries not to send us minerals we need. Our industries cannot survive without those vital minerals from the African nations. I think the time frame would be about six weeks.

I don't know if our administration had thought that through and found answers for these consequences. If they did and had reasonable assurance that we would not face such a disaster, fine, but I am not sure we had that foresight.

I have been asked if the Persian Gulf war settled anything. Yes, indeed. First of all, it restored Kuwait to its sovereignty. And secondly, it stalled for the time being Iraq's aggressive attitude toward its neighbors. And thirdly, it gave some semblance of dominance of the United Nations over Iraq's irrational conduct.

President Bill Clinton was acquitted recently after a trial in the Senate on charges of lying under oath. His trial grew out of his repugnant and atrocious personal conduct. But regardless of circumstances, whether the head of our country was a Democrat or Republican, I insisted that the *Globe-Democrat* respect the office of the presidency–if not the office holder. Clinton, I believe, is not equal to the image of the office.

Frequently, power is in the perception and not in its reality. We are perceived as the most powerful nation in the world but we have to have a leader who exudes power and respect. It goes with the territory. When a U.S. president is dealing with a foreign leader and is thought to be a despicable individual, he will not receive much respect for what he wants done.

President George Bush frequently visited St. Louis. Football hero Dan Dierdorf is between us, and Air Force One is in the background.

If an individual doesn't have character, he can't deal as well for us. Clinton has repeatedly demonstrated that his basic character is terribly flawed.

He appears to be a utilitarian—a person who believes the end justifies the means. That is morally wrong. The Clinton issue has nothing to do with sex, in my judgment. If he withholds information, if he is inducing people to lie, or lies himself, especially when he lies under oath to a grand jury, that is where the immorality comes in.

From what I know of Kenneth Starr, the independent counsel, I like him. I don't know him personally, but I do know St. Louisans who have a very high regard for him as a federal judge and as an individual. I reflect that attitude until I find out something different.

If I had still been publishing a paper during the impeachment hearings, I would have printed every word of the Clinton story. It was a disgrace to America. The media have a duty to uphold the public morals and I think it is wrong to demean them.

One of the many wonderful experiences during my life as publisher was the annual Gridiron dinner in Washington, D.C., which was staged by the Gridiron Club, an organization of about fifty working news people, print and electronic. It is a white tie affair for about 250 to 300 guests.

Club members put on a show of some ten acts, satirizing officials who, in an evening of fun and good sportsmanship, enjoy the jokes about themselves (or at least act as though they do). The president and his wife, the vice-president and his wife, most of the president's cabinet, most of the Supreme Court justices, most ambassadors, prominent government heads such as leaders of the CIA and FBI attend. The audience is made up of a large segment of the nation's business and political life outside Washington.

It is customary for the president to respond. This, of course, is a highlight and always done tongue-in-cheek, as is the show. There isn't any question among the older gridironers that the presidential response which outshone all others was in 1970 when Nixon and Vice-President Spiro Agnew had a sort of piano duet. Nixon played many of the then-popular songs while Agnew did his part with similar memorable songs. For some reason, probably Agnew's choice of songs and presentation, the vice president seemed to top the president.

On another occasion at a Gridiron dinner when Agnew had an opportunity to respond, he spoke for a couple of minutes and then reached under the podium and held up a bow and arrow which he prepared to shoot. Everyone in the audience in front of the podium ducked. In 1982, Nancy Reagan did a song and dance in costume.

The president of the Gridiron Club is the evening's toastmaster. We were pleased in 1981 when Edward W. O'Brien, head of the *Globe-Democrat's* Washington bureau, was the toastmaster. It is the custom for the head of the club president's newspaper, TV or radio station, to sit at the head table next to the president.

This posed a real diplomatic problem for me. Although, as publisher I was in control of the *Globe,* S. I. Newhouse owned the paper. Since he had died, his two sons, Si and Donald, were now the owners. I suggested the two brothers sit at the head table in my place and O'Brien agreed. Si was to sit to the right of President Jimmy Carter and Donald at O'Brien's left. Two days before the dinner, Si called to ask if he and his brother could change places halfway through the dinner and this was done.

I was particularly interested in seeing Carter because Ed had called me earlier to say that the president was refusing to wear the customary white tie and tails. I told Ed to get word to the president, in person if necessary, that the club really wanted to preserve its traditions and would disinvite him if he wouldn't wear white tie formal dress. O'Brien talked with him and he showed up in formal attire.

On the night of this particular Gridiron, I had invited Jack and Bill Danforth as my guests. Imagine our surprise when Bill showed up in white tie and tails, but without a collar. I never did understand the couture oversight.

Another guest of mine was also involved in a fashion matter at one of the Gridiron dinners. Lt. Gen. Robert (Dutch) Huyser, commander of the Military Airlift Command at Scott Air Force Base in Illinois, whose friendship Nora and I cherished, was standing with her at the reception which precedes the dinner when Andrei Gromyko, Russian Ambassador to the United States, approached.

Huyser had known the ambassador when he was vice-commander of NATO under Alexander M. Haig. He greeted the ambassador in Russian and introduced him to Nora.

After a few pleasantries, he asked, "Why are you dressed in a military uniform?"

The ambassador—the only man in the crowded room not in white tie and tails—flushed as red as a tomato, glared at Huyser, turned on his heel and walked away.

Huyser was not the least flustered or embarrassed. Actually, I think he was pleased.

Huyser once told me that when he was vice-commander of NATO, he received a call from President Carter in his office in Brussels. Carter said he wanted Huyser to be in Iran by 2 P.M. the following day and that he should do everything he knew of or had the power to do to maintain the shah of Iran in power. This was the time when Iranian dissidents were gaining in their efforts to remove the shah from his throne, a threat to America because the shah was friendly to the United States.

Huyser told the president there was no way he could close his office in time to get to Iran by two, principally because he had to arrange for the safekeeping of a large number of classified documents in his office. The president insisted until Huyser, knowing he was talking to his commander-in-chief, agreed. He got to Iran by the appointed hour.

There, he felt his first duty was to inform the U.S. Ambassador to Iran of his presence and his orders. Ambassador Sullivan was astonished, commenting, "My orders from the State Department are to do everything I can to help remove the shah from office."' Each man worked his own objective. Huyser lost when the shah abandoned his throne and fled his country.

Huyser had risen from the rank of private to lieutenant general in the air force. He enlisted in the army in the 1930s from his home in Colorado. Alongside him in the enlistment line was a boyhood friend.

When Huyser retired from service in a dinner ceremony at Scott Air Force Base in the 1970s, we were fortunate to be present. After dinner, as the usual laudatory comments began, Huyser interrupted the program and asked his school friend, whom he had invited to the ceremony, to come up front and sit with him.

The friend had remained in the service as a career and had made sergeant, but that night he shared the glory with a high-ranking officer to whom friendship meant more than rank.

- 9 -

DESEGREGATION IN ST. LOUIS

The issue of desegregation is so fraught with emotion, prejudice, and ignorance that I am convinced very few white Missourians, or Americans for that matter, have any real appreciation for the agony, suffering, indignity, denial and frustration of life's goals experienced by millions of blacks due to segregation.

One simple measure enacted by the Missouri legislature is a starting point for understanding the almost bottomless chasm into which blacks in this state were cast. Apart from being born healthy, one of the most important elements in a human being's life is an education. It is difficult to comprehend now, but in 1847 the Missouri legislature passed a bill prohibiting any black person from learning to read or write. It was a crime for a white person to teach a black or even to allow blacks to get an education. Beyond the actual harm inflicted, think of the savageness of such an act by one group of human beings against another group of human beings.

Fortunately, this rule did not last long until reason again prevailed, however inept the results. On February 20, 1865, the law forbidding black education was repealed. In the fall of 1866 the board of education of the city of St. Louis opened its first schools for blacks. On June 22, 1954–one month and five days after the U.S. Supreme Court's historic decision negating the "separate

150

but equal" doctrine—the St. Louis Board of Education under Superintendent Phillip J. Hickey initiated a three-year desegregation program.

Earlier, in 1947, Archbishop Joseph Ritter announced that henceforth parochial schools under the archdiocesan control would be desegregated. After the discouraging and puzzling experience with the inexplicable and implacable attitude of Archbishop John Glennon who openly and dictatorially refused to allow black children to attend white parochial elementary schools and Catholic high schools, Cardinal Ritter's orders were welcome. There was little more than an undercurrent of opposition. One person, a prominent political leader named Jack Barrett, tried to fight the measure. His opposition lost its steam when the Vatican declined to respond to his protestations and the St. Louis chancery made it clear that opponents of desegregation faced possible excommunication.

Gradually through the 1950s public facilities operated by the city of St. Louis were also desegregated, particularly the parks and other recreation centers. St. Louis County followed suit. During the course of time there were a few incidents which attracted public attention, most notably at Fairgrounds Park, but no real violence.

For some reason which I have never understood and certainly will not accept, many in the black community and some white liberals have erroneously contended that the *Globe-Democrat* was anti-black. That was an ignorant and prejudiced characterization—a myth—and I deny it absolutely.

As I pointed out earlier, observing mistreatment of blacks in my childhood and young adulthood, coupled with beliefs inherited from my parents led me to my own lifelong concern with the dignity of every human being. In this, I have followed the heritage of the *Globe-Democrat* which in its earliest days took a strong stand against slavery in a divided Missouri.

During my tenure, especially after I became publisher, the paper gave equally strong editorial support to desegregation efforts, to the individuals who made singular contributions to those efforts, and to the political aspirations of qualified blacks seeking public office.

I believe that of all the progressive steps our society has taken in the twentieth century, none is more important than desegregation, the erasure of barriers to freedom imposed on minorities.

It has not been easy. Prejudice—racial or religious—dies hard, but progress has been brought about through the efforts of many individuals and organizations. Unfortunately, for whatever reasons, some people tried to prevent integration, delaying the process for years. Some were overt, powerful and persuasive; some worked surreptitiously.

Following World War II, many communities in America, especially urban areas, made serious efforts to further desegregation, fulfilling a duty which had existed since the Civil War. But not much was achieved, as there was little organized or concentrated effort. Sporadically, federal and state governments enacted enabling legislation and individuals and organizations worked on the problem.

Progress throughout the nation in the 1960s and 1970s was agonizingly slow and often painfully ineffective. In many instances, violence erupted, occasionally resulting in death and extensive property damage from fire and looting. Washington, D.C., Los Angeles, Chicago, and Detroit are memorable examples. Many other cities suffered but not so grievously.

Granted, we in St. Louis have not been totally without conflict, roadblocks or attacks on desegregation efforts. And we have not been free of false or irresponsible claims of credit for desegregation's success in St. Louis.

I have been offended in recent years by public claims by some individuals that they were responsible for desegregation. That effort was not the result of a single individual or organization, and the lack of violence was not the product of a single individual or organization. The equally preposterous conclusion in a recent feeble *Post-Dispatch* article that the lack of violence in St. Louis was "pure dumb luck" is insulting to every St. Louisan, black and white, who worked for racial understanding and harmony.

Why did St. Louis not suffer the violence other cities did in the 1960s and 1970s? It was not "pure dumb luck." There were countless reasons, but it boils down to the fact that St. Louisans worked together, black and white, in good faith to achieve a goal. Fair employment and fair housing regulations were put in place. By the 1960s and 1970s there were a significant number of young people, black and white, who had gone to school together and who knew each other as individuals.

The lack of violence in St. Louis was most likely the inevitable result of the heartfelt, individual, uncoordinated effort which had its roots in every segment of our community. There were few places where the seeds of violence could germinate.

As early as 1947, a group of young people, most from Washington University, led by Irvin and Margaret Dagen, followed the nonviolent philosophy of Mahatma Gandhi when they conducted peaceful sit-ins to open the doors of public accommodations to those of all races. Incidentally, their seniors, members of the board of aldermen, did not pass a public accommodations bill until 1961, after failing to pass it on several votes.

The universities, Saint Louis and Washington, were in no hurry to open their doors to blacks and, in the case of the Jesuit school, Saint Louis University, to women either. On Lincoln's birthday in 1944 the Rev. Claude Heithaus, S.J., publicly criticized his university for not enrolling women and blacks in a homily at the College Church. Rev. Paul C. Reinert, S.J., president of Saint Louis University, went to Rome twice in the late 1940s to get permission from the Jesuit order and the Vatican to open the university to minorities.

St. Louis Archbishop John Glennon opposed it. He didn't have much to say about the university because it is not subject to the archbishop's orders, but the fact that he opposed desegregation did have some impact on the administration's views.

At the insistence of Dean Benjamin Youngdahl, the Washington University School of Social Work admitted its first black students in 1948, but the remainder of the campus remained an all-white world until the trustees quietly approved desegregation on May 9, 1952.

Few unions in the 1960s and 1970s welcomed black members, and the newspaper unions were among the worst offenders. Until the day we tried to close the paper in 1984, there were no black employees in the mechanical departments. This was because of closed shop contracts which required us to hire persons through the union hiring hall where there were no black members. The Newspaper Guild, which represented news department and business office employees, did welcome black members and we had black employees in those departments.

There was no significant black attendance in mainline white

Protestant churches throughout most of this century. Some white congregations, while not arbitrarily reserving a back row for blacks, nevertheless quietly and subtly directed them to the rear of the church. Clergy and lay leaders were among those who actively or passively objected to the idea of integration. I was not aware during this period of any black priests or nuns either in diocesan posts or in religious orders.

Several white ministers did call for desegregation, especially those active in the Metropolitan Church Federation. Among the most outspoken was Episcopal Bishop William Scarlett.

One of the very few public organizations then working publicly for desegration was the St. Louis Chapter of the National Conference of Christians and Jews (NCCJ). Others included the Urban League and the National Association for the Advancement of Colored People (NAACP).

Activists in the NCCJ included Virgil L. Borders and Myron Schwartz. Al Fleishman, founder of the now worldwide public relations firm of Fleishman and Hillard, and Irvin Dagen lent their support. But the NCCJ did not have whole-hearted public backing and especially lacked strong corporate and citizen leadership support.

The sole corporate leader who took a leadership role in the NCCJ and by his mere presence provided a persuasive role in the corporate world was Russell L. Dearmont, president of the Missouri Pacific Railroad in St. Louis. Many St. Louisans supported the NCCJ only half-heartedly and some frequently talked of dropping their support.

One day I asked Dearmont to explain to me his interest in the NCCJ. He told me that as a boy in Southeast Missouri, where prejudice was at as high a level as any place in America, he had seen the evils of segregation and from that experience tried his best to help eradicate it. He said that his worst experience was in 1928, when Al Smith, then governor of New York and a Catholic, ran for president. The vicious, hateful, and demeaning attitude against Catholics in that campaign shaped his philosophy for the rest of his life. The result was an unwavering support for the NCCJ in St. Louis, whose work against prejudice included not only that toward blacks, but against any group of Americans, including Jews and Catholics.

Other individuals made their own stands on desegregation in

radically different ways. Among the most prominent was activist Percy Green, who chained the doors of such major businesses as Laclede Gas and caused other attention-getting civil disturbances. Once he or his followers started a fire on the newsroom floor at the *Globe-Democrat* but it was extinguished before any damage was done. One of his colleagues, Gena Scott, interrupted the Veiled Prophet Ball in 1972 by swinging down from the balcony during the traditional proceedings. He objected to the order's use of city property for its all-white festivities, even though it paid the customary rental fee.

Other individuals, both black and white, responded in a quieter manner. I recall an act of kindness by a white man on behalf of a black friend which surely helped heal a bit of the divisiveness between races.

In recounting it, I am paying tribute to a distinguished and obviously sensitive corporate leader, Dr. Charles Allen Thomas. With his partner in a Dayton, Ohio, laboratory, Dr. Carroll Hochwalt, Thomas invented the ethyl additive for gasoline. Subsequently, their laboratory was bought by Monsanto and, ultimately, Dr. Thomas became chairman of the company.

At a luncheon at the Log Cabin Club, Nora sat next to Dr. Thomas. During the luncheon, she reported to me that he had been in tears. A black man who had worked for him for many years had died the preceding day, but the pastor of St. Mary Magdalen Catholic Church had refused to bury him because of the priest's concern about the man's right to have a Catholic funeral. She said she had told him that "Duncan will take care of the problem."

I called Cardinal Carberry and explained the situation. Within an hour, he called back to say that the church would have the funeral the following day.

One of the longest steps forward was taken when Civic Progress organized its Dialogue Committee, which met regularly with representatives of the black community to work on potential problems and, in some cases, prevent trouble from erupting into crisis situations. I have long been convinced, and have yet to hear persuasive arguments to the contrary, that this committee had a major role in the generally peaceful progress.

Early one summer, when Hal Dean, Ralston Purina chairman, was Dialogue Committee chairman, some black members of the

committee reported that they had heard that a few violence-in-
clined blacks planned to stage a demonstration on July Fourth. It
was feared the demonstration could lead to a riot.

The committee put its influences, black and white, to work,
and the violence never came to pass. The *Globe-Democrat* knew
of this threat and did not print a word about the upcoming danger, in accordance with an agreement. During the course of the
desegregation struggle, a group of citizens asked both newspapers not to print news in advance of potentially violent demonstrations so crowds would not be attracted. We followed this agreement and I am sure the *Post* did also.

We did print news of conflicts after they occurred. The acts of
civil disobedience in St. Louis were short-lived and did not result
in fatalities or critical injuries.

I was sorry, more recently, to learn about an unfortunate occurrence involving James Buford, who succeeded Bill Douthit as
director of the St. Louis chapter of the Urban League.

Buford became widely known in the St. Louis area and earned
much help and attention. My first contact with him was when
Ranken Technical College made a concerted drive to interest
black youths in attending. We called on him to assist us in attract-
ing them, and he was most co-operative and helpful.

However, he publicly criticized the Civic Progress Dialogue
Committee. This criticism, coming from an admired black leader,
caused the committee, at least for the time being, to abandon its
work. This doesn't appear to bode well for the community's future. What other forum is there in the community where issues
of such consequences can be discussed openly with a potential
for resolution?

The concern of the white leadership shown through the policies of the United Way and its predecessor organization was also
important. My first service with the United Way began in the
very early 1950s. I know from firsthand experience that the United
Way provided financial assistance to black social agencies during
this time. An example: the Urban League asked for an increase
in its annual allocation. The committee, of which I was a member, honored that request with an additional $300,000. The in-
crease probably doubled, or close to it, the League's annual budget.

Many corporations were genuinely conscious of the vital effort and contributed in countless ways to its progress. Again, at the risk of overlooking a worthy name, the program was helped by the policies of Anheuser Busch, Ralston Purina, Monsanto, Mallinckrodt, Southwestern Bell, Famous-Barr, Stix-Baer-Fuller, Sears, the banks and many, many others.

But most of all it was the people who made the difference between violence and nonviolence. Black leaders like David M. Grant, an attorney and widely admired civic leader, worked diligently on the issue from his post in the St. Louis City Hall. One of his jobs was director of legislative research for the St. Louis Board of Aldermen, which was integrated.

St. Louis and the entire state had long benefited from the inspiring leadership of Theodore D. McNeal, initially a vice-president of the Brotherhood of Sleeping Car Porters, who was the first black man elected to the Missouri State Senate, the first black member of the board of curators of the University of Missouri and the first black president of the St. Louis Board of Police Commissioners. He was appointed by Governor Christopher (Kit) Bond to the police board February 2, 1973, during the height of agitation for integration. The *Globe* supported McNeal in his race for the Senate and his work on the board of curators.

Another who helped materially to set the stage for St. Louis' nonviolent transition was James E. Hurt, Jr., who inherited the Employees Loan Company from his father. Hurt was supported by the *Globe-Democrat* when he ran for a post on the St. Louis Board of Education and won a seat. In the spring of 1969, he organized Central City Foods, a supermarket on the east side of Grand Avenue just north of Delmar. Unfortunately, the market closed in September 1974. Hurt occasionally hosted meetings of a black ministers' group at his loan office on Easton Avenue and he invited me. I was privileged to learn a lot about the frustrations of the black community and their efforts to further desegregation.

Black ministers in St. Louis are one of the most potent forces in the city and in the black community. Time and time again I have seen issues put before the voters which have been approved or defeated according to the position of the black ministers. Obviously during the tough desegregation push in the 1960s and 1970s black ministers gave sound advice and support to their congregations and they were a potent force in the resulting nonviolence.

Jack Dwyer, longtime Democratic power in St. Louis, brought Fred Weathers, a black man, into St. Louis city government. Dwyer wanted to know how the *Globe* would treat him and Weathers about this. I told him it was long overdue to have black representation in the city leadership and that we would certainly be fair and not critical, unless there was a reason to be. Governor Teasdale appointed Weathers to the St. Louis Police Board in May 1980.

Amberg was among a group of St. Louisans who lobbied for the appointment of Scoville Richardson, a noted black legal scholar, law professor and practicing lawyer in St. Louis, to be appointed to a judgeship on the federal bench in St. Louis. He would have been the first of his race there. While he did not make the St. Louis bench, he was appointed to the U.S. Custom Court in New York City where he served for many years in the 1950s and 1960s.

Ina Boon, an NAACP official in St. Louis and with the national office, was made a *Globe-Democrat* Woman of Achievement for her contributions to our community and the nation. Her son, Gentry Trotter, a good friend of mine who had made a name for himself as a radio personality and public relations man, at one time showed great courage in defending me and the *Globe-Democrat*, for which I will always be grateful.

I was a guest at the head table at the annual NAACP dinner. The speaker claimed that I was the organizer of the resurgence of the Ku Klux Klan in St. Louis, an outrageously untrue statement. Gentry was the NAACP treasurer. When it came time for his report, he cut the financial part short and gave a ringing defense of me, the paper, and our editorial policies which, he pointed out, had been of great help to the black community.

Howard Woods had long been associated with the *St. Louis Argus*, a black weekly newspaper, when he aspired to be associated with the nation's radio broadcasts to the Iron Curtain countries through the U.S. Information Agency (USIA). With a good deal of white support, including Dick Amberg and the *Globe-Democrat,* Howard was appointed. After a few years he returned to St. Louis to start his own newspaper, the *St. Louis Sentinel.* I introduced him to a major advertiser, Russell Savage, general manager of Sears, and asked Savage to give Howard some business, which he did. Unfortunately Howard died shortly after founding the *Sentinel,* but his widow continues to operate the paper.

Fredda Witherspoon was an energetic doer who will never be forgotten for her community dedication and bubbly personality. A schoolteacher who earned a doctorate, she accepted civic responsibility whatever the burden and did well at it. Her husband, Robert, was also an effective member of the community.

At one time, I asked Fredda to serve on a special task force for the St. Louis Police Department chaired by George Capps. After the first meeting she called to say, "What in the world have you gotten me into? George called our meeting on a Saturday at seven o'clock in the morning!" I had forgotten to warn her that George slept only about four hours every night and was often at his desk by dawn.

John B. Ervin, Ph.D., a member of the Washington University faculty since 1965, was exceptionally persuasive in the desegregation movement. He was highly respected in whatever circle he moved, largely the more sophisticated, multi-racial groups. He became dean of the School of Continuing Education and was also dean of the university's summer school. He left the university in June 1977 to become vice-president of the Danforth Foundation. He died in 1992.

Attorney Frankie Freeman got her legal education when it was not common for women to attend law school and certainly not common for black women to attend law school. Her leadership during the troubled times was rational, balanced, and effective. President Lyndon B. Johnson appointed her as a member of the U.S. Civil Rights Commission and subsequently she served as an inspector general of a federal cabinet department. She was part of counsel in many early civil rights cases. She also served on many social agency boards, and, as of this writing, is on the Ranken Technical College board.

Frankie was an original member of the board of the Herbert Hoover Boys Club, founded by Dick Amberg. The club's director, Carl Wood, wanted to discharge his assistant, also black, in a move authorized by the board. The assistant filed a complaint with the EEOC, the government agency which looks into unjustified discharges because of age or race.

I appealed to Frankie for advice. She said, in effect, "Let me handle this."

Obviously she did because we never heard another word from the complaint and the employee was dismissed, not because of age or race, but because he wasn't doing his job.

Margaret Bush Wilson was appointed a member of the board of directors of Monsanto Company in 1977 by Jack Hanley when he was chairman of Monsanto. As such she was undoubtedly one of the first black women in the nation to be a board member of a major American company. Wilson, who was also the national head of the NAACP, retired from the Monsanto board in 1987.

A key element in St. Louis' nonviolent desegregation was the participation of the St. Louis police department. One cause for violent social discontent is fear—fear for both individual or collective safety. If a large portion of a local community feels its members do not have security in public or are being abused by the public authority, that segment can be encouraged to express its discontent by public protest, occasionally with violence.

The black population in St. Louis, figuratively or literally, may have had more confidence in their city's police department than blacks elsewhere. And they had good reason.

Many residents are unaware that the St. Louis Police Department, like the St. Louis Election Board, is controlled by the state but the cost of operation is paid by the city. Statutorily, both departments submit an annual operating budget to the city government which is mandated to provide funds. Life being what it is, the mandate is rarely, if ever, followed and the final budgets are the result of negotiation.

Blacks were recruited into the police force beginning with the turn of the last century. In 1901, J. Gordon and A. Wilkinson became the first blacks appointed to the St. Louis Police Department. In 1936, the department had twenty-five black officers; in 1943, thirty-six. In 1960, a significant date in terms of civil rights, there were 400 black officers; in 1999 there are 480, or almost thirty percent of the 1600-man force.

The first black appointed to the St. Louis police board was Clifton Gates, in 1963. Clarence Harmon was the first black chief of police, a post now held by Ron Henderson, also black. Charles Mischeaux, a black vice-president of NationsBank, president of the St. Louis NAACP and former police board member, was instrumental in the choice of Henderson to succeed Harmon.

During the restive civil disturbance era, the St. Louis police department had superlative and reliable information sources which alerted them to impending or potentially inflammatory actions. The department acted promptly and authoritatively to prevent trouble.

On August 31, 1963, the first step took place in what would turn out to be one of more visible and memorable steps in the desegregation effort in the St. Louis area. It was an order by Circuit Judge Michael Scott ordering a number of militant black leaders not to interfere with the business of the Jefferson Bank, then located at Jefferson Avenue and Washington Avenue.

The judge's order followed information that black militants picketing the bank demanding more black employees intended to enter the bank and sit down in the lobby hampering normal business. The militants learned of the court order and held a meeting on the bank's parking lot where they voted to ignore the order and enter the bank. The bank's attorney, Wayne L. Millsap, again appealed to the judge and the judge responded with an order to attach, meaning that the sheriff was directed to find and bring before the court those who voted to defy. That included the militants' attorney, Ray Howard.

The activists were not easily found but on Sunday, August 31, following the order to attach, they began slowly to make themselves available for arrest. They included William L. Clay, later to become St. Louis' Congressman from the northside. Those surrendering were ordered to jail, but they appealed the order and the Missouri Court of Appeals found in their favor, ruling that they had been improperly jailed because they had not had a proper hearing.

At subsequent hearings, the defendants were again found guilty of violating the court order and sentenced to sixty-three days in jail. Judge Scott placed the defendants on probation for two years.

The picketing over the month-long period of the dispute did indeed threaten the security of the bank and kept customers away. Business institutions in the area made substantial deposits in the bank without drawing on them to show their support. James Hickok, chairman and president of First National Bank in St. Louis, was one of the principals in arranging the deposit program.

Dillon Ross was the chairman and owner of the bank. Through his business life he had been an unwavering citizen supporter of good government and public officials. He was known throughout the state as a leading Democrat. Today the bank, now located on Market Street near Jefferson and more successful than ever, is headed by Michael Ross, Dillon's son.

It has always been interesting and encouraging to me when individuals who have been total opposites in a point of view change their perspectives 180 degrees and become partners in seeking a common goal.

This happened in a significant way in late 1995 and early 1996 when Norman J. Tice, executive vice president of Boatmen's Bank and in charge of its government relations, induced Senator Lacey Clay, son of Congressman Bill Clay, to introduce a bill in the Missouri Senate which was in the banking industry's interest.

Tice sought Missouri legislation to increase the percentage of total bank deposits in Missouri which a single bank could hold to more than the then-limit of thirteen percent. Boatmen's could not grow by acquisition in the state unless the limit was raised.

Obviously the larger banks would benefit by this measure, but Tice needed the support of smaller banks for his bill. He persuaded Michael Ross to be a witness with Senator Clay before the Missouri Senate to support the bill. Many small banks opposed raising the limit, however, and there was not enough support from the larger banks for the bill to pass.

Clifton Gates, an outstanding business man, obtained the Miller beer distributorship for St. Louis and was heavily involved in the development of the first black-owned bank in St. Louis, the Gateway. However, when he ran against Congressman William Clay in the Democratic primary, he was disastrously defeated. Bill White, a successful radio station owner, also tried his luck against Clay and experienced a similar defeat.

There were many aspects to segregation which hurt the black community and made it more difficult for the community or individuals to progress. One was the disinclination of banks to make loans to blacks, individually or for business needs. Too, the banks during this period rarely made loans to white people living in areas of the city where banks mistakenly thought property would decline in value—areas in the Central West End, such as Westmoreland and Portland Place.

In the late 1940s two brothers, David and Phillip Lichtenstein, owned the controlling interest in the American National Bank at Gravois and Kingshighway. Philip was the operating head of American and David headed one of the nation's large consumer loan companies.

Philip's banking philosophy contained the principle that the bank should make loans to all borrowers whenever possible because in many instances they became successful and. loyal customers. This theory included loans to black churches.

Over a period of time the two brothers established the Brentwood Bank at Highway 40 and Brentwood Blvd. and the City Bank at Lindell Blvd. and Euclid. Philip Lichtenstein, shortly after founding City Bank, lured Norman Tice away from a post at Boatmen's Bank to become president of the new bank. City Bank board members included Stan Musial and his business partner, Biggie Garagnani, who ran their restaurant.

City Bank became the first bank in St. Louis to make loans to residents of Portland and Westmoreland Place, causing many more hesitant bankers to question the bank's judgment. City Bank also extended loans in significant volume to residents of north St. Louis. The basic banking concept was that loans were being made to individuals whose credit was good, no matter where they lived. Soon City Bank had a major volume of loans to West End and northside residents. They did not have a single foreclosure on a loan made to northsiders.

City Bank also established a checking account for people of low income, which provided six free checks a month to the depositor. The theory was that many times the cost of a bus fare to pay a bill in cash was an unjustified burden on someone who wanted to maintain a good credit rating.

Ultimately the City Bank sold itself in succession to Charter of Kansas City and then to Boatmen's of St. Louis. Boatmen's had not been making loans of any significance to persons living in north St. Louis. When Boatmen's acquired City Bank it had to meet government banking rules which required a bank to prove it was making a certain number of loans to low-income residents. City Bank's acquisition provided Boatmen's with a ready-made portfolio. Boatmen's continued the City Bank policy and the last I knew had a northside portfolio unmatched by any other St. Louis bank, in the range of $80 million.

All of this to the credit of the Lichtenstein brothers, Philip's son, Gayle W., and Norman Tice.

In the late 1970s many St. Louisans were aware of a need for the Veiled Prophet Order to modernize. Attendance at the annual parade was down substantially, financial problems loomed and there was rather wide criticism of the order's place in current life

The *Globe-Democrat* called this to the attention of the order's leadership in a private meeting with the Veiled Prophet. Robert R. Hermann, then in an influential role in the order, was alarmed at the almost fifty percent decline in membership, at its perilous financial condition, and declining public interest. Like many others he felt the order had been and should continue to be a significant factor in the cultural history of our community. He set about to do something about it.

He visited five cities—New Orleans, Pittsburgh, Chicago, Indianapolis and Baltimore—to study successful public activities. From this research he concluded that a July Fourth celebration on the Arch grounds sponsored by the Veiled Prophet Order would be attractive and reflect credit on the organization.

He presented the idea to the order and it was approved. The name, VP Fair, was coined. Within weeks, Hermann had a support crew of six or eight civic leaders backed by 10,000 to 15,000 volunteers. The VP Fair tradition began in 1981. It became evident that black participation was crucial to the use of the Arch grounds, which is federal property. Hermann enlisted the support of two prominent black leaders, Dr. Jerome Williams, a physician, and Dr. Donald Suggs, an orthodontist, who became members of the Order.

John Peters MacCarthy, chairman of St. Louis Union Trust, asked me to suggest other members of the black community who might be invited to become members. I suggested Wayman Smith III, a lawyer now with Anheuser-Busch, son of a well-known black politician and a third or fourth generation resident of St. Louis. I visited Smith in his home and issued the invitation and he was delighted to accept.

The fair still is supplemented by its impressive parade, led by the Veiled Prophet and the VP Queen. It gained national attention for St. Louis with an ABC telecast for several years.

As a member of the board of the Missouri Historical Society I was asked once to serve as chairman of the nominating committee. I was aware, as were other members of the board, that the society was in truly desperate plight, financially. It was so short of funds that it was dipping into what few trust accounts it had. This was a violation of the trust agreements, and significantly immoral, because the donors had given this money with the condition that it would be held in trust and only the interest used for the benefit of the society.

The leadership decided, wisely, that the Society should ask for permission to join the Metropolitan Zoological Park and Museum District to gain tax support for the operation. The district is a taxing body which levies property taxes on citizens of St. Louis and St. Louis County to provide operating funds for some of our major cultural institutions. The founding members were the Zoo, the Art Museum, and the Science Center.

The board set about to organize the election. The voters of St Louis County have to approve a new district member by fifty-one percent; voters in St. Louis City by the same percentage. A defeat in either of the two jurisdictions defeats the proposal.

The Historical Society at that time had never shown any notable interest in the black community. Obviously, the North St. Louis black voters would be a key factor in getting approval for the proposal. There had been few black members of the board. I convinced the members of the committee that we should nominate at least one or two blacks. One was Missouri Senator Jet Banks, a legislator who effectively controlled the vote in North St. Louis.

I asked Banks if he were made a member of the board would he support the admission of the Society to the Zoo District and he agreed to do so.

Two were—reluctantly—approved by the board as candidates, but someone arranged for a write-in candidate who subsequently was elected over Banks. I am glad to say that Banks, although he must have been disappointed, did not avenge his defeat by working against the proposition.

The board also chose a new public relations firm, headed by Ed Finkelstein, who had long experience in running community election campaigns. The proposition won, although by the slimmest of margins, and the museum became a member of the district with great financial gains, permitting the development of exciting programs—including, a fine representation of Black History in St. Louis under the leadership of its president, Robert Archibald, Ph.D. With the addition of the Historical Society and the Botanical Garden, the Zoo District now helps support five major cultural institutions.

There are hundreds of others, white and black, who should be given credit for St. Louis' remarkable nonviolent progress through desegregation to whatever level we may have reached. It is impossible to remember them all. The references I have made have been essentially to those I knew well and whose efforts I knew about personally.

The entire exercise here is to dispel the concept that any one person was responsible for the desegregation effort in St. Louis, as some have claimed, and that the nonviolent road was not "just pure dumb luck," but the result of the good will of thousands who worked seriously and thoughtfully to achieve the end.

The white population of St. Louis cannot deny its shame for the historical mistreatment of black citizens, but when awakened to the need, I believe that the responsible white population has responded with purpose to the development of desegregation in St. Louis.

Because of the determination of thousands, working in big and little ways to create racial understanding and harmony, I believe we are, indeed, a better community. I like to think that the *Globe-Democrat,* following the pattern set by its founders, played a major role.

- 10 -

"SIGNIFICANTS"

S ome of the thousands of people that I've met stand out in my memory for one reason or another. I've already mentioned many of these "significants," as I've termed them. Here are a few, only a few, of those who have meant so much to the progress of St. Louis and to me, as colleagues and friends.

Among the most memorable are the late Gussie Busch, his former wife, Trudy, and their children.

Gussie met Trudy in Switzerland where Trudy, her mother, and brother were operating a guest house in Lucerne. When Trudy and Gussie were married, they lived in an apartment in the Barnhoff at Grant's Farm. Gussie told me that his mother urged him and Trudy to move into the "big house," the mansion at Grant's Farm built by his father. Gussie told his mother he couldn't afford to furnish it, but his mother prevailed, and Trudy and Gussie did move into the mansion.

They had seven children. The youngest was Christina, dearly loved favorite of Gussie. She was coming home from school one day in a car driven by the Busch family chauffeur when an accident occurred on I-270 and the little girl, then nine, was killed. Her older brother, Andrew, was injured but not severely. It was a wrenching loss for Gussie and Trudy.

Gussie converted to Catholicism and was baptized by Rev.

Paul C. Reinert, S.J., at the private chapel on the home grounds. He was confirmed by John Joseph Cardinal Carberry, also in the chapel. The Busch family was not Catholic and Gussie's conversion was, I believe, because of Christina's death. I was very pleased that he did it.

Gussie built a chapel for Trudy near the big house. Trudy is a devout Catholic, very serious about her faith. The chapel had seating for maybe sixteen people. Almost every Sunday Mass was said in the chapel with the Busch family attending. One of the sons—Peter, William, Adolphus, or Andrew—would usually serve at Mass. We would be invited perhaps once every six weeks and it was an occasion which we always cherished.

The notable sense about the service in the chapel was the closeness, the intimacy, since there were so few worshippers. Father Reinert, then president of Saint Louis University, Cardinal Carberry, or Monsignor Jerome Wilkerson of St. Joseph's Church in Clayton, frequently said Mass.

After the 9:30 Mass, the custom was for everyone to go up to the house for a wonderful breakfast, always a memorable occasion. After breakfast there was champagne and conversation, and a very good time. In good weather, Gussie liked nothing better than to get out the coach and four, the one on which guests ride on top, and drive around the grounds. Of course, the coach rolled and swayed and the passengers were very high off the ground.

Gussie would drive those rough roads through the estate at top speed and with great glee. It scared me to death from time to time. It reached a point where Nora didn't want to ride and I didn't blame her.

One Saturday morning, Gussie called me at home to say he and Trudy were separating. I was shocked. I had no foreknowledge of this. During the conversation he told me that he would continue to follow his Catholic faith. He said that Trudy would have to leave. Within hours, Trudy called to tell us about the impending separation.

Gussie said their basic disagreement was because she was violating her obligations to do only certain things with her brewery stock, plus the fact that she spent too much money. I guess he didn't remember that she used to debate with the children about whether they should buy new shoes or economize by having them half-soled. For a while, Trudy lived in the small house which had been built for Gussie's mother, three or four hundred feet from the big house, but subsequently, Gussie asked her to leave the premises, which she did after much notoriety and press attention.

It was an unfortunate period in their lives when both received negative publicity regarding their differences. This bothered me considerably because each was a significant individual, and it just wasn't in keeping with the traditions of the Busch family or with Trudy's or Gussie's character to have this nasty public dispute.

Gussie was in Barnes hospital for surgery on his hip in the midst of all of this. One day Nora and I went to visit him. I told him I wanted to speak to him alone, whereupon Gussie, with his usual authoritative, gruff manner, ordered everyone out except me. I told him I thought his public attitude toward Trudy was detrimental and unbecoming to the image and the traditions that the Busch family had built up during the years. I emphasized the damage the public vendetta was doing. I said the thing for him to do was to get in touch with Trudy and their attorneys and settle the matter, get the divorce and not do any more damage to the picture of the Busch family as great and caring citizens of St. Louis.

Shortly after that, there was a divorce. That was a sad occasion for so many of us. A year or so later he married his long-time secretary Margaret Snyder, but she died within a short time and Gussie was alone until his own death. Trudy has never remarried. She lives in her home in St. Louis County and takes great interest in her children. Several years ago she lost both her mother and brother, who still lived in Switzerland. Monsignor Wilkerson went to Lucerne to participate in her mother's funeral, a wonderful gesture which I'm sure was deeply appreciated.

During their marriage, Gussie and Trudy liked to give parties, very elaborate affairs. In good weather, Gussie would bring out some of the animals from their private zoo, the elephants and the camels and others, to perform on the terrace in front of the house.

Gussie, as one would imagine, had a genuine and knowledgeable interest in politics relative to the brewery's vast operations throughout the United States. He had employed effective lobbyists and for many years, he had one of immense skill, a close friend, Tony Buford. Tony was an attorney whose family had a

One of St. Louis's most important assets is its Cardinals baseball team, for years headed by Anheuser Busch patriarch August A. Busch, Jr. He is shown here with actress Carol Channing taking a lap around Busch Stadium behind a hitch of the brewery's Clydesdales during the 1982 World Series.

long history of active participation in Missouri politics. His father was a state senator and at one time Tony was in the state legislature.

Tony told me this story. Franklin Roosevelt ran for his first term as president while Prohibition was still in effect. Gussie asked Tony what could be done to persuade the future president that Prohibition should be repealed. Tony said it would be helpful, and perhaps gain Roosevelt's allegiance, if they'd raise some money among members of the Busch family. Gussie agreed and Tony raised a great deal of money for those days, something around $30,000 or $40,000. Tony asked Gussie to go to New

York with him and see the candidate. He did so, met with Roosevelt and handed him the bag of cash. As the record shows, Congress did pass an amendment to repeal Prohibition in 1933, immediately after Roosevelt was sworn in. The states quickly ratified it.

The Busch divorce put me in an awkward spot because both Gussie and Trudy were friends and I could not take sides. That embarrassment was made even worse when some members of the Anheuser Busch board—many of whom were also my good friends—decided that Gussie should retire from active leadership of the brewery and August III should take over. I found myself squarely in the middle.

Once Gussie made up his mind about something, nothing would stand in his way to get where he wanted to go. He never deviated from an objective. For him to have to leave the brewery was unbelievable to him, but the board wanted him to leave. Edwin S. Jones and Wallace (Buck) Persons, directors, said that young August would do a tremendous job.

Naturally, this decision created a lot of animosity on Gussie's part and he wouldn't speak to his son for over a year. There were many occasions or meetings where both were there and it created a really awkward situation. I called one meeting where it was necessary for both of them to attend. I went to the brewery to see August III first. He said, "Duncan, invite us both and I will speak to my father whether he speaks to me or not."

That was the atmosphere in which August took over. But I'm grateful to say that he was reconciled with his father long before Gussie died.

In retrospect, August III has done many times better with the brewery than his father did. He has been tremendously successful. He is a tireless worker. I wanted to see him a couple of times after he took over and his idea for an appointment was seven o'clock in the morning. I have been concerned for his safety with him flying his helicopter to work every day. He is an intense disciplinarian for himself and for those who work for him.

I have been asked if the brewery's sale of the Cardinals was justifiable. Absolutely.

Many people have invested in brewery stock. They want to earn a return on their investment. When the brewery operates every day, it is using its shareholders' money. As a shareholder, I would not want my money dissipated at the rate of $12 million a year in something that was a losing enterprise. I want the brewery to use my money to make more money for me.

I think August had to make a very difficult decision. I knew from personal experience that the Busch family is very conscious of the image of the family and of the brewery, a historical factor in St. Louis. Many times when I asked Gussie for money he would weigh how that gift would affect his public image. I am sure that August does the same thing

Gussie told me twenty years ago that high salaries would ruin baseball. That's when he was paying Stan Musial $100,000 a year.

This is the man who occasionally at Christmas would call and say, "I have a little money to give away," and would ask my suggestions about agencies to whom he should give it. That "little money" would be in five figures.

There are so many things in our community that would not be here if it were not for Gussie's devotion to St. Louis—for example, Busch stadium. Not a penny of government money went into that project. It was all raised by donations. Gussie put $5 million into it.

During the course of their later years, Louis Susman, a highly respected lawyer, became Gussie's attorney. Gussie and Lou made a deal to give some of the Busch paintings from the Busch home to the St. Louis Art Museum. Trudy had a fit and arranged to get the pictures back.

After she left the house, she didn't go back until after he died. Within a reasonable time after his death, she had a dinner party at the house, the first one she had had for many years. We had the pleasure of being there. I made a toast respecting Trudy's diligence in holding the family together, and other things she had done to make the family coalesce.

There were many other reminiscences. Percy Orthwein, Gussie's cousin, then an elderly man, told of his boyhood days playing in the house and yard with Gussie and how much he enjoyed that. He was very grateful to Trudy for inviting him. He said, "I haven't been back since my boyhood until tonight."

Now August IV is becoming more involved in the brewery. This is one of the few families that I know in America where the family has maintained quality leadership through so many generations.

In 1960 Martin Mathews, a man devoted to serving his fellow man, founded the Mathews-Dickey Boys Club. He started the club with nickels and dimes he collected from his neighbors in north St. Louis and the club initially met under a tree in a north St. Louis park. He didn't have any money of his own; he had only a deep desire to help the young people in his area. He worked days as a janitor in a north side plant and nights as an elevator operator at 625 S. Skinker.

Even though Martin was not a man of means, he didn't think small. His first indoor location was a rundown storefront on Natural Bridge near Newstead but he dreamed of something far better than that. He asked me to head a $2 million campaign to build a new building for the club. It was an ambitious project and he needed capital.

Earlier, the *Globe-Democrat* through Martin Duggan and me had helped the club gain admission to the United Way. I told him I did not have the time for such a large fund-raising drive, but would endeavor to find someone who would. I subsequently visited Charles F. (Chuck) Knight at his office at Emerson Electric, where he was chairman. I told him what a fine administrator Matthews was and asked Knight to raise the funds. He first wanted to make sure that the club was helping underprivileged black youngsters on the north side. I assured him this was true and suggested he make inquiries on his own to verify this.

He did and found that Mathews-Dickey would be beneficial to hundreds of black youngsters in north St. Louis. He had one other request, one other caveat. He said he would raise the money if he could get August Busch III, Gussie's son, to help.

Within a few days Knight called me and said August had agreed. In ninety days the two had raised nearly $2 million and today there is a magnificent facility—the Matthews-Dickey Boys and Girls Club—due entirely to the kindness and dilligence of Chuck Knight and August Busch.

Did I say that Martin Mathews didn't think small? When he wanted a speaker for his new club home, he went right to the top. He invited Presidents Reagan and Bush—both accepted and made personal appearances.

Later, with a sharp eye on the financial returns and a desire to let his own young charges see and, perhaps, meet some professional athletes, he arranged for the St. Louis Rams to use the club as a temporary practice facility for a fee.

Harold E. Thayer, who was named Man of the Year in 1972, was chairman of Mallinckrodt Chemical Co. where he did an outstanding job bringing what had been a small family-held company with local status to worldwide recognition.

Thayer aspired to be chairman of the Barnes Hospital Board. He had been a member of the board for some years. There came a time in the middle 1970s when an opportunity arose for him to run for that post. He was opposed by a man equally distinguished in St. Louis, one who had mightily built up Emerson Electric during his tenure, Wallace (Buck) Persons. Both were equally attractive to many people on the board.

Thayer called me one day to explain that the support for him and Persons was about equal. He thought there was one more vote available which might swing the election in his favor. That was John Shepherd, a distinguished St. Louis attorney who became president of the American Bar Association.

Thayer asked if I knew Shepherd. I knew him well and volunteered to call him. Shepherd's secretary explained he was in England. I asked for his number there and called him. He agreed immediately without reservation to vote for Thayer. So that is how he became chairman.

In the late 1950s or early 1960s, Robert Hyland, vice president of CBS and general manager of KMOX Radio, convinced the membership of the University Club after two membership votes that they should move to new quarters in Richmond Heights on Brentwood Boulevard, south of Clayton Road. He proposed that the club occupy the three upper floors of a new high-rise office building which was about to be built. The club was then on the top floors of a high-rise office structure on the northwest corner of Grand and Washington.

A consortium of business people and investors, including, but not exclusively, Hyland and the Rallo construction family, tried to raise the money to construct the office building. Financing fell apart and many of the early investors suffered losses, including the Rallo family and their flourishing business. Their future was preserved, however, by an exceptionally unusual act of friendship. Gabe Alberici, owner of another major construction firm in

St. Louis and a Rallo competitor, told the Rallos to use his credit until their credit was reestablished.

The University Club now occupies the top three floors of the building in attractively decorated quarters. Its membership flourishes. Hyland's vision to move was justified, even with the travail involved.

When Dick Amberg died unexpectedly in New York City in 1967, Dave Calhoun called me with the request that he have an opportunity to talk to S. I. Newhouse when Newhouse was here for Dick's funeral. I told him Newhouse's policy was not to meet St. Louis people but I would try to set up a meeting. As I expected, Newhouse protested vigorously, but I finally persuaded him to talk with Calhoun.

The two met briefly on the church grounds following the service. Later, Newhouse told me that Calhoun had been concerned about the resources which Dick had left for his widow, Janet, and their three children. Newhouse assured Calhoun the family would be taken care of and they were.

Calhoun, during his prominent business career was chairman of the St. Louis Union Trust Co. and deeply interested in the community. There was scarcely a civic development or need which did not have his attention. He was regarded by many—and appropriately so—as Mr. St. Louis. An exceptionally handsome man, he always looked in public as though he had just dressed, with not a wrinkle in his suit or shirt or tie.

As indicated by his voluntary attention to Amberg's widow, he did have a genuine concern for the city and people. And so far as I know he did not have detractors, at least none received publicity.

Tragically, on a business trip to New York he fell dead on the floor of Grand Central Station. By the time police arrived, thieves had stolen his wallet, his money, his watch and cuff links. He lay unidentified for many hours in the New York City morgue. Nothing could have been more demeaning to this gentleman of distinction. When at last his identity was established, the body was returned to St. Louis for the proper ceremonies.

Oliver L. Parks was not a household name in St. Louis but he may have been one of our city's and nation's most valuable citizens.

As a youth he was intensely interested in aviation and became a licensed pilot. He had a serious flying accident on the grounds of St. Stanislaus Seminary in Florissant, which cost him one of his eyes. Feeling that he survived only because of the prayers of the Jesuits who rescued him, he converted to Catholicism and became deeply devout. More and more he spent his time serving the needs of the poor and those needing assistance in life.

Lafe, as he was known, gave up a career in aviation and became a businessman, an automobile dealer among other interests. When he had sufficient funds he established a flying school adjacent to Parks Airport, which he owned, on the immediate east side. This was in the 1930s and the school, Parks College, flourished.

With the threat of World War II he established two other schools for pilots, in the South and Southwest. When America became involved in the war, his schools were engaged to train the nation's fighter pilots, preparing some of the pilots who saw duty in the war.

He did not neglect his skill for business and he founded Parks Airline, which later became Ozark Airlines. It expanded to a regional airline of major proportions and was bought and absorbed by TWA.

In his fifties he gave Parks College to Saint Louis University, practically divesting himself of the benefits from a lifetime of work. He lived the remainder of his life in a devout atmosphere with meager financial support.

The university has continued to raise the level of education of Parks College and only a few years ago moved the academic segment of the school to the Grand and Lindell campus.

People give of themselves or their means to their fellowman and his needs for reasons as varied as the stars in the sky. Included in the motivation is always a question: was the gift from the heart or from peer pressure or for some other mundane reason? There was one person in St. Louis about whom there was utterly no doubt that the motivation was from the heart. That person was Joe Simpkins.

He was not born with a silver spoon in his mouth. His parents did not have wealth. Joe liked to refer to his parents and to what they had taught him. One teaching was to be generous. Joe accumulated significant wealth and was very generous. Maybe that lesson from his parents was his own special silver spoon.

In young adulthood, Joe owned a Ford automobile franchise in Wellston. From that substantial beginning, he invested heavily in the Illinois oil field development and realized enormous returns. He branched into varied business ventures including an office furniture manufacturing company and a firm to teach improved farming skills to natives of a number of South African countries. This was truly vexing to Joe because of what seemed to be a cultural tendency on the part of the nations' leaders to forget to keep their word when it came to paying the bills.

Joe made no distinction as to religion, race, or color when he made gifts. He was generous in responding to needs of his own Jewish faith and to Catholics and Protestants, black and white.

St. Joseph's Church, on St. Louis' near north side, had been marked for abandonment by the archdiocese because its parish population had dwindled to almost nothing. The church had been built in the early 1800s and was the site of one of the few recognized miracles in American Catholic history. A few of the older parishioners who had moved away were distressed by the potential loss of the church, which for many years had been served by Jesuits.

Some parishioners made a deal with the archdiocese. They would pay the cost of restoring the building and the cost of its operation, including the salary and expenses of a priest. The archdiocese agreed it would assign a priest to attend to liturgical duties.

Mayor James Conway asked Gabe Alberici and me to raise seed money for the project. I called on Joe Simpkins and asked him for $25,000. He pledged that amount, then he asked if we could wait a couple of months and he would give $50,000. I agreed. We talked a long time, then suddenly he said, "If you will wait until after the first of the year, I will make that $100,000." I agreed in a hurry. With Joe's gift, Gabe and I raised a bit over $300,000.

When the *Globe-Democrat* closed, a number of long-time, gifted employees elected to retire. Ted Schafers, who had been our financial editor, was one of these. He dedicated himself to restoring St. Joseph's, renamed St. Joseph's Shrine, which resulted in a virtual rehabilitation of the structure. A new roof, new electrical wiring, new plumbing, refitted windows, redecorating and renewal of the facade were completed. Ted begged from everyone. He obtained funds and donated labor from unions, as well as private and corporate gifts. All in all, I estimate that Ted and his friends have raised more than $2.5 million and he has spent practically every day working at this lovely, revived religious center only a few blocks from the skyscrapers of downtown St. Louis. Its interior is startlingly beautiful. A visit is rewarding

Simpkins' philanthropies took many forms and benefited thousands of St. Louisans. When he learned that officers in the St. Louis police department did not have bullet-proof vests, he organized a campaign, raised the funds and bought the protective vests for every police officer, undoubtedly saving many from serious injury or even death.

Years ago, he became interested in the St. Louis Variety Club, a group of citizens whose common bond was a love of show business. Variety raised money each year for charity. Joe developed the annual Variety Club Telethon, which brought in hundreds of thousands of dollars for disabled children.

Unfortunately, a member accused Joe of not fulfilling his own financial pledge which totally disenchanted him. He brought cancelled checks to me and these proved that the charge was false. Even so, he was so hurt that he withdrew from the club.

However, he had enlisted the aid of a young businessman, John Londoff, a prominent Chevrolet dealer. With his enthusiasm, energy and salesmanship, Londoff took the annual telethon to almost $3 million. Working with unsurpassed dedication, Londoff begged and gave. He talked star entertainers into performing in St. Louis for their expenses only. He talked unions into charitable participation. He induced suppliers and hotels to provide services and suites and enlisted top St. Louis civic leadership to become a part of Variety. As a personal contribution, each year he provided a Corvette for Sammy Davis, Jr., the telethon star for many years.

Under Londoff's leadership, Variety paid almost nothing. KMOX donated the time, a huge gift. They donated the salaries of the employees who worked on the telethon, the electricians, the behind-the-scenes people.

John would go to the hotel and say, "I'm not going to pay this bill. You donate it." They did. He would say to the stagehands. "'You give the time." They did. He went to Emerson Electric and said, "I want to borrow your airplane to bring Sammy Davis and the other stars here." Emerson sent its plane out.

He was a remarkable salesman, all in the spirit of doing good for his fellow men. The result was that the expenses were very low, about fifteen to twenty percent of the total. But as the post-Londoff group moved in, they started paying for everything, which meant that the net dollars for charity were reduced and the children for whom the telethon was created didn't receive all the help they had formerly received under John's leadership.

Londoff was unique in St. Louis. He has probably raised more money for one children's charity than any other individual. Because of his endeavors, Londoff was selected as a *Globe-Democrat* Humanitarian of the Year.

John had the idea that for Variety to grow it had to develop from an average middle-level citizen agency to a leadership citizenship body. I tended to agree with him at the time, so he sought out some leadership appeal. One I recall well was Zane E. Barnes. He became chief barker (president) and did immensely well for Variety.

Southwestern Bell, of which Barnes was chairman, provided free office space which took Variety from back alley storefronts to front row offices. Meeting rooms, offices, even the equipment, were free.

Zane served several years and really put it on its feet. But when it came time for succession, some of the leadership maneuvered Londoff out. It absolutely crushed him. He no longer participates.

George H. Capps, a true entrepreneur, probably was known by more St. Louisans, talked about by more St. Louisans and sought after by more St. Louisans than any individual I've known.

He attended St. Louis schools and Washington University. Both of us graduated from Washington University Law School.

George was a gifted card player. He and I were part of a bridge game every Saturday at the Bogey Club, where he usually won. When he teamed with Helen, his wife, the two were even better.

They had seven sons and daughters: Robert, Ken, John, Tom, Mary Jo (Sauer), Julie (Ahlring), and Kathleen (Short). Every one was a true achiever. They were a close and caring family.

George had an inherent, unquenchable urge to succeed and to help others, usually the less fortunate or those who had suffered illness or affliction. It was rare when he read of an unfortunate occurrence that he did not call me and ask the *Globe-Democrat* to help. He was a willing part of every important civic endeavor.

His father had built a prosperous business, Capitol Coal Co. After a stint with the FBI following graduation from law school and after marriage, he took over the operation of the family business building it into a worldwide operation in coal, automobiles, and land development. His interests were so numerous and widespread that often we would drive by a property, and he would say, "I think I own that place."

Once when we complained that we couldn't get a convenient hotel reservation in Phoenix, he told me, "I think I own a hotel there." The next day he called to say we had our room.

However, he never sacrificed his family to his business. For years, until the children were older, he and Helen seldom accepted social engagements.

His sense of humor was ever-present. After his home was burglarized twice, he placed two $100 bills on the dresser with a note, "Dear Burglar: Take this and leave."

George usually slept less than three hours a night and he was at his office practically before dawn.

When Dr. William H. Danforth was chancellor of Washington University he asked George to head a fund-raising committee for the school. I think the goal was $200 million or $250 million. I told George that would be difficult and I didn't think he could do it. But George and Bill not only met the goal, they surpassed it. They brought in $600 million, the largest amount ever raised in a single campaign for a single university in America.

George was a staunch conservative and worked diligently to support conservative causes and political figures, including former Senator Jack Danforth.

His instinct was to trust people, but sometimes he trusted too much. When a son of Robert Kennedy was in St. Louis his car broke down. George and Helen not only arranged for repairs but paid the bill. The Kennedy family never paid it back.

Most of all—best of all—George Capps was my friend.

I don't believe I am wrong in saying that in the history of the city there have been few citizens who have contributed so uniquely, singularly and beneficially to St. Louis as Howard F. Baer, onetime chairman of A. S. Aloe Co., manufacturers of medical equipment.

Baer's incomparable contribution to St. Louis life is the conception, development and successful creation of the Metropolitan Zoological Park and Museum District, usually referred to as the Zoo District. It is a taxing body authorized by a referendum approved by voters of the city and St. Louis County which levies a real estate tax on all property owners each year for the benefit of St. Louis area cultural institutions: the Zoo, Art Museum, Museum of Science and Industry, Missouri Historical Society and the Missouri Botanical Garden.

When Howard proposed the Zoo District concept in 1969 I don't believe many people thought he had any chance of success. In order to create this beneficial tax it was necessary for a majority of the voters in the city and county voting separately to give approval by a simple majority.

What voters want least is to levy additional taxes on their property; but Howard pursued his vision diligently and effectively and the voters did approve the tax. Now we realize its value. Without it, some of our favorite cultural institutions might not be here.

During this period, Howard was chairman of the Zoo Commission. He was a devoted and dedicated zoo chief, originating many good things for the popular St. Louis attraction including the train.

Howard also was interested in art. At one time he decided to present two large sculptures of bears to be placed at Lambert St. Louis Airport. They were huge, probably eight to ten feet long and four feet or so high, weighing several tons. The sculptures were in a modern vein, and there was significant criticism. But they were placed at the airport, near the main entrance to the terminal's departure gate. They remained there until Howard moved them, one to the Missouri Botanical Garden, the other to the St. Louis Art Museum.

Howard was an Easterner by birth, a widely read and literate individual. After coming to St. Louis he married the daughter of A. S. Aloe. Howard and his wife and her family presented one of

St. Louis' best known pieces of art to the city, the Milles "Meeting of the Rivers" fountain across Market Street from Union Station.

Lon Hocker was a man who was blessed with great talents. An
attorney, he succeeded his father as legal counsel for the *Globe-
Democrat.* One day he came afoul of Gussie Busch.

The Princeton Club of St. Louis planned to be host to other
Princeton Clubs from around the country. Bob Hermann, Gussie's
former son-in-law, was president of the St. Louis Princeton Club.
He arranged to have the party at Grant's Farm in the Barnhoff.
There were 200 or 300 guests. Bob invited Gussie to come and
went over to the Big House to get him.

Meanwhile, Hocker, a former club president, and his wife,
Esther, were having a great time. Hocker loved to play the guitar
and sing. He also liked to wear garish costumes. That night he
was in yellow knickers. Some time before this, Fred Saigh, who
sold the Cardinals to Gussie, had employed Lon to file a lawsuit
against Gussie. Saigh thought the shareholders at Anheuser Busch
were being shortchanged because of spending by Gussie on what
Saigh claimed were personal advantages. Gussie, of course, was
furious.

When Gussie saw Lon at the party, he raised so much hell that
Lon and Esther were personally escorted by Busch private guards
from the grounds. Also, Gussie called many people who he knew
used Lon's legal services, including me, demanding that we fire
him. I couldn't do that. The *Globe-Democrat* had relied on him
and his father before him for probably seventy years and they
were very good lawyers. As far as I know, Gussie didn't hold it
against me for not firing Lon.

Lon and Esther had two children and made their home in
Clayton. His parents had a lifelong interest in politics, supporting the Republican party. His mother survived his father and to
the day she died in her nineties, she actively supported conservative issues.

Lon's talents were so varied and at such a high level of skill
that I find them almost awesome. He was a one-in-a-million lawyer who could always find a precedent to support his client's
need, or if he could not find one in past law, he invented a cause
of action and nearly always won. In my memory, he lost only

two cases and one of those was reversed by the United States Supreme Court in his favor after nearly twenty years.

He was a poet, a musician and singer, a carpenter, plumber, electrician, marble finisher, yacht builder and a beekeeper. He bought a Lyon and Healy harp for Esther, a superb musician. When it came time to tune the instrument, Lon couldn't find anyone in St. Louis with the skill to tune such a harp. So he bought a book on harps and tuned it himself. The couple had an old-fashioned foot pump organ in the entrance hall of their home. Lon found an old vacuum cleaner motor, installed it, and they had an electric organ.

Lon and Esther inherited a summer cottage at Sugar Tree, a private resort about 100 miles southwest of St. Louis. It needed extensive repair. Lon qualified with the county to certify his work on the house as a carpenter, electrician, and plumber, then did all the repair work himself. He learned that Mercantile Bank in downtown St. Louis was selling a beautiful marble railing, which enclosed a stairway to the bank basement where the safety deposit boxes were located. He bought the railing, and installed it to enclose the patio at his Clayton home.

A sailor at heart, he built a thirty-five-foot ketch in the garage of his home. Then he discovered he could not buy a trailer large enough to haul the yacht from St. Louis to their summer home at Woods Hole, Massachusetts. So he built his own trailer and hauled the ketch to Woods Hole where he sails it to this day.

When he decided to raise orchids he converted the entrance foyer to his home into a greenhouse. Friends couldn't enter by way of the front door without threading through a profusion of orchid plants, so they customarily used the kitchen door. His bee-keeping hobby never seemed to fluster Esther even though at times the ground floor of their home was covered with bees.

Lon's penchant for politics inspired him to run for governor of Missouri and U.S. senator. He lost both races. During one of his campaigns Dick Amberg wrote an editorial accusing Lon's financial manager of mishandling campaign funds. Lon asked Amberg to run an answer in the *Globe-Democrat's* mailbag, where we printed letters from readers. Dick refused, so Lon bought a full page ad to respond. (He did not lose his post as legal counsel for the paper.)

Through his active legal career, Lon was not easily defeated.

Joe Sansone, the brother of Tony Sansone, a commercial real estate developer, is a tax reduction specialist. He undertook to get a tax reduction for the Teamsters' high-rise retirement apartment buildings at Grand and Highway 40. He was successful, but when he submitted a bill for $40,000, the Union declined to pay.

Joe engaged Lon who was also unsuccessful in getting the money. So Joe and Tony, who had an interest in the case, directed Lon to file suit. Lon was to receive as his fee one-third of what was recovered. He won a judgment against the Union. The Union had not defended the suit, so the judgment was by default.

Again the Teamsters refused to pay. So Lon executed a lien against the buildings and took possession. The Teamsters did not defend, and because the buildings are part of the union's business headquarters and all the property is designed with a single heating system, the union was compelled to furnish heat for the new owners.

After several years of this, the Teamsters negotiated for a return of the title. They got it back, but Lon, Joe, and Tony profited far beyond Joe's original bill of $40,000.

Gen. Leif J. Sverdrup was a St. Louis titan in every sense of the word, a genuine hero, a professional and business success and a concerned human being. Jack, as he was known to his friends, immigrated from Norway to Minnesota as a youth and graduated from college there. His original architectural and engineering firm was a partnership with one of his professors, John Ira Parcel. The firm became Sverdrup & Parcel, a major St. Louis enterprise.

After graduating with an engineering degree, he decided to establish his company where he could more easily obtain construction projects from the state. He chose Missouri and as one of his first projects, built the bridge across the Missouri River at Hermann. Later, in an even more spectacular achievement, he built the Chesapeake Bay bridge which combined spans with tunnels.

In World War II as Gen. Douglas MacArthur's chief engineer, Jack liked to comment that he walked from Manila to Tokyo, a reference to the countless islands he traversed in the course of building airfields in the Allies' move from the Philippines to Japan. Their friendship lasted through the general's life and he felt proud and honored that MacArthur's widow, Jean, asked him to be one of those who arranged MacArthur's funeral services.

During his business life his company expanded to include offices around the world. He built many huge facilities in Saudi Arabia and designed and operated many properties for the U.S. government, particularly military facilities.

In St. Louis, there was scarcely a civic need in which he was not an active participant. He never asked anyone to help on a project until he was deeply involved and he never deserted those who agreed to help. One day he called to say that Sandy Zimmerman, chairman of Famous-Barr, whom he did not know, had asked him to lead a $6 million campaign for Webster College, then in perilous financial difficulties. I urged him to accept. He did so and may have saved Webster. One of his contributions was to induce Leigh Gerdine, then a Washington University professor, to become Webster's president.

He never forgot his roots and for a long time served as Norwegian Consul in St. Louis. He and Molly, his wife, enjoyed life to the utmost. At social events, if the party should drag a bit, they would stand up and sing a duet. Molly had been trained as a singer and was quite professional. Jack was a party tenor but he loved to sing.

Aviation was one of his hobbies. He bought a DC-3 for the firm. The plane had given an enormous advantage for the Allies during World War II. Shortly after the war, new planes made the DC-3 obsolete. Despite the urgings of his associates to buy a newer plane, Jack was reluctant to give up on the DC-3. It was nicely furnished inside and had new engines. With all, it probably cruised at no more than 130 miles per hour with a tail wind. We enjoyed riding with him. But in the last months of his long life he bought a twin-engine Cessna jet.

He never became pretentious. He and Molly lived most of their married life in a comfortable but far from luxurious home in Hampton Park. Jack Sverdrup was a great role model for American youth.

Homer Sayad was for many years one of St. Louis' more prominent citizens. He was much sought after for civic leadership roles which he often accepted and discharged effectively. He was a C.P.A. who had been born in Iran and who came to St. Louis by way of London and Chicago. In St. Louis he married Elizabeth Gentry.

One of his appointments was as president of the St. Louis Police Board. During that year, I was asked by a high-ranking Washington official to inquire of Homer whether he would accept responsibility for transmitting information about his country to the CIA. This was during the time when the United States was desperately trying to preserve the regime of the shah. On occasion Homer and Elizabeth had been invited to social events in Iran by the shah.

Homer acknowledged my proposal and promised to consider the matter. I heard no more.

Many years ago, probably in the middle 1950s or early 1960s the United Way decided that some member agencies receiving benefits really did not qualify for membership. Edwin S. (Ted) Jones, then head of First National Bank, was chairman of the United Way Allocations Committee. His committee was given the responsibility for reviewing agency qualification. I was a member of his committee.

The result of the study was that a number of agencies lost their United Way membership and support. Most of those who lost out were not social agencies, but offered most worthy services in the public interest. Many related to art or medical services.

Margie May, then wife of Morton (Buster) May, chairman of the May Company (the parent of the Famous-Barr Department Store), was distressed at the loss of support for many community art activities. She initiated an effort which culminated in the formation of the Arts and Education Council, a group designed to provide the same financial support for art agencies as the United Way supplied for health and welfare agencies.

Quality leadership more often than not produces a quality product and in the instance of the Carpenters' Union and the Carpet Layers' Union in St. Louis this certainly was the case. The carpenters were led for years by Oliver (Ollie) Langhorst; the carpet layers by Perry Joseph.

Langhorst demanded responsible and quality work from his members and he led his union with a deep sense of community and national responsibility to his members and to St. Louis. For his members he achieved good wages and benefits and few strikes. The same was true of Joseph, who had a unique rule for his members: if they did work which was shoddy and unsatisfactory, the workmen responsible were required to do the work over at their own expense.

Both men enjoyed community respect and enjoyed working in the civic arena. Both were unique among labor leaders in that they did not blindly follow labor's traditional devotion to the Democratic Party, in fact they were Republicans. Certainly there were others in the labor movement who were also independent thinkers, but the only two I knew who publicly espoused the GOP were Langhorst and Joseph. They endured more than a modicum of public criticism from their fellow union leaders but they maintained their political independence.

A family named Bangert was prominent in St. Louis County in construction, especially road building some years past. The member most often in the public eye was Bill Bangert.

He was a huge man, some six feet five inches or so tall and quite heavy and muscular. He lived with his wife and daughters in a home on the bluff on the south side of Highway 70 as one drove west and down the hill into the valley to cross the St. Charles Bridge. He was a visionary who dreamed of developing the bottom land between the bluff and the Missouri river along Highway 70 into what he called the Village of Champ, a commercial district.

His public persona centered on his athletic skill in throwing the caber, which looks like a telephone pole. It is an ancient athletic event popular particularly in Scotland where Bill participated in numerous caber events. In the 1950s or early 1960s he managed to induce the annual AAU national track and field meet to hold its contest in St. Louis. He arranged to stage the affair in the St. Louis public high school stadium. He honored me by appointing me the chief timer.

He tried to the best of his ability to make his dream a reality, but he failed for lack of financing. He gave up and moved out of the area. Now the area, known as Earth City, is developing well as a commercial center and entertainment venue.

Any history of St. Louis during the 1930 to 1990 era would be incomplete without an account of Morris L. Shenker, an attorney and Jewish community leader.

Morris came to America when he was eight years old from Kiev, Russia, not able to speak a word of English. He had an insatiable appetite for an education. The Jesuit community at Saint Louis University was the only academic institution which would help him and made his education dream come true. He never forgot the Jesuits. After finishing law school he began a practice which ultimately established him as one of the most noted criminal defense attorneys in the United States.

How Morris chose his career is not known, but soon his name as a criminal defense attorney in St. Louis was well known. His clients included the anonymous and those with national reputations. He devoted a specific portion of his time every day to defending the poor without charging a fee.

If anyone did not know Morris Shenker prior to the hearings on organized crime held in St. Louis and directed by U.S. Senator Estes Kefauver, his name was certainly known afterward. Shenker defended a number of his clients in the televised hearings.

His multitude of clients included not only criminals, but many high-profile labor leaders, such as Jimmy Hoffa, boss of the Teamsters union, and Harold Gibbons, St. Louis Teamster chief. Many people ignorantly attributed some of the characteristics of his clients to Morris' character. I never found this to be true. To the contrary, I found him to be an exceptionally compassionate and caring man who served his fellow men well.

He was a prodigious fund raiser for Jewish causes and many non-Jewish activities as well. He had a special interest in Bonds for Israel and was outstanding at organizing Bonds for Israel dinners.

He decided that released and paroled convicts deserved a better opportunity to regain an acceptable place in the community than they were experiencing, so he and several friends, including Harold Gibbons, established Dismas House in an abandoned elementary school building at 10th and Cole. He recruited a Jesuit, the Rev. Dismas Clark, S.J., to run the function, one of the first in America. Recidivism, the rate of return of released or paroled convicts to prison, is close to fifty percent.

A recognized reason for the high return rate is the plight of persons released from prison. In many cases they have lost their families, they have lost their wives and children, they have very little money, few clothes, food, no place to live, and no job. Society does not welcome them. Dismas House provided the parolees or released persons with shelter, food, and clothing, and most often found a job paying enough money to support themselves. Most importantly, Dismas House via Father Clark, provided sound spiritual counseling. The facility's clients returned to prison at the astoundingly low rate of about five percent.

Board members—and I was one—began raising money to supplement the operating costs. When the Cole Street building became inadequate, we sought other facilities. The Roman Catholic Archdiocese of St. Louis owned a large residence on Cote Brilliante just west of Kingshighway which had been the residence for the Marianist Brothers who taught at McBride High School at the same location. It was then closed. After months of negotiation Dismas House paid the asking price of $94,000 and moved in.

Tony Sansone was exceptionally important to the facility in raising money for the new house and dealing with the city on an occupancy permit. When Father Clark died, the Jesuit order assigned another Jesuit, the Rev. Fred L. Zimmerman, S.J., a carbon copy of Father Clark. During the course of a personal meeting with Archbishop John May, I told him of Dismas House and my conviction the place could not be effective without a priest-director. The archbishop pledged to me that he would provide a priest when we needed one. I called upon him when Father Zimmerman died, and he sent us the Rev. Joseph Kohler, a great successor.

Through the years, government entities such as the Department of Justice and Internal Revenue Service investigated Morris Shenker several times. No charges were ever filed.

In the late 1940s Nora and I went to Sunday Mass at the Saint Louis University College Church, St. Francis Xavier. It was the only Catholic church with a Mass that met my work schedule. I left work at 3:00 A.M. Sunday morning and I had to be back at the paper at noon on Sunday.

I picked Nora up about 4:00 A.M. and we drove from our home

on Rosebury to the College Church at Grand and Lindell. Our route was east on Lindell, crossing Kingshighway. One Sunday morning a driver named Martorelli ran the red light going south on Kingshighway and hit us broadside. It threw Nora out of the car and she was seriously injured.

Henry Morris filed a suit for damages for us and we won the case, with an award of $5,000. We tried on a number of occasions to collect, but the man who hit us was a hoodlum who had a record a mile long, including a murder or two. He hid his assets and we failed to collect.

I was bemoaning our inability to collect to John Doherty who was then chief of detectives in the St. Louis police department. He commented he'd be happy to collect the debt for us. I declined his offer. I knew that Doherty would collect by physically beating up the hoodlum and we'd get our money. But I had to come home in the middle of the night and park my car in our garage, which fronted on an unlighted alley. I didn't want the constant concern that the hoodlum would retaliate in his accustomed fashion in the dark alley.

Prejudice, bigotry and discrimination have existed probably since the world began and unfortunately we've had our share of it in America, to our national disgrace.

The practice of these ideas have irreparably damaged and in some instances ruined the lives of many Americans. Some individuals and families have beaten the denigration and created inspiringly successful lives. We've had our share of the successes in St. Louis. One of them is Eugene P. Slay and his family.

Gene Slay is a second or third generation Lebanese. It's been my experience that the most dedicated examples of good citizens frequently are sons or daughters of immigrants, irrespective of the nation of origin. And, it's been rare that members of any immigration group to America was welcomed with open arms, from those who arrived before the Revolution to the Germans, the Irish, the Negroes, and the Latinos.

Certainly the Lebanese in St. Louis had difficulty in being accepted–they were never favorites of the dominant WASP faction. So, when Gene Slay inherited a small, local trucking company from his father and set out on his life's work he did not have a ready acceptance.

But from the small, local company he built the business into a $100,000,000 company, doing business virtually nationwide. There were many reasons for this success, but notable among them was an unswayable determination to keep his word and pledge when he made a business deal, a contract or a political pledge.

In the 1970s, Harold E. Thayer, chairman of Mallinckrodt Chemical Co., experienced the woes of a strike by a St. Louis Teamsters Union. He could not get his product delivered to his customers. Someone referred him to Gene Slay.

Slay offered Thayer a trucking contract. Thayer accepted and Slay performed without a hitch, which was and still is a mystery to me because his drivers were also Teamsters. Slay kept the Mallinckrodt business and still has it.

Like many Lebanese in St. Louis, Gene became interested in politics, as had his father. Through the years, through his personal effort and time and contributions, he became a significant factor in Democratic party activities in the city and the state, helping Joe Teasdale upset Kit Bond in his first governor's race. As his company grew, he needed land on which to build warehouses, which he used both for trucking and barge operations. Some of the locations were city property and he had to negotiate purchases or leases with the city.

As with any businessman he made the best deal he could in his own interest. Some of the city employees less astute than he who negotiated these deals were later disappointed in the arrangements they had made. These contracts were subject to criticism by politicians and the press. Never did anyone produce evidence that Slay's contracts were made at less than arm's length, to my knowledge.

He did his stint as a civic supporter and was always willing to lend a hand in a worthy charitable endeavor. His specific interest has been the Southside Boys Club. He was a worthy fund raiser for the club and served as president for some period.

He and his wife, Joan, raised seven children, four boys and three girls. His sons participate in the business with him—Gary, Glen, Guy, and Jeffrey.

A contract he recently worked out with the Bayer Company has been a source of great pride, and a lot of new business. Apart from being a good businessman, Slay never wavered from a characteristic which was probably a significant factor in the growth of his company. When he gave his word, for whatever reason, he never reneged.

I. A. "Zack" Long, a very distinguished St. Louisan in his appearance, actions, and speech, was widely known as a top vice-president of Mercantile Bank.

He was asked one day by the then-governor whether he would serve as president of the St. Louis Board of Police Commissioners. Long lived in the city, one of the prerequisites to qualifying as a member of the police board. He consulted with his superiors at Mercantile and they assured him that his position at Mercantile would not be at risk if he accepted the appointment. Long accepted the appointment, and the governor announced it. Shortly, Mercantile announced his "resignation." Subsequently he located at Southwest Bank where he became president.

As president of Southwest Bank, Long was recognized nationally for his acute sense in changing interest rates in a timely manner, often before interest rate changes were announced by the Federal Reserve. Frequently, more often than not, Long led the nation's bankers in adjusting interest rates upward or downward. He was frequently quoted ahead of any other industry decisions.

Long took Southwest Bank from a somewhat obscure place to a prominent position in banking, especially in St. Louis, and to some extent nationally. He remained with the bank until a few years before his death. He did better and was more widely recognized for his work at Southwest than if he had stayed at Mercantile.

We had in St. Louis for many years, a very capable doctor by the name of Richard A. Sutter. He decided early in his life as an M.D., that he would be an industrial surgeon. He was a doctor who served the major companies in St. Louis, advising them on the health of their employees. Many companies had occupational accidents, injured hands, injured feet, injuries of other natures associated with the employees' working conditions. Sutter treated employees for these injuries. He also did preemployment physicals. Where employees had health problems, and the company was willing to pay for medical attention, he treated the illness so an employee could return to work. This type of practice was not always acceptable to many members of the profession.

The *Globe-Democrat* used him for pre-employment physicals and other modest medical advice which employees needed. His offices were downtown in a three-story building, most of which he occupied. He had an enormous practice because his clients included the major companies in the city. He gave his patients attention and good care.

Since he was a graduate of the Washington University Medical school, he longed to be a member of the medical staff at Barnes Hospital. Despite repeated applications, he did not succeed until late in his practice life. He told me that he knew for certain that there was one doctor on the committee responsible for appointments who declined to grant him privileges to practice at Barnes. When that doctor left the committee, Sutter instantly was given permission. Later he donated a seven-figure gift to Washington University Medical School.

Zane E. Barnes, longtime chairman of Southwestern Bell Telephone in St. Louis and one of our city's most dedicated civic participants, was one of a long line of telephone company leaders from whom St. Louis benefited immeasurably. Few of St. Louis's top corporate executives did more for our community than the Southwestern Bell chairmen.

When it became necessary to build a second major building in St. Louis to house Southwestern Bell management, Barnes decided to build a high-rise office building downtown on Pine Street immediately east of the original Bell building at 1010 Pine. In keeping with the utility's legendary reputation for doing things right, the new building was a magnificent addition to the downtown skyline.

The company's executive offices would occupy the top floors of the new building with the chairman's office and the board room on the top floor. Well along in the construction of the building Barnes discovered that the executive elevator which he had specified to run nonstop from the parking garage to the top floor was not in place. He notified those responsible and corrections were made to include the elevator. This was after the interior of the building had been roughed in.

Further, to his dismay, he discovered that the special Mexican marble which had been specified to cover the lobby walls was being set in place in what he believed was an unsatisfactory manner. He ordered this work redone.

St. Louis' downtown got an outstanding new building and more people working downtown. Mayor Cervantes had pushed Barnes to build the building out west near the Union Station and others pushed him to build it on the north rim of downtown, probably along Delmar.

He made the decision to place it adjacent to the original building. Later, after his retirement, still a third Bell building was built on the east to make three huge Bell properties in a row.

It should also be noted that when a community need arose, Southwestern Bell could be counted on to be a major player in pushing the problem to a successful conclusion, with financial contributions or executive leadership, usually with both. Thus, the departure of the headquarters function to Texas made a deep wound in community development.

Andy Craig's adventure into St. Louis was a notable event in St. Louis' history, especially its economic and cultural development.

Until the time of Don Brandin, Boatmen's Bank had been a sound institution and a great place to do business, but certainly not the front runner in the banking community. Its leaders had always been strong in civic responsibility, such as Harry Harrington. Then Brandin appeared on the scene and all this changed.

He began the expansion of the bank and it grew in an astounding manner. At Brandin's retirement Andy Craig took over and the bank continued to grow. In the course of time Craig manipulated the sale of Boatmen's to NationsBank, causing great consternation and great joy. Some did not like having the bank lose its local identity and some were tremendously happy over the profits they enjoyed from the increase in the bank's stock value.

St. Louisans often worry about how a new chief operating officer will respond to civic needs and to what extent he will continue his institution's historical commitments. Craig thrilled the watchers. He became immersed in everything available that his time would permit and showed his dedication in countless ways. His wife, Virginia (known as Jake), did likewise. The two were a boon to St. Louis in the last few years.

When St. Louisans became genuinely excited about the return of a professional football team to St. Louis, Craig joined the effort at a crucial time and provided the financial acumen and leadership. He served a most productive term as president of Civic Progress and he continued his community service as a NationsBank officer until his recent retirement.

Without Ben Wells and his wife, Katherine (Katch), the cultural environment in St. Louis, especially the music world, would have been notably poorer.

Ben migrated to St. Louis in his early adulthood and began a teaching career at John Burroughs School. His wife-to-be, Katherine, was a daughter in the Gladney family, her father a lawyer with the Jones, Hocker and Gladney law firm. Gladney had the wisdom to invest in 7-Up stock. Ben became president of Seven-Up and was at the time the company was sold.

He and Katch contributed generously and kindly to the St. Louis community, especially to CASA and the Saint Louis Symphony. Once a year Ben would buy out the symphony performance and Katch, who was an accomplished musician, conducted a new work which she had composed. The auditorium was filled with the Wells' friends and it was always a superb evening.

Ben, a member of the Bogey Club, initiated a never varying menu for his Bogey Saturday birthday party luncheon—mutton, cooked to a New York restaurant recipe. And he always gave each guest a memento of the luncheon.

In the early 1970s or late 1960s Dr. William H. Danforth was vice president of Washington University in charge of medical affairs, meaning the medical school. I'd gotten to know him when I was chairman of the Bi-State Regional Medical Program. Danforth represented Washington University.

One day Danforth suggested we have lunch together. At the Racquet Club on Kingshighway he told me that he had been offered the position of chancellor of Washington University, and asked me if I thought he should accept the position.

I told him that I had had some modest familiarity with the sacrifices which people make to become doctors, particularly the sacrifices that their wives and children are called upon to make, as the young doctor makes his way in the profession. My sister's husband was a radiologist, a graduate of the University of Illinois medical school, who took his radiological training at Barnes and Mallinckrodt under Dr. Wendell Scott. My sister and her husband lived with Nora and me during that time, so I had some knowledge of the sacrifice.

Later, when my brother-in-law took an internship at Grant Hospital in Chicago, his salary was $75 a month.

In any case, this prompted me to ask Dr. Danforth why he even gave any consideration to giving up the practice of medicine, after putting his wife, Ibby, through all the rigors with which I was familiar. He, too, had made sacrifices in long hours of study and long hours of work to reach the peak of his medical career.

He answered that he thought he could do more good for more people during his lifetime as chancellor of the university, than he could as a doctor. That's a pretty lofty goal, and of course it was one that Dr. Danforth could seek, because he had the financial resources that made him independent of the need to earn a living.

How can anyone suggest that he not take the position under those conditions? So, our conversation ended as he repeated that he was pretty sure he would accept the appointment, and he did.

Danforth turned the university around, both in academic standing and financial support. From a school of modest recognition, Washington University became a school of wide recognition and national ranking.

Danforth not only carries a wondrous family history with his name, but he also has delivered tremendous contributions to St. Louis, not only at the university, but in other areas as well.

For example, when the federal government's medical programs were getting underway, the state of Missouri had to pass supportive legislation to provide Medicaid for Missourians. Twice, Governor Hearnes had vetoed that legislation. I was president of the Health and Welfare Council at the time. I asked Bill Danforth to chair a committee to study the need for Medicaid in Missouri. He did that and submitted a report, which we in turn passed on to the governor. The next time around, Hearnes signed the legislation, providing for Medicaid for the state's medically indigent. Bill Danforth thus is responsible for the presence of Medicaid in Missouri—a major achievement.

Ed Schnuck was the second generation in his family in the retail grocery business in St. Louis. His parents started and operated a mom-and-pop grocery store in north St. Louis. Ed left school after the fifth grade. When he got into the business, he decided to expand and built every single display fixture in the new store by hand, himself alone.

By the time Ed died, he and his brother Don had pushed the Schnuck Markets in St. Louis to being the dominant grocery retailer in our community. Despite his limited formal education, he had a phenomenal business acumen, best illustrated perhaps by his appointment to the board of the Federal Reserve Bank of St. Louis, which he served as chairman for many years.

He also was a consummate community participant. I remember well his service on the board of directors of the Backstoppers, an organization which pays the debts of widows of policemen and firemen killed in the line of duty. Ed became enamored of this organization and its function and was a most effective president. He was a tireless worker for causes that he found worthwhile.

He died in 1987 and was survived by his wife, Marilyn, and his daughter, Stephanie. His younger brother Don took over the business. Don was in the same pattern as Ed, and carried on with the Schnuck traditions in the public arena and the development of the stores.

Before Ed died, he decided to will half of his stock in the Schnuck markets in equal shares to Don's children in order to encourage their interest in the business. They are now running the business following Don's death in 1991: Craig is chairman and CEO; Scott is president and COO; Terry is chief legal counsel; Mark is president of Desco; Todd is vice-president and chief financial officer for Schnuck's; and Nancy Schnuck Diemer is director of community relations, also for Schnuck's.

Hal Dean came to St. Louis in his young days to begin a career with Ralston Purina. He became chairman of the board of Ralston and took the company to even greater heights of corporate citizenship. When the St. Louis Blues hockey team was thinking of moving out of town Dean motivated Ralston to buy the Blues to keep them in St. Louis, probably in the afterglow of his illustrious basketball life as a student in his native Minnesota.

When St. Louis was experiencing the agony of trying to rehab residential neighborhoods to keep people from moving out of the city, Ralston gave the city $3 million to help with rehab work in the LaSalle area, south of the company office buildings on Chouteau just west of Broadway. Dean's predecessor, Ray Rowland, had been just as committed to the community.

Like most St. Louis corporate executives, Dean was personally involved in numerous projects, not the least of them being the rehabilitation of the Grand and Lindell area.

After he retired, he visited me in my office to ask the support of the *Globe-Democrat* in the development of a light rail transportation system for St. Louis. Since a similar program had been tried twice previously and was unsuccessful, I told him I didn't think light rail could be built and I declined to pledge our support.

I couldn't have been more wrong and I am continually embarrassed at my shallow thinking which caused me not to support him.

One of the principal reasons for his success was a change in the economic life of our railroads. Light rail is helped by using existing rail lines. During the earlier proposals, the lines were being used constantly. When Dean advanced his plan, usage of the tracks had declined.

My discouraging words did not deter Dean. Like Jerry Clinton and the football stadium, Dean moved ahead. Virtually alone he lobbied the railroads and got tacit agreement to use their lines; he lobbied Congress and won preliminary approval for the federal approval and financing; he lobbied local interests, wherever and whenever and for whatever need. Finally he put it all together.

Light rail became a reality from Lambert Municipal Airport through downtown to East St. Louis and is successful, with operating support from the city and the county. An extension is now being built to Belleville and Scott Air Force Base. Plans are being prepared for an extension through Clayton.

J. S. McDonnell was the founder of McDonnell Aircraft, which became McDonnell Douglas and later a division of Boeing. It was my supreme good fortune to have enjoyed his confidence, even though I don't think either one of us ever thought of the other as a close friend. On occasion he would call and ask that I meet with him in his office to talk. This usually followed an unfortunate incident in the life of the company, such as after the airplane crashes in Paris and Chicago. I did play a round of golf or two with him.

Known as Mr. Mac, he did two exceptionally memorable things for my wife, Nora, and me. One was inviting us to the state dinner in Los Angeles honoring the astronauts.

The second reveals a detail of his character which will cause a great many to blink. A week or ten days after my mother's death in 1971, I received a phone call from the Rev. Gerard Glynn, the director of the Newman Chapel at Washington University. He asked me if I knew a man named McDonnell, a J. S. McDonnell. I responded that I did, and asked why.

Father Glynn said he had a check in his hand payable to the Newman Chapel from J. S. McDonnell for $5,000 in honor of my mother. I was surprised and immensely gratified. I am not sure Mr. Mac ever met my mother and we certainly had never talked about her, nor had he ever indicated any interest in the Newman Chapel.

It was a heartfelt, magnanimous gesture and underscores why I love St. Louis: People care about each other here and prove it in so many wonderful ways.

- 11 -

AWARDS

M uch of the success of a community relates to the quality of its environment—its educational facilities, cultural advantages, health care system, leisure time opportunities, and other public amenities. These attractions do not appear by spontaneous generation. They are the product of the thoughtfulness and leadership of people willing to give their time and means to create them.

St. Louis has been blessed manifold with volunteer leadership to satisfy community needs. When older leadership disappears— in retirement, relocation, or by death—others rise to take their place.

Almost no one who has taken a leadership role in St. Louis has done so to receive acclaim or personal benefit, but recognition is the least the community can accord those who work for its betterment. For that reason, the *Globe-Democrat* established a number of programs to recognize those who helped and, by example, encourage new leadership. We were proud of our awards programs and are proud today that some have been validated by being continued in their basic concept, even though the *Globe-Democrat* has exited the scene.

Foremost among these continuing projects are the Man of the Year and the Women of Achievement. Both are ideas that Dick

Amberg brought to St. Louis when he became publisher in 1955.

The Man of the Year award was presented to a distinguished community leader chosen by past honorees. I am proud to have been given that cherished honor in 1983. *Globe* feature articles about the recipients were collected into Mary Kimbrough's book, *Movers and Shakers: Men Who Have Shaped Saint Louis* (Patrice Press, 1991). As the book jacket states: "The character of a community is measured not by the stone and steel of its buildings, but by the sinew of its people."

The Globe-Democrat *annually honored significant St. Louisans with a "Man of the Year" award. Here are the past honorees during the 1979 luncheon honoring Armand Stalnaker. Seated from left: Bill McDonnell, Stuart Symington, Stalnaker, Tom Curtis, and Howard Baer. Standing: George Capps, Harold Thayer, Rev. Paul Reinert, S.J., Charles A. Thomas, Dr. William Danforth, Edwin Jones, Lawrence K. Roos, Hadley Griffin, and Bauman.*

When it was announced that the *Globe-Democrat* was closing, former Men of the Year, led by George H. Capps and Harold E. Thayer, decided that the significance of the award in the community was such that they wanted to continue it on its own initiative. This was a tremendous compliment to the *Globe-Democrat*.

The Men of the Year decided that they would assess themselves whatever funds were necessary to carry this on, and they did. Fortunately one of the Men of the Year, Lee M. Liberman, former chairman of Laclede Gas, contacted the *Post-Dispatch* and induced it to pick up the program.

At first, the *Post's* participation was minimal, amounting to publishing the story at the first of the year. Through the years, Liberman and Cedge Barksdale, who is now the head honcho, have convinced the *Post* that it ought to do the whole job, and it is now paying for the total project.

Recently, Barksdale and Liberman became disenchanted with the *Post's* rather indifferent treatment of the project. They hit the *Post* again, and the paper agreed to do better. As part of "doing better," Mike Pulitzer, *Post-Dispatch* chairman, now serves on the selection committee, but he does not vote. The Man of the Year continues as the Citizen of the Year. The name of the award was changed in 1998 when Chancellor Blanche Touhill of the University of Missouri-St. Louis became the first woman to be so honored.

The annual *Globe-Democrat* Women of Achievement award originated in the 1950s. Each year, ten women, all of them community volunteer activists, were honored at a luncheon which attracted an audience of several hundred friends and well-wishers. Top government executives from the city and St. Louis County gave their special commendations to the recipients.

This tradition also has been kept alive by the past honorees—now numbering more than 400 since its founding. News coverage appears in the Suburban *Journals* which, with radio station KMOX, have assumed sponsorship of the event.

As we conceived it, a committee of citizens appointed by the *Globe-Democrat's* publisher solicited nominations of St. Louis area women thought to be worthy of identification as a Woman of the Year. The qualifications were that a woman would have contributed her talent and skills to aiding the community in an extraordinary manner. This work was not to have been a part of her work or profession if she was in the business world. The achievement was to have been a contribution to others.

The award for years was a sterling silver engraved plate, ten inches in diameter. Additionally the recipient received a sterling silver charm. In the 1970s, when the cost of sterling went through the roof, increasing as much as ten times, we felt the need to go to silver plate. The paper paid all the costs except the luncheon, and it absorbed a portion of the that cost, too, to make it somewhat easier for the less affluent friends of the nominees to attend.

The selection committee was carefully chosen to represent the major elements in our area—black, white, Catholic, Protestant, Jewish, non-faith, social and non-social, affluent and low income. The publisher of the *Globe-Democrat* was a member of the committee, and I can attest that I never railroaded a candidate to selection.

We received some five or six hundred written nominations each year. A staff member or two reviewed the nominations and produced one-page summaries of each nominee. An assembled package of all the nominee summaries was mailed to each committee member a week or two before the selection meeting. The summary was important for several reasons: some nominations were elaborate, some very simple; some bore with them numerous letters of recommendations; some were very persuasive, others were just lists of achievement; some had pictures, and so forth. It was necessary to standardize the nominations to be fair.

The committee met once and made its choices. In the more than twenty-five years of its work under the hand of the *Globe,* we don't believe we ever named an undeserving woman.

For years the presentation was made in the Khorassan room at the Chase Hotel. The room accommodated more than one thousand persons comfortably for a sit-down luncheon. The room was always packed to overflowing. For years the nominees, by their own choice, wore white gloves. Each nominee was presented with a corsage.

It was one of the greatest pleasures of my life to make the presentations. It's always been my philosophy that it's a lot more rewarding to make complimentary remarks about an individual when the person is alive and can hear, and in front of an audience of friends, rather than at a funeral. I had the good fortune to know some of the nominees from year to year and the paper's staff gave me details about the nominees I didn't know personally. This allowed me to make appropriate comments, with great fun. Perhaps one of my most memorable comments was to tell the audience how one of the nominees was taking belly dancing and was doing well with the course.

When Amberg was publisher, he received a phone call from Lewis Apple suggesting that the *Globe-Democrat* establish an annual award for the person who had done the most in a public way for his fellowman. Apple offered to fund the award with $1,000 each year which would be given to the honoree. The paper would bear the rest of the cost associated with the program.

Dick thought well of the suggestion and put it in our program in 1959. We called it the *Globe-Democrat* Humanities Award, and it honored "the person whose lifetime exemplifies best the universal ideal of the Fatherhood of God and brotherhood of man."

He appointed a selection committee consisting of the Roman Catholic Archbishop, the head of the Rabbinical Association, and a representative of the Metropolitan Church Federation. Dick also sat on the committee.

Each year we asked for nominations and usually received in the range of fifty nominations. The committee was given copies of the nominations and met once a year in the publisher's office to make a selection. The award was presented in an environment of the honoree's choice at the expense of the *Globe-Democrat*.

We gave the honoree a framed 14" x 24" inch handcrafted scroll outlining the basis for the selection and the $1,000 check from Lewis Apple. Some of those receiving awards seemed to be more moved or inspired by this presentation than by any other. It was a wonderful experience to see the appreciation and happiness of those who received these awards for unselfish service, service for which they expected no reward.

When John Londoff was presented with the Humanities Award, his handicapped daughter, Jackie, rushed from her seat in the audience to the stage to hug her father—he wasn't the only one there who broke into tears.

Historically, going back at least to Civil War days, the *Globe* consistently supported our country's national defense program. President Abraham Lincoln is quoted as saying he would rather have the support of the *Globe-Democrat* than a division of troops. Amberg served during World War II under Gen. Douglas MacArthur and continued the paper's pro-defense policy during his career.

It occurred to me after I became publisher that the men and women who served in National Guard and Reserve forces ought to be recognized since they represent more than fifty per cent of our military strength. It is important that our country attract competent members of the Armed Forces Reserves and National Guard. In the event of a national emergency we would have to depend on them to defend our country, in contrast to the standing armies which we formerly maintained. When Congress approved higher salaries for members of the military as a volunteer force, it became necessary to reduce the regular force and increase the Reserve and National Guard, because they could be maintained at much less cost and we could still maintain our ready strength.

Wanting to honor Amberg's service to the community and to the paper, I came up with the notion that we would give awards to a member of every Reserve and National Guard unit in Missouri whose service during the prior year had been distinguished and beneficial. We asked the units to make their nominations and we accepted their recommendations.

The honors were identified as the Richard H. Amberg awards. The *Globe-Democrat* designed a magnificent plaque for outstanding members of the guard, the Navy Reserve, Army and Air Force and Marine Reserves throughout the state. I presented the awards in front of an assembly of the unit's members in different locations around the state each year and shook hands with every member, sometimes as many as 200 in a given ceremony.

It was a very rewarding experience and one extremely appreciated by the recipients. Tears and lumps in the throat were common. On later occasions when I met recipients elsewhere, they would thank me again profusely. One young woman tearfully told me it was the most memorable day of her life.

A year or two ago, when Lucy and I were guests at an art show in Scottsdale, Arizona, someone in the audience sought me out to tell me what an eventful occasion it had been for him to receive the award. I'm sorry to report that when we left the paper the awards were discontinued.

The paper also established an award for members of the Missouri legislature which was highly thought of by the recipients and meant to express genuine appreciation in behalf of the community to legislators whose work exemplified the best in public service. It was called the *Globe-Democrat* Legislative Award and went to both senators and representatives, ten every two years.

The recipients were selected by a committee of our news department employees, including Jack Flach, the political editor, Martin Duggan, editor of the editorial page, George Killenberg, managing editor, myself, and usually another reporter with knowl-

Globe-Democrat *military awards were made annually to outstanding guardsmen or reservists in every unit in Missouri. Attending this ceremony were, from left: (later Maj. Gen.) Henry Mohr, Maj. Gen. William Branson, Bauman, and Congressman James Symington.*

edge of the legislature. The awards were made at a dinner sponsored by the *Globe-Democrat* in Jefferson City, usually at the Jefferson City Country Club.

Political notables and spouses of the awardees, sometimes parents, children, or others close to the recipients were guests. Almost without exception the governor and his wife attended.

The award was a sterling silver plate suitably engraved—afterward it always occupied a highly visible place in the legislator's office or home.

We at the *Globe-Democrat* were convinced that the award motivated many of the legislators to do the best they could for their constituents and to find pride and satisfaction in their work. Many of them expressed this conviction in letters or in personal comments.

Even as the *Globe* was giving awards, it was also receiving them. Its list of journalism honors places it among the foremost newspapers of America. Because they are so numerous, I am quoting an article in our "Final Edition."

"The *Globe-Democrat* has won every top award in journalism during its history . . . . Excellence in investigative reporting and in public and community service were recognized by the awards."

Listed were:

1952 Pulitzer Prize to Louis LaCoss, our editorial page editor, for an editorial entitled "The Low Estate of Public Morals" critical of the student body at West Point, which had been caught in a pervasive scheme to cheat in the classroom. It was the first scandal of this nature in the history of this great school.

1969 Pulitzer Prize to reporters Denny Walsh and Al Delugach for their three-year investigation exposing a million-dollar pension fund fraud and illegal political spending by the Steamfitters Union.

University of Missouri Award for Community Service in 1958 by a member of the Inland Daily Press Association for a wide range of civic projects. Eighteen were cited specifically, including a series of stories on how St. Louis was falling behind in airline service; a campaign to raise $65,000 to buy the city's first heart-lung machine for open heart surgery at Children's Hospital; a series on the mentally retarded that led to legislation which improved treatment; a long and arduous campaign which led to Missouri banks paying the state of Missouri interest on state deposits; and the construction of the Poplar Street Bridge across the Mississippi River.

National Headliners Club Awards to Ted Schafers, for stories about a McDonnell Douglas jet plane fiasco that cost taxpayers at least $122.2 million (1956); to Schafers and Louis Kohlmeyer for a series on problems in the railroad industry; to editorial cartoonist Don Hesse for outstanding editorial cartoons (1964), and to Beulah Schacht as outstanding feature columnist (1964).

Sigma Delta Chi Public Service award, again honoring Walsh and Delugach for their Steamfitters Union expose (1969).

The brain trust of the Globe Democrat *photographed in 1984, from left: Martin Duggan, editor of the editorial page; Bauman; and George A. Killenberg, executive editor.*

Roy W. Howard Public Service Award to Steve Higgins and Richard Krantz for a series on traffic ticket fixing and other types of corruption in the city courts (1973).

American Bar Association Awards to Higgins and Krantz for their city courts series; to Mary Scarpinato for articles on the revised Missouri criminal code (1980), and to Scarpinato and Thomas L. Amberg for their series of Missouri's parole system (1983).

University of Missouri Honor Award for Distinguished Service in journalism in 1967, to the *Globe-Democrat* for "its unrelenting assault upon the blight of civil disorder, crime and stagnation of purpose, with the goal of revitalizing the city's pride and heritage."

American Legion Fourth Estate Award to the *Globe* for distinguished public service in the field of communications in 1967.

Alfred P. Sloan Award for Distinguished Public Service in Highway Safety, for articles and editorials on highway safety in 1971.

National Allstate Foundation Safety Award in 1970 to Sue Ann Wood for a series on drunken driving pointing to a flaw in the state law that hampered enforcement and conviction of offenders.

International Association of Fire Fighters News Media Contest. First prize to Steve Higgins for a series on arson-for-profit.

National Association for Mental Health for a series by Marguerite Shepard on the treatment of mental illness in Missouri in 1974.

Variety Club International Communications 1981 Media Award for the *Globe's* coverage of Variety Club efforts on behalf of disabled and underprivileged children.

In addition, the newspaper was a finalist five times for the Public Service Award of the Associated Press Managing Editors Association and was named a finalist in the nationwide competition four consecutive years.

It was never a puzzle to me, and it's entirely possible that my surmise could be utterly wrong, why the St. Louis *Globe-Democrat* received so few Pulitzer awards, only a total of three for many outstanding journalistic achievements. But for that matter the St. Louis *Post-Dispatch* didn't receive an extraordinary number of Pulitzers either, which tends to confirm my uninformed opinion.

Since the Pulitzer Prize was established by a Pulitzer, a publisher of the *Post-Dispatch*, I think the award committee leaned over backward not to name either St. Louis paper because of the desire not to be subject to charges of favoritism. This is an understandable position for the committee to assume in order to protect its integrity. But be that as it may, the *Globe-Democrat* received its share of journalistic honors.

One of the *Globe-Democrat's* public events of which we were most proud was Old Newsboys Day, held each fall. Amberg recognized that the allure of the newspaper business might be put to use for the benefit of the community. He reasoned that giving adults, men and women alike, a chance to play in the newspaper business once a year could raise money for the needy. Many adults remember fondly the days when they sold papers on the street or delivered papers to homes.

The *Globe-Democrat* invited St. Louisans to participate in Old Newsboys Day and literally thousands responded. On occasion

In 1974 Peter Bauman assists his son during the Globe's *highly successful promotion, "Old Newsboys Day."*

there would be four to five thousand "Old Newsboys" on the street just before Thanksgiving selling a special edition of the paper for whatever amount buyers wanted to give. They came out sometimes in bitter cold, drenching rain or heavy snow. The *Globe* took not a penny from the street sale income that day.

A special committee allocated the receipts to various children's charitable agencies. The intent was to provide some extra cash to an agency, not in its annual budget, for a special need. Allocations to a single agency were small by design, so that as many agencies as possible could benefit. About $200,000 was distributed each year.

We always felt one of the appeals of Old Newsboys Day was that someone could give whatever he wanted—twenty-five cents or five dollars—and feel good. Somehow it symbolized our relationship to the community, a relationship that established that individuals and institutions which give of themselves are, in turn, richly rewarded.

- 12 -

IT'S A CRIME!

Dennis McCarthy, one of our finest investigative reporters came into my office one day in the spring of 1981 to talk about the case of Dr. Glennon Engleman, an alleged murderer. He was convinced that Engleman, a South St. Louis dentist, was guilty of seven or eight murders, one on the east side, but he never could get confirming information to justify the *Globe-Democrat's* publication of the story.

We had to be absolutely sure of our facts. Dennis was ninety-nine percent certain, but needed one piece of irrefutable evidence. After several years of work, he told me he thought he had found that piece.

He had discovered evidence that $35,000–the exact amount of a victim's life insurance benefit–had been deposited in Boatmen's Bank in Engleman's name, leaving an easily-detected paper trail. Engleman's modus operandi was to persuade a woman to marry a man he selected for her. He then would murder the bridegroom and he and the bride would split the insurance money.

Dennis had asked the bank for confirmation of this particular deposit but was refused. I told him that this was proper on the bank official's part, that details of a customer's bank account cannot legally be revealed to a third party. However, I said I'd do what I could to help. I went to see Don Brandin, the bank chairman, whom I knew pretty well.

He said, "Duncan, you know I can't give you that information."

I said, "That's what I expected but we feel this man is guilty of seven or eight murders and this time I think you ought to make an exception."

He repeated that he couldn't tell me. I said, "Are you saying you will sit there and let this man go free to commit more murders?" Then I had an idea. I said, "'You don't have to tell me. There is a datebook on your desk. When I come back tomorrow, if that datebook is turned around, I will know the answer is yes."

Dennis McCarthy

When I went back the datebook was turned around. I told Dennis the deposit was confirmed and we followed up with a series of stories.

With the information police investigators had found coupled with McCarthy's findings, federal prosecutors took over. Within a few days, the U.S. District Attorney called me. He said we should get Dennis out of town because Engleman was going to kill him. He explained they had a microphone on Engleman's girlfriend. Engleman had told her at dinner the night before that he would kill Dennis the next day.

The U.S. attorney said the FBI would pick up Engleman in the next twenty-four hours and the danger would be over. I told Dennis we would pay to take his wife and their ten children out of town. Dennis refused to go.

I'm grateful to say that Engleman didn't carry out his threat. He was arrested the next day and at his trial was convicted of murder and sent to prison for life. He served that sentence in the Jefferson City Correctional Center until he died in 1999 of numerous ailments. Toward the end, he was in a wheelchair, both legs amputated at the knees because of diabetic complications. He still bragged about his criminal career as a serial killer.

At the *Globe-Democrat*, our staff dug into many alleged crimes, solved some and uncovered crucial information which gave law enforcement officials enough to bring the criminal to justice.

Among our top investigators were McCarthy, Jack Flach, Ted Schafers, Les Pearson and the two who shared the Pulitzer Prize, Denny Walsh and Al Delugach. But this, perhaps more than any other area of news gathering and writing, had to be a team effort. Many other staff members—reporters, editors, reference librarians—supported the investigators' efforts and supplied information.

I was involved sometimes, as in the Engleman case, hands-on.

When I joined the paper, the city was still talking about the Nellie Muench case, although at the time she was serving a prison sentence in connection with a notorious baby hoax. The story had so captivated the St. Louis press that one of its last mentions rated larger headlines than the nomination of President Roosevelt for a second term. Perhaps, that was due to some extent to the tenor of the times.

The 1930s were rather quiet in St. Louis. An exotic crime as that perpetrated by Nellie—a well known owner of an exclusive west end shop patronized by high society—was rare. No one was murdered, although one man was kidnapped. The public could eat up the news without feeling overly outraged at the moral state of humanity.

In 1936 Nellie, the sister of a Missouri Supreme Court justice, was convicted of attempting to extort money by mail from a prominent St. Louis physician by claiming that she had given birth to his child. The baby actually was the illegitimate child of a servant girl.

I had joined the staff too late to help cover the case. However, Aaron Benesch, city editor of the old *Star-Times,* who came to the *Globe* when the *Star-Times* folded in 1951, led that newspaper's investigative staff who found the real mother of the baby. The paper published her story in serial form.

We did send Marguerite Shepard, one of our top reporters, to interview Nellie when she was released from prison in 1944 and moved to Kansas City to begin a new life as a practical nurse. She refused to talk with Marguerite, but her detailed story of the case brought the once-glamorous extortionist back into the spotlight.

Again in 1960 her name returned to the headlines when Carl Major of the *Globe* revealed that she was a minor stockholder in a corporation which proposed to build skyscrapers at the corner of Lindell and Kingshighway. The plan didn't materialize but, as

Ernest Kirschten wrote in *Catfish and Crystal,* "this hardly was necessary to recall the Mitzi shop and Nellie Muench to St. Louisans . . . It is the west end's Number One conversation piece."

Ted Schafers was responsible for many of our scoops over the *Post-Dispatch.* One involved Andrew Brinkley, the state's witness against three officers in the case of Edward Melendes, who was fatally beaten in his jail cell at police headquarters in September 1942. Brinkley was sentenced to seven years in prison for perjury. In his testimony he blamed the *Globe-Democrat* and Ted for tricking him into admitting perjury.

He called Ted to his cell after the verdict and told him, "I'll be out someday, and the first one I'm going after is you."

I can understand Ted's relief when he heard that shortly before he was due to be released, Brinkley, who had made many enemies during his stay, "fell" on the prison grounds and was killed by a prison farm wagon.

One of the biggest investigations Ted worked on was the Bobby Greenlease case. And one of his greatest scoops came about as a result of his story on a minor misdemeanor–making an illegal left turn.

Bobby, the six-year-old son of a wealthy Kansas City automobile dealer, was kidnapped and murdered on September 28, 1953, despite payment of $600,000 to preserve the boy's life. His killers, Carl Austin Hall and Bonnie Brown Heady, fled to St. Louis, where they were arrested on October 6. They were tried in St. Louis, convicted and sentenced to death for the crime. They were executed shortly after their conviction.

But the story turned out to be a dual mystery. The first, identifying the killers, was quickly solved, but the second–the disappearance of half the $600,000 ransom money–set the investigative reporters on an avid chase which would last for many weeks. Although the second mystery was never solved, Detective Lou Shoulders and his driver, Elmer Dolan, who were suspected of stealing the money, went to prison for perjury.

In his book, *A Grave for Bobby* (1990, William Morrow), *Post-Dispatch* reporter James Deakin, discussing the missing money and suspected police involvement in its disappearance, wrote:

> The news media, the public and the St. Louis police department were not aware that the FBI had withheld some things Hall had said in his confession. These things, and the FBI's subse-

quent investigation, raised the nagging question.

However, the two Teds were on the job, which meant the government secrecy was not complete. Theodore C. Link of the *Post-Dispatch,* and Theodore Schafers of the *Globe-Democrat,* both nicknamed Ted, were tough, persistent investigators, and both were trying to crack the remaining puzzle in the Greenlease case. The missing $300,000 put the newsrooms of both papers on a war footing.

Ted Schafers won a major victory because of a minor traffic incident which had happened before the Greenlease story broke.

Joe Costello, head of Ace Cab Co., got into trouble for trying to turn from Washington Avenue onto 18th Street. He thought he was right. A traffic cop said no. Ted, on duty at police headquarters, wrote a light-hearted story and Joe Costello called to thank him. He said, "If you ever need help on anything, just call me because you are the first reporter to ever give me a fair shake."

Not long after that, Ted, with every other crime reporter, wanted to interview John Hager, a driver for Costello, who had driven Carl Austin Hall around town for twenty-four hours before his

Arteaga Photos

Globe *reporter Ted Schafers interviews John Hager, the Ace Cab driver whose tip to police led to the arrest of Carl Austin Hall.*

Arteaga Photos

Ted Schafers, right, interviews Greenlease kidnapper Carl Austin Hall, in handcuffs. Hall and Heady went to the Missouri gas chamber in December 1953.

arrest. He remembered Costello's promise and tracked him down. At 4 A.M., Ted got his interview with Hager in Costello's home.

He asked Costello to keep Hager under wraps until the *Globe-Democrat* came out at 7 P.M. that day. Costello sent Hager to a hotel room and told him not to stick his head out of that room "until Schafers turns the key."

Incidentally, on October 8, 1982, long after the Greenlease tragedy was a dim memory in the minds of most readers, Sue Ann Wood, who had worked on the case twenty years earlier, and Edward W. O'Brien, then head of our Washington Bureau, obtained a six-and-a-half page confession by Dolan, an unsigned statement which appeared to confirm his and Shoulders' guilt. It was headlined, "FBI Files Unlock Mystery of Greenlease Ransom."

That was one of the last references in the files of the *Globe-Democrat* on what was the most infamous crime in Missouri history and the unsolved mystery of the money.

One of the dozens of rumors, true and false, swirling around the case was that Frank (Buster) Wortman, the East Side rackets boss, was involved. A prostitute, with a greedy eye on the ransom money, was said to have gone to East St. Louis after midnight looking for a friend who could put her in touch with Wortman, and together they could help themselves to the cash. However, reporters learned that she found neither the friend nor Wortman.

In a special story prepared for the final edition of the newspaper, Ted wrote of another scoop—which he lived to regret.

> Sometimes a reporter is placed in an awkward position when information is offered about alleged misconduct involving someone who has been a good tipster or a long-time friend.
>
> That happened when a city jail warden, a friend of mine, was accused of permitting steaks and fresh bakery goods to be smuggled into the cells of Lawrence Callanan, a convicted labor racketeer, and some other big shot prisoners.
>
> The warden, as far as I knew, ran a good jail but I waited one night until the prisoners' dinner hour before requesting permission to tour the jail. The warden gave me a personal tour but insisted on going to the top floor and working down. By the time we got to the third floor, where Callanan was housed, there was a smell of broiled steaks but no steaks—the evidence had disappeared. It was obvious I had been had.
>
> I warned the warden that if special meals were being allowed, he had better stop. He insisted that, even if it were going on, he saw nothing seriously improper because "guys like Callanan help keep the young punks in line."
>
> Two weeks later, a prisoner-clerk was at my desk with the names of the guards involved and how much they were being paid for doing those favors. My inclination was to bow out and let someone else do the digging, because I had been told the warden had a heart problem; a major expose could be harmful to his health.
>
> Instead, I went calling at the home of one of the accused guards. He denied the accusation but his wife, who had been eavesdropping, burst into the living room, shouting to her husband, "I told you not to get in that mess and take that money."
>
> The grand jury investigation did prove too much for the warden who had a fatal heart attack. I still wish I had walked away from that story.

A minor jurisdiction judge in Sikeston, Lloyd Briggs, was known to be abusing defendants, particularly women who were before him. It was alleged that he would demand sexual favors for a favorable decision from the bench.

Jack Flach, one of the ablest investigative reporters on any newspaper, heard of this. He always had a quick sense of indignation. Without this sense, a person cannot be much of a newsman.

One day Jack came into my office to tell me what he knew about Briggs. He had been tipped off by Judge Robert Dowd, member of a distinguished family of lawyers and judges, that the Missouri Bar Association was inquiring into Briggs' conduct. We agreed that he should investigate. First, he called Joseph Teasdale, then governor, who planned to appoint Briggs to a circuit court judgeship. Teasdale listened, but did not promise either to take action or defer, even though Jack knew many had questioned the appointment before it was made.

Flach had discovered that when the appointment of Briggs to the circuit court was pending several people called or wrote the governor and advised him that Briggs was not of good character and should not be serving on the bench. Flach told Teasdale what he had heard about problems associated with Briggs' conduct. The governor listened, said okay, and that was the end of the conversation. He went ahead and appointed Briggs, but the *Globe* pursued a campaign for his removal on the basis of his poor conduct.

In 1980 Briggs was charged by the Supreme Court's disciplinary committee with numerous counts of misconduct. This was upheld by the Missouri Supreme Court and the judge was removed. In 1985, he pleaded guilty to tax evasion associated with illegal drug trafficking.

Another case involving Jack Flach was regarding Clyde Orton, the sheriff of Pemiscot County in southeast Missouri, and his apparent "blindness" to illegal gambling and violations of liquor control laws.

When two liquor control agents from the state of Mississippi came into Pemiscot County to investigate activities by some Mississippi citizens, Orton had them arrested. His deputies escorted them to the Missouri border and told them to leave the state and never to return without his knowledge and permission.

After Jack Flach and the *Globe* disclosed this, the Supreme Court of Missouri ordered Orton removed from office on March 9, 1971. He tried to run for re-election shortly after his removal from office and the Supreme Court issued an order forbidding him to do so. Orton's wife then ran for sheriff, but she was defeated.

Ten years later, Orton called Flach to say he had "learned his lesson" and wanted desperately to run again for office. He asked if the *Globe-Democrat* would campaign against him. Flach, convinced that Orton was sincere and would run a clean office, told him to go ahead and file. But he told him, "If you are elected, we'll watch you like a hawk and if you make a single error, if you allow anything wrong to occur in your office, the newspaper again will seek to remove you from office." Orton said that was all right with him. He did run and he was elected. I heard no more about it, but I'm sure Flach kept an eagle eye on Orton and Pemiscot County.

These stories demonstrate the power of the newspaper. No single individual could bring down a public official because one person's influence is so limited, but a newspaper has tremendous power to right wrongs. Granted, that power brings its risk.

Both Dick Amberg and I received death threats. Dick received his by telephone and he believed to the day of his death that he could identify the person who called and threatened him. The individual was reasonably prominent in St. Louis civic circles. Dick reported the threat to the FBI but nothing came of its investigation. Dick refused to talk with his believed enemy and tried several times to have him removed from a responsible post, but never succeeded. I am not sure that the man Dick suspected of threatening was the one who actually made the threat.

I was also threatened by telephone and twice by letter. The caller told me he planned to bomb my house and my car. We lived in an apartment with an alley garage and this was a real vexation, especially since I parked in the same space every day at the paper and had an identifiable license number. I parked my car for several weeks at a friend's home at night and walked some distance to my house. The police provided attention for several weeks at my home.

I thought it would be helpful, not only to me but others, if a remote control similar to a garage door opener could be made to set off all of an automobile's electrical circuits from a distance. It would ignite a bomb attached to an automobile's electric circuits and explode it before anyone was close enough to get hurt. I was not successful in interesting any manufacturer in developing the item.

One letter-writer threatened to set my apartment on fire. I was concerned, sure. But what can one do? One becomes very apprehensive about safety, whether walking on the street or walking into a house or a theater or turning on the ignition of the car.

The press isn't just a medium for gathering and reporting the news. It must also be a partner of the police, a protector of the people, turning a spotlight on society and forcing miscreants into its glare. Investigative reporting has been a part of our work for centuries. Rooting out evil and evil-doers is a major duty.

One of the biggest problems in America today is crime, not only murders and rapes and other brutal physical attacks, but, also white collar dishonesty, a lack of integrity and principle. If we do not solve the broad issue of crime, ultimately the American people will make a choice. They will give up some freedoms to solve crime, and that means we will have a more oppressive government without some of the freedoms we cherish.

We are breeding too many criminals. We have to find a way to stop this. One of the weapons in our arsenal is technology.

In the early 1980s, Mayor Vincent Schoemehl and County Executive Gene McNary appointed me chairman of the REJIS Commission—Regional Justice Information Service—a government body created by joint action of the St. Louis city and county. Its purpose is to collect criminal justice data and distribute this information as requested by its 150 clients. Data includes court records, arrest records, warrants, stolen guns and cars, wanted persons and crimes of all description.

An example of its service: If an officer stops me while I am driving, he radios REJIS and within seconds, before he approaches my car, he knows a lot about me—whether I am a known felon wanted on a warrant and if the car has been reported stolen. This helps him a great deal in determining how he approaches me.

REJIS has a six-member board, three from St. Louis city and three from the county. Customarily, they represent criminal justice functions and are appointed by the mayor and the county executive for two-year terms. The chairmanship is a joint appointment, also for a two-year term.

REJIS is mandated by its city-county charter to operate on a break-even financial basis. If it has a financial surplus at the end of a year, it returns the surplus in equal portions to the city and county. It generates revenue for its $6 million annual budget by charging small fees for information requests, ranging from a few cents to more than $100.

In the early 1990s, REJIS installed an electronic system for identifying fingerprints, known as AFIS. It supplanted the tedious print-by-print, hand-worked visual comparison which sometimes took weeks, while AFIS did the work in minutes. There are about 300,000 prints in the St. Louis area police files. The system is now integrated with the state system.

REJIS recently was asked by St. Louis County to consider taking over the operation of every computer function used or operated by the county government. REJIS agreed to do so, for a fee. St. Louis city and county governments revised the agency's charter to include the enhanced function, expected to save the county more than $1 million a year when the changeover is up to speed.

During much of its history, at least since the late 1970s or early 1980s, REJIS has been managed by Paul Newhouse. He has done a uniquely effective job and has managed to constantly improve the service REJIS renders, year after year, and give annual wage increases to employees without raising prices charged for services. Price increases have been required only about once every two or three years.

Police departments and other elements of the justice system have always depended on information. REJIS makes it possible to aggregate information from many sources and share it among many agencies. As the electronic exchange of information grows, REJIS will play an important role in helping government use technology to deliver services.

The press has been condemned by readers for publishing *only* bad news. That is an unfair criticism. They ask, "Why can't you give us some good news?"

We do. Look through any major newspaper today and you will find many stories about heroes, about innovative school teachers and responsive students, about community improvements, about racial concord, about churches and food pantries and neighborliness. These are a major part of our reportage and they deserve the spotlight.

We printed at least one good news story on page one of the *Globe-Democrat* every day. But we must also focus attention on the bad news. When crime and other evils become so commonplace that they are no longer news—when a good deed is so rare that we must shout it to the heavens and emblazon it on page one—then we are in real trouble in our society.

- 13 -

THE HEALTH, EDUCATION, AND RELIGION BEAT

America unquestionably has the highest quality of medical care of any nation in the world and St. Louis fortunately offers that same high quality of care. We have two fine medical schools, Saint Louis University and Washington University, which always rank very high. They both lend inestimable service to medical care in our area. The BJC Hospital System, comprised of Barnes-Jewish, Christian, Missouri Baptist Medical Center, and Children's Hospital, has a direct association with Washington University Medical School. By contract, the medical school supplies all the doctors who serve patients at Barnes-Jewish and Children's.

What counts to patients is not the ratings, but the service and results they get from the doctors, nurses, and other health-care professionals. Few communities have been as fortunate as St. Louis in the number of skilled and devoted doctors who practice here. One can serve as an example for all.

That is Dr. Everett R. Lerwick. Born in Washington state, he worked as a logger as a youth and earned the confidence of his boss who helped him financially to attend school. He graduated from the University of Missouri School of Medicine and began his surgical practice at Missouri Baptist Hospital, then located at Enright and Taylor. He chose vascular surgery as his specialty, which proved to be the salvation of countless patients.

When the hospital decided more than twenty years ago to move from the city to Ballas Road and Highway 40, Lerwick was among the foremost of the physicians in promoting the move. By then he was a leader of the medical staff and most likely the influence which prompted a recalcitrant but important board member to change his mind and support the move. He also motivated doctors to make substantial financial contributions to help pay for the new building.

Lerwick's skills developed a huge practice. Customarily he would be in surgery from before 6:00 A.M. to late in the evening. His office hours always began late in the evening, after he had finished surgery, more often than not starting after 8:00 P.M. and running to midnight. It was not uncommon for him to visit his hospital patients after midnight to check on their condition. He maintained a six-day schedule, occasionally seven days. The results of his work were legendary and in later life he lectured to groups of surgeons all over the world.

An outstate Missouri teenager was in an automobile accident in which one of his hands and lower arm were severed. An ambulance brought him to Missouri Baptist, along with his arm and hand which had been picked up in a field. Lerwick reattached the arm and hand, which function perfectly today. Lerwick became interested in his patient and arranged for a job for him with Southwestern Bell. The young man has since had two promotions.

After his retirement, Missouri Baptist named its surgical department after Lerwick. I once described him in a speech as an angel in the delivery of health care. I still think that's apt for him and hundreds of others who deliver health care, the best in the world.

The opportunity to serve as a board member and officer of the Missouri Baptist Hospital for nearly thirty years has been an exceptionally valuable learning experience and a rewarding opportunity to serve the community. I was at one time the only Roman Catholic and the only non-Baptist on the board.

I enjoyed many years of friendship with Philip F. Lichtenstein and his brother, David, who was a major factor in the consumer loan business in America. David and Don Barnes began making small loans when they were students at Saint Louis University. They built this business into American Investment, a major corporation.

In 1959, David and Phil asked if I could persuade Dick Amberg to chair a fund-raising campaign for a new Missouri Baptist Hospital in West County. It had been in the city for nearly a century. At the time, we were in the midst of the Newspaper Guild strike, but Dick agreed to head the campaign after the strike was over. He followed through and raised some $2 million or $3 million. In appreciation, the hospital board named a street in the hospital complex for him.

Dick received some money from Anheuser-Busch and Falstaff. The Missouri Baptist Convention, the policy-making board for the Baptist church, sent word to the hospital, which had a loose but non-binding affiliation with the convention, that brewery contributions were unacceptable because of Baptist policies forbidding the use of alcohol. Dick sent back word that if these were unacceptable, he would return all the money to every other donor. That was the end of the quarrel. The brewery money was accepted.

With the evolution of Medicare, Medicaid, HMO's and PPO's and with the change in payment policy for health care it became evident to the Missouri Baptist board in the early 1990s that stand-alone hospitals would inevitably lose financial support to the point where they would have to close. The board made the choice to seek an affiliation with a hospital group which would meet the needs of the developing health care system in St. Louis.

Our first venture was with the Saint Louis University system which I thought would be a superb alignment because the philosophy behind the delivery of health care in the Saint Louis University system and that in Missouri Baptist were so significantly alike.

The attempt to work with SLU was not what we envisioned, so when the Barnes-Jewish-Christian hospital group, affiliated with the Washington University Medical School, invited Missouri Baptist to become a full partner in 1994, Missouri Baptist accepted. BJC had been looking for an affiliate in the important central St. Louis County area and had earlier offered an affiliation to St. Luke's Hospital but St. Luke's declined.

For the 125 or more years that Missouri Baptist has been delivering health care in the St. Louis area, it has done so with an unswerving determination and insistence that no abortions could be done at the hospital and no euthanasia could be provided.

The board felt that the BJC affiliation warranted committing its policies on abortion and euthanasia to writing because of a potential conflict with BJC over abortion and euthanasia policies.

About the time of the BJC affiliation, Joyce A. Pillsbury concluded that he should relinquish the board chairmanship to a younger person. So Dr. W. Joseph Privott, chairman of the Novus Company, a Monsanto spinoff, succeeded him. Privott, as chairman, also is a member of the BJC board and the BJC executive committee. Each constituent member of BJC has four members on the BJC board and one member on the executive committee. No major corporate decision, such as changes in the bylaws, can be made without seventy-five percent board approval.

This is important to each constituent member because each member retains an element of individual authority which it cherishes. Thus Missouri Baptist can control the ethics behind the delivery of health care at the hospital and full, unquestioned authority to credential physicians who may practice there.

It was a special joy and privilege for me to serve on the BJC board, which I did at the urging of Chuck Knight, Emerson Electric board chairman and the founding board chairman of BJC. Joe Privott has been a staunch anchor for Missouri Baptist on the executive committee and board, giving literally hundreds of hours to the assignment, an especially arduous task during the formative years of BJC.

Prior to closing City Hospital, Mayor Vince Schoemehl set up a committee headed by Lee Liberman and Bob Hyland to plan a delivery system for the medically indigent. The result was St. Louis Regional Hospital, located in the old St. Luke's Hospital facility on Delmar just west of Union. The county closed St. Louis County Hospital and picked up a share of the cost, as did the city after closing City Hospital. The hospital was run by a board on which Liberman and Hyland served and was conceived to be financially self-sufficient.

Through the years Schoemehl and County Executive Gene McNary were able to persuade the U.S. Department of Health, Education and Welfare to provide supplemental money, in addition to Medicare and Medicaid payments, to support Regional Hospital. Eventually, according to Liberman, St. Louis city and county authorities did not make their payments to support the hospital because they thought the HEW supplemental money was enough to enable the hospital to operate. This turned out not to be true. The hospital foundered and faced closure.

BJC was aware of the community obligation to the medically indigent and its own obligation thereby. BJC administrators worked diligently with executives of several private, not-for-profit hospitals to help find a solution. From these efforts came a consortium of St.Louis hospitals, six to eight, who agreed to provide medical care for low-income city and county residents for a fee to be paid jointly by the city and county, plus the state of Missouri. Regional closed and the care began to be provided by the consortium.

Maybe Schoemehl's refusal to reopen Homer Phillips Hospital turned out to be for the best. Certainly the indigent now have unquestioned access to the best medical care available in the St. Louis area.

Health care has become political in recent years. If I were still in the newspaper business, one of the obvious subjects I would be writing about is health care and the wrangle in the Congress about Medicare and Medicaid. These would be substantial editorial issues. Our problem is to find a way to preserve the delivery of quality health care in America at a cost patients and third-party payers can and will pay.

Churches, temples and meeting halls of all religious faiths have been a major force for good in St. Louis since our city's founding. Its Roman Catholic heritage, reflected in the historic Old Cathedral on the riverfront and the grandeur of the cathedral in the Central West End, gave the city a solid foundation of ethical standards and spiritual aspirations. That foundation has been strengthened and enriched by the establishment and growth of many faiths–Protestant, Jewish, Muslim, and others.

The churches through their leaders and followers have spurred our progress and brought into our community consistently higher concepts of human conduct and charity. We have learned to work together to respect our differences and achieve unity in sectarian programs.

One of the greatest satisfactions of my life as a newspaperman was the experience of a close friendship with John Joseph Cardinal Carberry.

The friendship originated when the *Globe-Democrat* gave me the wonderful assignment of accompanying Archbishop Carberry to Rome for his investiture as a cardinal by the pope in April 1969. It was an unforgettable experience. Since the group which accompanied him to Rome consisted primarily of friends whom he trusted, much of his reserve as a bishop was discarded. He was just another human being. One evening he entertained the group by playing the violin.

Monsignor Robert Slattery, a St. Louis priest who was along with us on the trip, told me he could get a better ticket to the investiture ceremony than I had if he had $50. I gave him the money and we took a cab to the Vatican, to the backdoor of the pope's housekeeper's apartment. Slattery met her at the door, gave her the $50, and got a ticket to the ceremony. It was not quite as good as mine.

John Joseph Cardinal Carberry with me and my mother, Mae Bauman, in 1970, shortly after he became a cardinal.

The cardinal called me one day to discuss a problem. He said he had become disappointed in the way some diocesan priests appeared in public, in sports clothes with long hair. He proposed writing a letter to his priests asking them to wear prescribed priestly garb in public and trim their hair and beards, but he was concerned about how such a letter would be treated in the media, especially at the behest of a few dissident priests.

I suggested that if he gave the *Globe-Democrat* a copy of his letter in advance and authorized us to print it the morning of its receipt by the priests this might help. I said the media tended to follow one another in they way they treated news stories. A favorable story about an incident usually bred other favorable stories, and vice versa. He agreed, we printed the story, and there was not a single media item in protest.

When Carberry was expecting to be the host in St. Louis for a visit from the cardinal primate of Canada, he asked if Nora and I would give a dinner for the Canadian cardinal and his entourage. We were pleased to do so and made the arrangements at the Bogey Club.

About a week before the dinner Nora asked if I thought the Canadian churchman might have a black person or two, in his group. I inquired of Cardinal Carberry and sure enough there were two black members of the Canadian's group. Since the Bogey had not to our knowledge ever had a black person in attendance at a party, we thought we'd better find out where we stood.

I called Fred Peirce, then Bogey president and chairman of General American Life Insurance Co., to seek advice. He commented that he did not foresee any problems but that we both knew two or three members each, about six total, who might possibly object. We each took three of the six questionable members and called them. Not one of the six objected.

Nora and I had our dinner and had a beautiful time. Cardinal Carberry was ever grateful for the occasion.

Carberry failed to get enough votes to pass an amendment to the Missouri constitution which was about as innocuous for a church-state issue to be. The cardinal had a carefully worded poll run to determine whether Missouri voters would approve a constitutional amendment which would permit public school buses taking children to school and bringing them home throughout the state to also pick up children attending parochial schools. The amendment specified that Catholic students would be picked up only if they and their school were directly on the established bus route. This would result in minimal extra daily expense.

The cardinal told me the poll showed that fifty-six percent of Missouri voters would favor the amendment. I urged him not to go to the expense of having the amendment put on the ballot because I was certain it would be defeated either at the polls or in a lawsuit challenging its constitutionality after it had been approved. I explained that Missouri has one of the strictest constitutional amendments governing church and state relationships of any state in the United States. I also advised him that I thought a Baptist coalition would doom the measure, since it had become known that Baptist activists would work against the amendment. He was determined to see it through and the question was placed on the ballot, where it was overwhelmingly defeated.

In terms of political clout I'm convinced that if Baptists in Missouri–a very large group–align themselves cohesively by way of the Missouri Baptist Convention or some other recognized Baptist group, they can be a persuasive or determining factor in any statewide election. I don't believe that the Baptist group organized itself well in a recent election or Missouri would not have river-located casino gambling.

Most of us have preconceived ideas of how people should act, especially doctors, lawyers, and the clergy. When one acts out of character, we become a bit disenchanted–a lot more so when the unhappy action is by a man of the cloth.

When Gabe Alberici and I were raising money for St. Joseph's Shrine, a fine friend of mine agreed to give $5,000. For weeks we waited for the check to come in the mail. By happenstance one day I spoke with a priest assigned to the shrine.

"Oh," he said, "'I got that check and I kept the money for myself.'"

I told him the money was a gift to the shrine. He was adamant and said he would not give it to us.

I told the donor the story. He agreed the money was intended for the shrine and showed me the endorsement on the check. It was by the priest and the money had been deposited in his account in a bank on North Grand.

On the other hand, when a so-called bad person turns good, it gives us a lift. My interest in Dismas House, the halfway house for paroled and released convicts, motivated my wife, Nora, to work with the institution also. In the course of time, she became acquainted with a recently released prisoner, Leonard V. He had committed an armed robbery to get food for himself. As with most of the Dismas House residents, Leonard was searching for a job. Nora asked me to put him to work at the *Globe* and I did.

Leonard had a high skill level in office work. We put him in charge of the department which handled our weekly pay insurance policies bought by our readers. We had about 75,000 policy holders in this ten-cents-a-week policy program. It was a job laden with detail but important to us and to the readers to have the records straight.

In a short period Leonard did a superb job of organizing the functions to near perfection. He was an enthusiastic, productive department head. The quality of his work became known to a few other employers in the St. Louis area. A purse manufacturer offered him a position in his main office with much more money than my salary scales could match. So Leonard resigned and went to work for the purse company.

In the meantime he had met and married an exceptionally congenial woman, divorced, with two children. She and Leonard had a son by their marriage, Leonard, Jr. Within a few years, Leonard moved his family to Florida where he owned and operated a gasoline service station.

Leonard, Jr., excelled in school and after graduating from high school was offered an appointment to West Point. Early on, however, he found he was not suited for the military school and resigned. He continued his education and wound up earning a Ph.D. in English and is now teaching.

What better example could you find of good coming from a good deed?

I was surprised one day to take a call from Sorkis Webbe, Sr. I had known Webbe, a Democratic political figure, for a long time and had a lot of respect for him. He never lied to me. He never even misrepresented anything to me. Some people speculated that he was not too clean, and that he associated with less than admirable people. At one time he had a major interest in the Aladdin Hotel and gambling casino in Las Vegas.

Webbe wanted to know if I would accept a substantial gift for Dismas House from Larry Callanan. Callanan and others in the Steamfitters' Union were not very friendly to the *Globe-Democrat.* Webbe explained that Callanan would give a check for $25,000 to Dismas if I would be willing to come with Webbe to Callanan's office to pick it up.

I told Webbe I would accept the check. He and I went to see Callanan. I got the check, gave it to Dismas House and never heard another word from him. No pressure, no request for favors, nothing.

Another good deed also had long-lasting effects. Tom Yates, a news department copyreader, asked if I would handle an adoption proceeding for himself and his wife. Although I'm an attorney, the only law I practiced was to use my legal training in operating the newspaper.

However, I undertook the responsibility and in a short time I learned that the baby they planned to adopt was virtually blind. Here was a young couple knowingly assuming the burden of rearing a virtually blind child.

When we appeared before Judge Noah Weinstein, St. Louis County's juvenile judge, recognized for his skills in handling such situations as this, the social worker representing the court urged him not to grant the adoption. Her argument was that the child would receive better care in an institution. I argued to the contrary and the judge granted the adoption.

We thought little more about this until seventeen years later when we received an invitation to a graduation ceremony at Fontbonne College. The Yates' blind daughter, we were happy to see, was graduating. But she was not blind. The Yates family had found treatment for her which substantially restored her sight. After receiving her education, she became a teacher.

Through the years, the *Globe-Democrat* steadfastly supported development of the state of Israel, following its founding by the United Nations after World War II. President Truman took a leading role in pushing the United Nations action.

On top of everything else Israel was the one nation in the

Middle East that this country depended on to help with a continued supply of minerals and oil from Middle East resources and minerals from South African nations friendly to Israel. When the Jewish people established the state of Israel in 1947, they turned barren, treeless, unproductive land into a prosperous nation, its beauty enhanced by green grass and trees. As a result of this, I supported many things the Jewish people of the St. Louis area did.

The *Globe-Democrat* gave generous news space to St. Louis Jewish activities. The St. Louis community appreciated the support and acknowledged it on a number of occasions. I have great admiration for the Jewish people. They teach charity, family loyalty, and good conduct in the home.

In appreciation, the St. Louis Rabbinical College presented to me a magnificent sterling silver Crown of the Torah. Such a crown rests atop the two poles of the Torah when carried in a formal ceremony.

I believe I am one of the few Gentiles to receive such a significant memento of friendship and respect. I have given it a prominent and honored place in the living room of my home.

Receiving the Crown of Torah from St. Louis Jewish leader and philanthropist Joe Simpkins. Nora is in the center.

It seems to me that during my lifetime, when there has been so much emphasis on education for everyone through the college level, evidenced by the construction of public junior colleges, the public forgets or overlooks the vital need in our socicty for skilled craftsmen. Parents, grandparents, aunts and uncles, and high school counselors almost universally encouraged young people to seek college degrees, especially professional degrees.

St. Louis can be forever grateful that one man had the vision years ago to realize the value of skilled craftsmen to our society. He was David Ranken, Jr., who provided the money to start Ranken School of Mechanical Trades. He had inherited a substantial amount from an uncle and was wise enough to enhance the inheritance through real estate dealings.

The first Ranken students entered the school in September 1909. It was located where it still is, on the west side of Newstead at Finney. The original building is a magnificently constructed stone structure of two stories plus a usable basement.

The school now occupies about forty acres and has numerous other classroom buildings, including a new addition to the original building named for W. Ashley Gray, president of the board and the most effective single fund raiser for a trade school in the history of St. Louis and probably the nation.

Gray took over the presidency of the school following Nicholas Veeder. Veeder was chairman of Granite City Steel. Gray succeeded him both as head of the company and of the Ranken Board.

I estimate that Gray alone, in about ten years of fund raising, raised more than $13 million. About $6 million of this went to the construction of the new classroom building. The rest has been used year after year for operating expenses. Wallace R. (Buck) Persons, former chairman of Emerson Electric, recently gave $600,000 and Desmond Lee, a retired manufacturer, contributed $500,000.

The school has an endowment fund of about $30 million. Some twenty-five years ago that fund was about $12 million and was being administered by a professional investment counselor. The board was dissatisfied with the advisor and began to look for a replacement. Persons, then a board member, volunteered to operate the fund temporarily. Under his tutelage it grew enormously. Finally, the board engaged the three major banks in St. Louis to handle the investments on a competitive basis. The bank which does the best job on an annual basis usually is given a bit more money to handle than the others.

Ranken awards a number of scholarships each year to needy

students. It teaches high school graduates the skilled trades and they graduate after a two-year course. Among its courses are carpentry, bricklaying, electrical work, plumbing and automobile mechanics. It graduates about 300 students each year, men and women, black and white. There are more than twelve job openings available each year for each student. They go to work the day after graduation for salaries in excess of $30,000 per year.

When David Ranken founded the school, he specified that students would be white males only. In the 1960s, the board realized that the policy had to be changed to recognize blacks and women. It was painfully evident to the board that the black community was sorely unhappy with the policy. With court permission, Ranken enrolled black males in 1963; the school opened to women in 1975.

Bringing blacks into the student body was a rocky road. It was difficult for the black community to send their young people to the school because of the long-standing policy, so the school administration and the board undertook a program to educate the community and encourage participation. Schools, parents, churches and community organizations were consulted and asked for assistance, which all gave. Now the black enrollment is promising.

But the school has had unfortunate experiences with the level of learning of some students graduating from the St. Louis public schools. Frequently they have a diploma but have not learned enough to qualify as a Ranken student. Perhaps the best example is that Ranken has encountered public high school graduates who cannot read a ruler. Monsanto Co. is the largest single donor to a remedial education program to which Ranken assigns otherwise qualified students. Usually when they finish the remedial course, they are admitted to the school.

Now known as Ranken Technical College, the school is accredited by the North Central Association and offers a two-year degree. It is recognized among technical schools around America as one of the best—if not the best. On its board are representatives of many of the major businesses in St. Louis, including those in the black community.

One day Missouri Baptist's Dr. Lerwick brought a doctor and

an educator to my office. They were proposing to start a medical school where a student could complete his medical education in six years instead of eight. They wanted to make this a branch of the University of Missouri at Kansas City. The two men were concerned about unfavorable public reaction and wanted to know what the *Globe-Democrat* would do. I assured them that the newspaper would support the program, so they set about to create it.

The medical school was thus established and has been operating since that day. The opposition in St Louis was fierce. Saint Louis University and Washington University besieged us to oppose the concept. Obviously we didn't, and the school has gone forward to become a successful teaching institution.

Another kind of request came from Rev. Ed Drummond, S.J., long-time head of the Saint Louis University Medical School, a marvelous man who was, incidentally, a director of Loyola University in Chicago, my alma mater.

Father Drummond said the administration had been negotiating with the U.S. Department of Health, Education and Welfare for a grant to the Medical School and that grant had been approved for $9 million. However, the university could not get its money and Father Drummond wanted to know if I could be helpful in getting the funds released in Washington.

I decided to call Pat Buchanan, a member of President Nixon's personal group in the White House and a daily influence on the president's decisions. I knew Pat well because when he had graduated with a master's degree from Columbia University, he had applied to many papers, including the *Globe-Democrat*. Dick Amberg recommended him for an interview and we hired him. Amberg wanted Buchanan to do editorial writing so, without any news experience (usually a prerequisite for an editorial writer) Buchanan moved into our editorial department.

He did a splendid job. Somehow, President Nixon became aware of his work and asked the *Globe-Democrat* to lend Buchanan to him to write speeches during his campaign for the presidency. We agreed and when Nixon was elected, Pat went into the White House as one of Nixon's closest advisors.

When I explained the problem to him, Pat said he would try to shake the money loose but had some reservations because George Romney, former governor of Michigan and then head of HEW, was not getting along too well with Nixon. Fortunately, however, he was successful and the university received its promised $9 million.

Two years later, Pat called me and asked sarcastically what planet the Jesuits at the university lived on. He explained that his brother, Brian, had applied for admission to SLU Medical School but had been turned down because his grade point average was a fraction below the required average—Pat said about a tenth of a point. I called Father Drummond and asked if he didn't realize the quid pro quo involved in matters like Buchanan's influence in the school's behalf, especially after he had jarred the $9 million from the federal government.

In a few days, Brian was admitted. He graduated in good standing and began a practice which is a credit to the medical school.

When residents, businesses, and Saint Louis University became aware that efforts should be made to stabilize and revitalize the Grand Avenue-Lindell Boulevard-Washington Avenue neighborhood, it was apparent to everyone that two strong forces in the area would have to get out in front and lead the effort—Saint Louis University and the Masonic Order.

The Rev. Paul C. Reinert, S.J., president of the university, had earned immense respect in the community. Along with many other well-known citizens he let it be known that the university was supportive. The Masonic Order, in one form or another, dominated most of the north side of the block of Lindell from Grand west to Spring and the south side of Olive from Grand to Spring.

The historical coolness between the Catholic Church and the Masonic Order obviously was shelved as the two most influential powers in the area worked together in the common interest of the community. A significant resurgence took place.

The university's building program under the direction of the school's new president, the Rev. Lawrence Biondi, S.J., adds remarkably to the developing rebirth of the neighborhood.

St. Louis was the only city of its urban status that did not have a night law school in the late 1960s and early 1970s.

Shortly after World War II, Saint Louis University closed its night law school. Several non-college-associated law schools in St. Louis, such as Benton, also had closed. Washington University never had a night law school.

Many bright, capable, ambitious and productive young people—and some not so young—decide after they have been out in the world for awhile that they want to earn a law degree. Many are already professionals, especially CPAs, but also doctors and dentists. The lack of a St. Louis night law school unjustifiably denied these individuals the right to earn a law degree.

A number of serious-minded St. Louisans decided that this was wrong. They organized a group to pick up the charter of a defunct night law school and founded the Laclede School of Law. John L. Davidson and Judge John (Jack) Kelly were among the founders.

After a short time they invited me to join the board and I accepted. I had finished my legal education at Washington University Law School after an eight-year hiatus. I worked as a reporter and assistant city editor until 3 A.M., went home, got about three hours sleep and attended day law school classes. It was tough but certainly worthwhile. I knew from my own experience the value of a night law school.

Classes were held for many years in rented space at Fontbonne College. The faculty members were outstandingly qualified. All were practicing attorneys or judges of stature. The students were dedicated and serious.

Soon the hammer fell. The practice of law in Missouri is regulated by the Missouri Supreme Court. The court told the Laclede board that its graduates could not take the Missouri bar examination. Essentially, the court told Laclede that its facilities, space, library and instructors did not meet the standards of the American Bar Association. Further, it said, students at Laclede sometimes worked full-time while they attended school. The ABA said a student could work only eight or ten hours a week and qualify for attendance at an ABA approved school.

Laclede said, "Let our students rise or fall by the results of the bar examination." But the court refused. Laclede ultimately filed suit against the Missouri Supreme Court, seeking authority for Laclede students to take the bar examination, pointing out that the Missouri Supreme Court had improperly delegated its responsibilities to the ABA.

Both Washington University Law School and Saint Louis University Law School joined litigation and opposed Laclede's request. The court ruled against Laclede. However, even with the knowledge that they could not take the bar examination and practice law, a number of students continued to study at Laclede.

Through most of the years of Laclede's existence, Noah Weinstein, retired juvenile court judge from St. Louis County, served as dean. His reputation and devotion were the glue that held the place together.

In the early 1980s or late 1970s, after Saint Louis University reinstated a night law school, the board closed Laclede but did not give up its charter as a school. The financial reserves were designated to provide law scholarships for needy students. The principal fund is not diminished; only the interest is paid out as scholarships.

This service is known as the Noah Weinstein Foundation in memory of the judge. It awards three or four partial scholarships a year.

- 14 -

THIS I BELIEVE

I am a middle-of-the road conservative just as was the *St. Louis Globe-Democrat.* While my personal philosophy jibes with the philosophy and policies of the Republican party, I consider myself a moderate and I have endorsed candidates of both major parties.

I believe in and have long supported civil rights. I believe in the dignity of every human being. I believe in America and in our government, as flawed as it sometimes seems to be. I believe in the concept of private property. I believe in restraints upon government.

I do not believe in abortion or euthanasia, and I am gratified that in this I concur with the moral and ethical philosophy and policies of Missouri Baptist Hospital and that my active association with that institution has enabled me to endorse that philosophy for what I consider to be the public good.

I believe in the basic integrity of the press, despite its failings, and in its inherent power to lead and to strengthen the moral fiber of our nation.

I believe a newspaper is a public trust and should be operated as such. Actually, it is part of the free enterprise economic system and if a paper cannot maintain sufficient revenue to pay its expenses it cannot continue to publish. There are no subsidies, nor should there be.

This is an element which makes newspapers so important to the freedom of this country, in the media environment, and to every citizen. Among the media, only newspapers are totally free. No one except the owner of a newspaper has any real control or influence. This is not true of the electronic media. They are licensed by the federal government and to the extent that threat of license removal is a deterrent to total freedom of expression, radio and television are victims of at least potential control.

I believe a newspaper should respect the office of the presidency and the person in that office, whether Republican or Democrat. But I also believe that it is the role of the press to keep a watchful eye on every office holder, to avoid cover-up, bias or misrepresentation, to support that which is good for the people and investigate that which is bad.

I believe if something is wrong, a newspaper should attack it but it should be on the basis of facts and not because someone on the paper doesn't like someone or something.

I believe that investigative reporting is a vital role of the press. But my rule was that the *Globe-Democrat* would not be critical without substantive reasons. If there were a substantive reason, such as a threat to public health or safety, we would be just as critical as anyone else. We supported what we felt was right and progressive for our country, criticizing what we felt was wrong and regressive.

I must add this, however. The media often has been guilty of forgiving or ignoring its own sins, including bias and bigotry, and is sometimes cruelly intrusive while spotlighting the sins of others.

It is very discouraging to me to see some of the press which have a duty to be accurate, fair, honest, and fulsome neglect that duty, largely in the case of fairness and fulsomeness. Some in the liberal press will give uncounted time and space to a favorite candidate and vice versa in the conservative press. That is not right. It is a violation of the obligation of the media.

At the *Globe-Democrat* we were concerned in the news columns with giving equal treatment to both candidates or both sides of a question. At times, in critical cases, we even measured with a ruler the number of lines to insure objectivity and fairness.

There is a wide gulf, of course, between the news pages and

the editorial columns. We can be as harsh or supportive or one-sided as we wish on the editorial page, but the news columns must remain a sacred territory, fair, objective and untouched by the opinions or philosophy of the editor or reporter.

I have often been disappointed in the leadership of the media. To allow what appears to be news space to be filled with biased information is outright wrong. It damages the media and during a political campaign it damages the ability of the candidates to make their points. The public is damaged because it doesn't have a clear explanation of the issues.

I believe in the responsibility of a newspaper publisher and staff to be community leaders. We had a duty at the *Globe* to serve the community and to serve it in the interest of the community's welfare. We should uphold the public morals and part of the upholding is not to demean the leadership. A newspaper should not be petulant, picky, and negative for no valid reason.

I encouraged our staff members to take part in community activities. This is contrary to the philosophy of many publishers and editors who believe reporters and editors cannot be completely objective if they are involved.

However, they and I had to walk a fine line between the need to keep certain matters confidential and a newsman's natural desire to break a story first. For myself, I can say that never did I come back from a civic committee meeting to give the news department a story so we could beat the competition; but once the reporter had the news, I could verify it.

In its role of a public trust a newspaper should be operated in the interest of the public and the interest of the community. At the same time, it has to make money to stay in business so there needs to be a balance and that balance must be achieved with integrity. That is a publisher's obligation.

1 believe the basic value of a good newspaper lies in providing the community with news of its own functions so that the citizens have knowledge of what is happening and can work together to create a good community for themselves, one which serves them in many ways, culturally and in terms of security.

There has to be a balance in newspaper coverage between the man next door and the man in Bosnia. I don't think a paper has to be characterized as local or national, as long as it is sensitive to local needs and meets those local needs.

The average individual is far more interested in what is happening in his own neighborhood than is what is happening overseas. He is interested in what the school board or his church or the local government does, whether streets are full of potholes, whether lighting is adequate for safety, whether his children are given a good education, how well the baseball Cardinals or the football Rams or local college teams are doing.

Citizens band together as a community principally for three reasons—security, culture, and education. The newspaper's prime service is to do for the community what the community cannot do for itself and to provide dissemination of knowledge which helps the community govern itself.

Community involvement, to me, is an essential role of a communicator. I do not believe a publisher can sit in an ivory tower, look out the window, and credibly praise or condemn or anguish over what is going on out there if he has no firsthand knowledge of it. He must focus simultaneously on the small, compact world of the city room, the composing room, the mail room, the press room, and on the massive world beyond the threshold.

Relationships between and among human beings on this earth and solutions to problems between and among people occupying the planet have become infinitely more complex than they were two or three centuries ago. Knowledge of issues helps us find equitable solutions. The media's role in life is to provide that knowledge.

I believe that America is in danger of becoming a nation of the uninformed. We cannot, we must not, let that happen.

It seemed to me that the media, particularly the TV members, went far beyond normal human interest in devoting such lengthy daily coverage of the recent sad death of John F. Kennedy, Jr., his wife and her sister in the plane crash into the sea. No one questions the interest anyone has in a death of a family member, a public figure, or a notable, such as a Kennedy. But was extensive TV coverage, virtually day and night from the time of the crash to the funerals justified? We don't think so. Neither did a number of nationally read newspapers.

One should not overlook the growing potential for genuine damage to our country under the guise of free speech in the misuse of the Internet and other modern forms of communication to undermine public confidence in our government. A high measure of a local, state, or national government's ability to govern and provide for benefits, including protection, lies in the acceptance of government as a good function. If the public ever totally disclaims the integrity of our court system, for example, and no one obeys a court order, only chaos can follow.

Discouraging and frustrating threats to effective government come from citizens who strive daily to distribute lies and deceitful information. A Missourian insists in conversation and letters that the U.S. government has allowed foreign soldiers, sometimes identified as United Nations troops, to occupy several military bases in the United States. These rumors say that a given time these troops will take over America and the United Nations will rule our country. Recognized authorities label the rumors nonsense, and it is, but some naive citizens believe it is true. The potential damage is obvious.

Another rumor is that foreign nations have established concentrations of troops in Yellowstone National Park, which are labeled "no fly zones" on aeronautical charts. Aeronautical charts of Yellowstone Park which I have studied do not show any "no fly zones" in that vicinity. The answers from the perpetrators of the lies is that the printing plant which produced the maps was compelled to elminate the "no fly zone" identification when printing the charts. This is preposterous on its face and an infuriating lie. Fortunately only a handful of Americans believe such gibberish, but the numbers could grow. The solution is exceptionally complicated, given our devotion—a proper one—to the Constitutional guarantees of free speech.

As the complexity of problems increases, there is a concomitant need for deeper knowledge. The media provides this, especially the print media. Radio and television are limited by time constraints and the inability of the human mind to absorb and retain information presented in only a few minutes or even seconds. Thus, only the print media can provide knowledge in depth and in an absorbable manner.

The human mind has its limitations, and one of those is the retention factor. It has been said by analysts that a casual viewing of a television item or casual listening of a radio item is retained by the human mind for about two minutes. Obviously, a newspaper, by its nature capable of being held and reread and studied, and to be kept in newspaper files and public libraries or on the Internet, has not that disadvantage.

The world is bound to become even more complex in the centuries ahead, and the need for reliable knowledge will increase. Because printed publications feed that knowledge to humanity most effectively of all the media, they cannot die. The print media have a sure and a challenging future—but only if they clean up their act and regain public confidence.

We in the print media—and I count myself, with pride, as a member of this fraternity—have lost much of that confidence in recent years. We have become overly intrusive on occasions; too protective and secretive on others. We have made senseless errors of inaccuracy. Even in our technological age, we have sometimes failed to put in place safeguards that would lessen the chance of error. As an example, a careless technician put on the air the announcement of a famed athlete's death. Properly, the news bulletin had been prepared in advance but when it went out to the public, the athlete was still living. Caution had given way to a desire to beat other media with the unhappy news.

Has competition taken away our professional integrity?

That example is not to denigrate the electronic media. Newspapers, radio and television are partners in the dissemination of news and entertainment. The print press, eldest of the trio, has made its share of mistakes, both careless inaccuracies and biased propaganda designed to influence public opinion. But even with the miraculous growth of technology—and newspapers have certainly taken advantage of that—the print press will survive. Historically, we know that it has been established; that books and periodicals, including newspapers, have contributed mightily to the development of civilization. Perpetuation of the printed word is a given.

However, if we want to survive, we have to find our way back to our original purpose, which is to inform the public and provide it with resources to equip it to govern itself.

Why have newspapers lost readership? Why have they lost public confidence? There are a number of factors.

Newspapers have become less interesting to the public. There is a tendency among some publishers and writers to become more vicious. Unfortunately, a large segment of our population has come to believe that government is made up of crooks and miscreants and the press, in its desire to uncover what it deems sensational news, has not always been willing and able to counteract this opinion.

I have heard highly educated young people say, "Every politician is a crook, so why should I vote?" What they are overlooking is so obvious it is shocking. If that generation multiplies and becomes a majority that has no interest in national government, what kind of government will we have? These are the kind of people who would benefit immensely by reading a newspaper and many of them do not bother.

As a publisher, I found that the hardest age for us to sell was eighteen to thirty year olds. Fewer people in this age bracket vote, despite the push to lower the voting age from twenty-one to eighteen. It is the smallest group to do volunteer work. A number of reasons are obvious.

They are trying to succeed in their careers, or even just to survive economically. They are trying to raise families. But this does not absolve them of the obligation to become good, well-informed and participatory citizens.

It is grievously disturbing to learn that significant numbers of young citizens—the moral, bright, effective leaders of America in a generation or two—have become so cynical and distrustful of government that they throw away their only means of effecting good by not having enough concern for the future to participate in government. Not voting is an ignorant and totally ineffective way of creating change.

It can be documented that countless elections have been won or lost by *one* vote per precinct. Notably, Richard Nixon lost the state of Illinois by less than one vote per precinct in one of his campaigns. And because of losing Illinois, he lost the presidency in 1960.

We have to hope that this promising group will recognize its responsibilities.

I believe the media plays a dominant role in strengthening the moral fiber of the country by holding up before the people the inspirational value of what is good. By publishing the bad news hopefully you show people what is wrong.

The value system in America has changed, the value system for families, for business people, for ministers, for bankers. There is a tendency among a lot of people, probably a majority, to live by subjective moral values, whereas we created a great country and nation and community, on objective as opposed to subjective moral values.

I guess the best definition of a subjective moral value is that the end justifies the means, which is totally wrong. It is a form of utilitarianism, which means that whatever serves me best is what I am going to do, not what is right. Truth is not relative. Truth is absolute. We have gotten away from absolute truth as an objective moral value. This underlies all of our problems.

Media leaders have an obligation to see that the media perform in the public interest. The public interest includes protecting, preserving, and promoting institutions of public good, such as churches, cultural organizations, schools, police who serve to maintain order in a community, government, and all other elements of our society that are essential to society's continued welfare.

It is patently not in the public interest for media to vilify, denigrate and seek to destroy public confidence and respect for individuals serving the public, by election or appointment, or public or social organizations without serious purpose or demonstrable need, but only for the purpose of displaying power. Some media members, particularly newspapers, seem to delight, without demonstrable or obvious need, in destroying public confidence.

Unfortunately, as Lawrence Grossman, former president of NBC News and PBS, said, journalism as a public trust is a "rapidly disappearing perspective."

How many of today's top journalists—in print or electronics—would emulate the late Fred Friendly, president of CBS News in 1966, who resigned in anger and embarrassment when the network chose a rerun of "I Love Lucy"' over a Senate hearing on the escalating war in Vietnam?

Compounding the problem which has led to the deterioration of the media and the loss of public confidence in the media is the character and lack of a sense of responsibility on the part of many individuals who head the country's most persuasive media. Sadly, it's not uncommon today to hear a media head disclaim responsibility for a questionable action by saying something to this effect: "I am not responsible for that. That was done by my staff. I didn't know anything about it."

Such comments are cowardly and display total ignorance of what a media head's duties are. He is responsible for establishing an operating policy and seeing to it that the policy is followed. An editor or publisher has to rely on the character of his employees. He doesn't have time to go out and research the material the reporter presents, and barring the obvious misstatement of fact, has to rely on the writer's integrity. But whether he accepts it or not, the buck stops at his desk.

For reasons I find unsound, some of today's publishers leave the authority over the product to staff members. This is a failure to understand that—whether they like it or not—as the authority they are responsible legally and morally for the product. To disclaim this is meaningless. They should accept this and act accordingly. If they did, today's media would receive more respect.

A significant part of the problem the media has created is the organizational structure which has developed since the days of our founding fathers. They held the media in such high regard that they incorporated safeguards into the Constitution to preserve the function against legal destruction. It must be noted that no other business in America has had or has been given Constitutional protection. Our Supreme Court has preserved and even enhanced the safeguards in countless decisions.

America's media had its beginnings decades before we became a nation. Citizens who had a fervent interest in creating America strove to arouse interest and support for their ideas with handwritten letters which they circulated as widely as possible. Some of the letter writers published pamphlets, many of which became newspapers. Some were free; others sold for a penny.

In those early days, citizens knew who was responsible for the letters and pamphlets, because the writers were their friends. The authors had no opportunity to deny authorship and they did not. As the first crude publications became newspapers, the citizens still knew the editors and the editors accepted their due. In the main, this continued until early in the twentieth century when some newspaper editors and owners sold the publications to entrepreneurs who began to develop chains of papers. Then emerged publishers who did not own their papers. They then began to disclaim responsibility.

It is an imperious misconception that press members are above the law and do not have to answer questions put to them by authorities investigating a crime or legal dispute because they assured a source of confidentiality.

I do not think the theory that reporters are privileged to decline as citizens to help maintain social order by refusing information to prosecuting authorities is either morally or legally defensible.

Some reporters and management refuse to answer, claiming the knowledge is privileged, either by outright pledge to the source or by inference. Some political jurisdictions have supported this position, either by statute or court decision. A pledge of confidentiality is voided when one party to the pledge commits a crime.

When law enforcement asked the *Globe-Democrat* or its employees for help, I always recommended to our staff that they cooperate, knowing full well the power of my office. I asked reporters to respond to requests for information. If pictures, which were our property, were requested, I directed that the pictures be supplied. It was my position that the product of a reporter's work, just like the product of the work by a General Motors employee on the production line, was owned by our paper.

Certainly the reporter or editor should maintain promised confidentiality against casual inquiry. But when an individual is being prosecuted for a crime and information crucial to the solution of the crime is sought by proper authorities from a media member who withholds information under a promise of confidentiality, it is my conviction that the reporter or editor has a moral and legal obligation to disclose such knowledge. Many media people disagree with this and have successfully obtained court rulings upholding their position.

The conditions under which the reporter agreed to confidentiality may have been changed since the pledge was made because the second party to the pledge committed a crime which voided the pledge. This removes a vital condition of the pledge. Further, if investigation giving rise to the need for information from a media member is motivated by a felonious act, this creates an obligation in the social order to respond. A distinction might be made if the wrongful act for which redress is sought is not a felony but a civil cause of action.

The argument that disclosure will destroy a news source is specious. The loss of a news source is insignificant in comparison to securing justice when a high crime has been committed against society and society's right to lead a secure life in a disciplined social order.

Whatever the validity of arguments on each side of the issue, the result is patent. It creates a further erosion of the public's confidence and support of the media.

If one can trust the world to handle its incendiary problems in the future, such as the bonfires in middle Europe and the Middle East, as it has over the years since World War II, there is hope that the world might have found a way to live in peace without the chance that it could destroy much of itself with a nuclear catastrophe. It is to be hoped, fervently and prayerfully, that world leadership will find a way to contain and eliminate the insane threats to peace by the Saddam Husseins or Slobodan Milosevics of the world.

As I write these words, we have just gone through another nightmare of suspicion, of wrong doing on the part of our trusted leaders, of partisan acrimony without seeming regard for the will and welfare of the people. We have watched cynicism seep into our thinking, turning millions away from the polls and a precious opportunity to speak up and be heard. We have seen many lose their faith in government and in the officials we chose to represent us.

In my lifetime, I have experienced war and the Great Depression, of growth and progress, of destruction and decay. I have seen increased violence in our schools and in our streets and I have watched good-hearted men and women try valiantly to solve our problems.

I have seen my beloved press struggle with its new ethics, its philosophy and practice of intrusive reporting. I can only hope I have helped keep that press stable and honorable.

I believe the press, by clinging to its original purpose, by supporting the right as it sees the right, without bias or bigotry, by condemning the wrong as it sees the wrong, with fairness and humanity, and most of all, by leading with integrity, can turn our national nightmare into the American dream and its promise.

I believe in the freedom of the press—freedom with responsibility.

I believe in democracy. I believe it will triumph over tyranny.

I believe in America and in her spirit. Yes, I believe in America. America, the troubled, but still so beautiful.

Index

Mary Kimbrough, like Duncan Bauman, lived in Tulsa as a child. She was a reporter for the *Tulsa Tribune* before moving to St. Louis and joining the staff of the *St. Louis Star-Times* as women's editor. After that newspaper closed, she went to the *St. Louis Post-Dispatch* and later became family editor and magazine feature writer for the *Globe-Democrat*.

She has received many honors for her journalistic skills, including being the first woman named as the St. Louis Press Club's Media Person of the Year. She has been a *Globe-Democrat* Woman of Achievement, a Missouri Press Women Woman of Achievement, and a Women in Communication National Headliner.

Among her many books are a history of the Muny Opera, a history of the Children's Home Society, a history of Family and Children's Service, and *Movers and Shakers*, a compilation of her articles on *Globe-Democrat* Men of the Year (Patrice Press, 1992). She is a popular writing instructor at several St. Louis insitutions.

68 Catholic Charities
   Dismas House

155 funeral